Learning to Teach, Teaching to Learn

Learning to Teach, Teaching to Learn

Reflections on Education as Transformation through Dialogue

DAVID RHOADS

CASCADE *Books* • Eugene, Oregon

LEARNING TO TEACH, TEACHING TO LEARN
Reflections on Education as Transformation Through Dialogue

Cascade Books
An Imprint of Wipf and Stock Publishers
199 W. 8th Ave., Suite 3
Eugene, OR 97401

www.wipfandstock.com

PAPERBACK ISBN: 978-1-62032-879-8
HARDCOVER ISBN: 978-1-4982-8809-5
EBOOK ISBN: 978-1-7252-4831-1

Cataloguing-in-Publication data:

Names: Rhoads, David M., author.

Title: Learning to teach, teaching to learn : reflections on education as transformation through dialogue / David Rhoads.

Description: Eugene, OR: Cascade Books, 2025. | Includes bibliographical references.

Identifiers: ISBN 978-1-62032-879-8 (paperback). | ISBN 978-1-4982-8809-5 (hardcover). | ISBN 978-1-7252-4831-1 (ebook).

Subjects: LCSH: Theology—Study and teaching. | Bible—Study and teaching. | Religion—Study and teaching. | Theological seminaries. | Clergy—Training of. | Parish education. | College teaching. | College teachers.

Classification: BS600.2 R46 2025 (print). | BS600.2 (epub).

VERSION NUMBER 02/23/26

Contents

Preface

Why This Book?

"If only I knew then what I know now" might be a pretty good explanation of my purpose in writing these reflections. Of course, when I began my career I couldn't know what I know now because I had to learn it by trial runs and experiments that were a mixed bag of successes and failures. Those of us who teach post–high school have spent years learning our field of expertise, but we have not usually had any courses on education. So perhaps someone still in graduate school or just starting out their teaching career might benefit from what I have struggled to learn.

This is a new age of digital learning, which has made distance learning possible and often quite desirable. AI will be further changing the challenges of teaching. I have no presumption that my suggestions for teaching will be useful in today's academic environments. Nevertheless, the basic ingredients of education are still in place: students, teacher, the relationship between them, the subject matter, and how they all work together to enable education to happen.

So, what you will find here occurs pretty much within the framework of old-school, person-to-person education, a teacher in a classroom with a group of students. There is hardly a word about online classes or the use of technology in the classroom or communicating with students via social media. During the majority of my years of teaching, most of these resources were not widely available. I admire those who use them. They open entirely fresh arenas in which to pursue an education. Perhaps some of the dynamics of teaching and learning discussed here will be relevant to relationships cultivated through electronic media.

And while this book is intended mainly for people starting out in teaching, in regular or adjunct positions, in colleges, seminaries, and graduate schools—some of these reflections may also be useful for seasoned teachers as well, perhaps to think about strategies of education you have not thought much about before. Or perhaps you will be prompted to decide how you would do things differently. You will likely experience affirmation of the way you already teach. Maybe it will suggest to "old dogs" like me some new tricks. And, of course, the reflections here may also prompt school teachers, pastors, and parish educators to find some ideas to enhance their vocation.

My career began at a time when teaching positions were more available and opportunities to move were more frequent. A position in a four-year liberal arts college, Carthage College, was available to me out of graduate school, a position I held for fifteen years. Then, an opportunity to teach seminary and doctoral students at the Lutheran School of Theology at Chicago presented itself, which lasted for twenty-two years, ending in retirement in 2010.

I began these reflections in the last several years of teaching and have continued to reflect back on my experiences in my retirement years. Looking back, I realize that one of the things we seldom do as teachers is to reflect openly on the process of education and learning. Students often have little idea what we are trying to accomplish as teachers or what our strategies are for doing it. They seldom hear us talk about our philosophy of teaching and how our personal experiences have informed the choices we make in the classroom. And we do not often invite students to reflect in any profound way about what they understand to be their vocation as learners.

My hope is that these ruminations will be generative in leading teachers and students alike to reflect on teaching and learning. Maybe they will stimulate conversations among colleagues about meaningful and effective ways to engage in the educational process. We *need* to talk with each other about these things if we want to deepen our personal vocations and if we want to fulfill our collective mission as teachers in an educational institution.

What I hope you find here are the reflections of someone who has made an honest effort struggling with a vocation as a teacher and with a personal vocation as a human being—struggling with my role, my relationships, my personal search for meaning, a set of values, and my efforts to respond to the abundance of grace from God that has blessed my life. The reflections clearly show someone in the process of "learning to teach." And because I love to learn, they also reflect a process of "teaching to learn" with the students.

I have been dependent on many people, first in college and then in seminary—able to exchange ideas and challenges with wonderful colleagues and friends. I have benefitted enormously from those with whom I shared a classroom in the experience of team teaching. I have also learned much from people who work outside the teaching profession. The line between the classroom and the world is permeable. I reckon that most teachers work hard to see the dynamics of their classrooms as a microcosm of life so as to prepare students to live in the macrocosm of the world.

There is no right way to read this book: forward, backward, or pick and choose what may pique your interest. The chapter topics have sometimes been clustered around a theme. But overall, after a few introductory chapters that orient the reader to an overall philosophy of teaching and learning, reflections about very practical matters are interspersed with more conceptual themes. There is some repetition, which I have sought to keep to a minimum. The bibliography includes books on teaching and learning that have been helpful throughout my career, some of which are referred to in the text.

Special thanks go to friends who have given such helpful feedback and much encouragement: Kadi Billman, Jerry de Jaeger, Jae Won Lee, Don Michie, Patricia Novick, Audrey West, Rob Worley, the group of LSTC students and faculty who over many years engaged in discussion about some of these reflections, and my amazing partner in life Sandy Roberts. This book is dedicated to the students, faculty, and staff at Carthage College and at the Lutheran School of Theology at Chicago, where I was privileged to teach and learn for so many wonderful years. What a great ride!

1

Transformation Through Dialogue

A LONGTIME FRIEND WHO used to teach at Carthage College is magical in the classroom. He has an astounding ability to engage students to think and learn for themselves as they seldom do in their other classes. He exemplifies in spades what is profiled in the study by Ken Bain about *What the Best College Teachers Do*. Yet when asked recently by another instructor at the college what he does in the classroom that makes his teaching so effective, he replied, "I don't know. I just teach." By contrast, you may well react to these reflections by saying, "Why does Rhoads *think* so much about everything? Can't he just teach?"

Unfortunately, teaching has not come so easily for me. I have had to work hard at it. Between the challenges of teaching college religion classes required of freshmen to teaching seminary courses and doctoral seminars, I had a passion to make learning meaningful. Therefore, it was necessary for me to think a *lot* about teaching and to experiment with many different approaches.

I find teaching to be most rewarding when students are empowered in their learning and in their lives, especially when their education is transformative. So, I had to be inventive in order to make the learning work. I could not tolerate it when teaching and learning was a matter of going through the motions in a kind of pedagogical charade, or when I was groping in the dark to get a discussion going with only two or three students participating in a class of twenty, or when I dispensed knowledge and the students were passive recipients coughing up what they had just ingested. Such experiences can be boring—not only for the students but also for the teacher!

In fact, my lifework as a teacher was, in part, designed to avoid boredom—the students' and mine. I have always been fascinated by the subject matter I taught. The challenge was to make the classroom engaging. One of my main goals was to organize classes so that they would be enjoyable, indeed fun. I figured that if I was having a good time, the likelihood was that the students would be having a good time as well. The joy of learning should be contagious. Sometimes at the end of the very first class period of a new course, I would comment to the students (tongue in cheek to turn the tables on their likely thoughts): "When I came in here today, I wondered if you would be boring, but I can see that won't be the case!"

I drew upon the skill and wisdom of many people in my efforts to learn about teaching. I have learned mostly from students, who know better than I how they learn and whose responses and involvement are the keys to what works. Also, from early on, it was a practice of mine to read books on pedagogy. In addition, I have garnered ideas from conversations with faculty colleagues and from many terrific opportunities to team teach with colleagues in different fields. I have picked up ideas from business leaders, middle school special education teachers, and kindergarten teachers. I would hear ideas, adapt them, and try them. I was a kind of pedagogical hoarder.

TRANSFORMATION THROUGH DIALOGUE

I have for many years thought of the educational experience as "transformation through dialogue." Education can be a way of engagement with ideas, with experiences, and with methods that transform our beliefs and values, our relationships, and our ways of seeing and acting in the world. Part of the reason we are not always transformed by learning (in any field) is the simple fact that we do not expect to be changed. We think of education primarily as accumulating facts and information rather than learning ideas that could change the minds and hearts and habits of ourselves and others. We think of education as someone else's opinion, which we listen to as we think of rebuttals from our own point of view, rather than taking in what we hear and expecting to be altered by what we learn. Or we think of education as passive activity in which a teacher pours facts into our heads, rather than the acquisition of insights that may well subvert our present worldview and generate new interests and actions. When we come to education with an open and an active mind, ready to engage learning in a profoundly personal way, expecting to be challenged by what we learn and expecting to think for ourselves, we will experience the transformation that education promises to bring. In fact, we will discover that transformation *is* the process of learning!

Transformation

We underestimate the power of education if we think it cannot transform us. Perhaps you can recall a course that turned you on to some subject and, in so doing, formed the entire direction of your career. Or maybe you can remember some insight you heard that has shaped so many of your subsequent attitudes and decisions in life. Just think about pieces of information you have gotten at one time or another that completely reoriented your views about something, enabling you to see things in a new way. Most of us can recall how the learning of some skill or method opened up many possibilities for our thinking. Or consider how certain memorable life experiences have engendered in us the capacity to cry or to experience awe and wonder. Think of the story you heard or the novel you read or the film you saw or the magazine article that led you to take a course of action or to adopt some cause in life. Or consider simply the accumulative impact of teachers who cared about you and taught you basic things about life that continue to inform the way you live today.

When I think about how people may change from learning, I remember, for example, what I heard from students when I taught about the ecological state of the world and its relation to the Christian faith. Some said they were changed because of a piece of information or a different way of seeing things that led them to experience, in an instant, an entirely new relationship with the rest of nature and a sense of responsibility toward it. As a result of such learning, I watched some students being led to profound repentance, a turning around, an abandonment of cultural attitudes and actions that are cavalier toward nature, and an embrace of actions that tread lightly on Earth.

In my field of study, I have seen students transformed by study of the New Testament. The New Testament is filled with people who witness to their own transformation and the transformation of others, with visions to transform the world. Just consider, for example, how we study the influence of Jesus in his role as teacher—putting forth such unforgettable sayings and such memorable proverbs, telling parabolic stories that reoriented people to think in entirely new ways, offering eye-popping insights on morality and our relationship with God. Jesus fulfilled the role of a *sage*—sharing unconventional wisdom that challenged the core values and the common cultural ways of his disciples and his people. Jesus's words were actions that produced results. They were events that turned the world upside down and opened up vistas for those with ears to hear and eyes to see. And the model of his life and death was his most profound teaching. The early Christian writings that followed upon his life are testimony to an explosion of incredible creativity, dramatically renewed lives, and startling experiments in alternative communities—all generated in the aftermath of his witness.

As a teacher of New Testament, my main task was to find ways to bring that early Christian material to life and to allow it to work its magic. This could sometimes be a challenge. Theologian Joseph Sittler once cautioned me with these words: "People no longer take something seriously just because it's in the Bible. We have to find ways to make it engaging and relevant." And once you get started down that path, the New Testament turns out to be an amazing subject to study—generative, puzzling, radical, mind bending, challenging, sometimes offensive, and transformative. As a colleague in theology at the Chicago theological seminary, Ted Jennings, once said of teaching New Testament classes: "This stuff teaches itself!"

It is critical to observe that transformation is not simply for the individual seated before you. It is also communal. The goal is not only for persons in a class to be transformed but also that their studies may contribute to the transformation of communities, workplaces, congregations, society in general, and the very educational institution of which the classroom is a part. The best way we can do this is to see the classroom itself as a community that is ripe for transformation and to cultivate that reality.

Of course, the question presents itself: Transformation into what? Transformation for what? I hope that the following reflections will make clear that the hoped-for transformations represent a committed and intentional movement toward becoming more humane individuals and communities with values that promote justice and peace and care of the Earth.

Dialogue

Not every field of study may lend itself to transformation as readily as biblical studies. However, I am convinced that in every field of study, transformation takes place most effectively in dialogue with others who can teach us, challenge us, draw out of us what we did not know was there, and share the excitement of learning. Transformation through dialogue is most effective when done with people different from each other, with people from diverse cultures, social locations, ages, career backgrounds. This dialogue amid diversity can occur among students (when the composition of the class permits) but also with guest speakers, with books we read, and with experiences and knowledge we each bring to the process. Efforts to incorporate diversity into the classroom and to make the most of it require effort and persistence; but the benefits to the educational experience are well worth it. When we get the challenge of many different voices in the mix, we all, including ourselves as teachers, find it hard to be in conversation without changing.

Such transformation through dialogue happens only if there is a genuine partnership in conversation. This means that there has to be some level of parity between teachers and students. Early on, I read the works of Malcolm Knowles, who argues for a shift in teaching from pedagogy to what he refers to as andragogy. *Pedagogy* literally means "words/education for children." Here the implication is that the teacher is the authority and the students are dependent, focused on absorbing information, and motivated by external rewards and punishments. *Andragogy* means "education for adults." Here the authority is shared by teacher and learners; and the students bring much to the learning experience—intelligence, creativity, knowledge, passion, life experiences, and perhaps previous careers or educational training in other fields. Adult students are motivated by their own desire to learn. The idea of andragogy is for the teacher to shift the responsibility for learning from the teacher to the students—so that there is created in the classroom a community in which all are active learners and teachers.

When teachers expect to learn and students expect to teach by contributing to the learning process for the whole class, then genuine dialogue becomes more likely to happen. The educational center of gravity moves from the teacher to the relationships among all the members of the class, with the teacher serving as facilitator, guide, and stimulus. Of course, such dialogue implies the need for a safe atmosphere of mutual trust and respect. Creating an atmosphere for dialogue becomes a central part of the vocation of teaching. The shift from pedagogy to andragogy in class planning and classroom strategies has made my life as a teacher so much more meaningful, and I believe it has created a much more effective learning experience for students. And this can be done while maintaining the appropriate student-teacher relationship.

The dialogue in many of my classes has also been generated by team teaching with faculty in other fields. At Carthage College, the dialogue was informed by opportunities to do cross-disciplinary teaching with faculty in psychology, economics, political science, and English literature, among others. From a teacher of psychology, we learned about "authenticity" and were introduced to *The Denial of Death*, by Ernest Becker. In class with a political scientist, students each chose a political hot spot from around the world about which to teach the rest of us. As a result of teaching together, English professor Don Michie and I wrote a book on the Gospel of Mark as a narrative. At seminary, I continued this tradition of team teaching. There, in addition to teaching with faculty from LSTC, I also team taught with faculty from nearby denominational seminaries on topics ranging from cultural anthropology to contemporary film to an ecology course that involved presentations by scientists from nearby secular institutions. The dialogues engendered in these classes were dynamic and unpredictable experiences both for the students and for those of us who were leading the class.

An Ethic of Dialogue with the Bible and with Each Other

Of course, significant dialogue partners were the writings of the New Testament. There is an ethic to dialoguing with something written, especially a writing that originates from another time and place. Thanks to postmodern theory, we now know that marks on a page or a manuscript have no life or meaning until readers bring them into play. When readers come into play, they participate in the creation of meaning. The writing has multiple but not limitless possibilities for meaning. Readers bring assumptions, experiences, diverse social locations, desires for certain outcomes to the reading, and, especially with the Bible, often a stake in what it may or may not say.

So there is a responsibility to be aware of what we ourselves bring to the exercise of understanding—that is, what may facilitate and hinder understanding—and to use methods and frameworks to seek the most faithful interpretations of what meanings a given writing might have had in its original contexts. This requires an ethical commitment to listen over and over with exploratory methods and to seek faithful understandings even when they counter what we may expect the Bible to say or even what we may want it to say. Then an additional step may be required in order to seek its potential implications for today in certain times and places—taking into account different contexts, the potential for harm, and the opportunity to promote human wholeness and well-being.

Of course, the same ethic that applies to dialogue with the Bible also applies to our dialogues with each other and with others, including secondary writings *about* the Bible—not to distort the words of others, to seek to understand faithfully, and to respond honestly and respectfully. It is our role as teachers to model such an ethic of dialogue throughout our courses.

From these experiences, I have learned that education can be profoundly invigorating and deeply personal as classroom participants engage with the subject matter and with each other. The diversity of points of view and of social locations has also shown me that education is profoundly political; that is, it has to do with the social order of things. The classroom is an educational institution that is embedded in a society and *is therefore itself part of* the social order. It can thus promote a humane order of things or it can dehumanize.

A diversity of perspectives and experiences was especially evident at the seminary, where students came from different colleges as well as different areas of the country and of the world. There was a mixture of ethnicities, career backgrounds, and a significant age range. In the doctoral program, there were international students from many continents and countries. Because of these factors, classes were often a global experience in which we mainly learned from each other and from the distinctive perspectives we each brought to the material under study.

Through this dialogue with one another, transformation moved beyond the personal to encompass challenges to cultural conventions, social mores, political perspectives, and economic worldviews. In other words, the transformations taking places in and with the class *were themselves* an expression of social transformation at work.

THE CLASSROOM AS WORKSHOP

For me, dialogue was most meaningful when there was time for the relationships among participants to develop, for the subject matter to deepen, and for the creative juices to flow. For these reasons, I valued seminar classes that met for three or four hours at a time, once a week. Such block courses enabled momentum to occur, as each part of the class could be built on what had been done earlier in that class period. I taught each class period as if it were a workshop. Although this model can also be used in hour-long classes, the workshop model in three-hour classes enables one to change class activities often, so that various approaches to a subject can be explored. The time moves quickly. This was sort of a Sesame Street approach to adult learning, because we were continuously changing patterns of learning, usually every fifteen or thirty minutes: I gave mini-lectures to initiate conversation; students worked in pairs or small groups; the whole class would do a plenary exercise on some problem; or students made presentations. The process took planning, from setting goals and designing assignments to managing class activities. I usually brought seven or eight ideas into each class period and ended up doing five or six (and sometimes interjecting components for which I had not prepared), giving me flexibility to follow the flow of the class. The transformational dialogue that resulted from the intensity of this model seemed to produce salutary results.

A SPIRITUALITY OF LEARNING

As I reflected on my own personal transformations through dialogue over the years of teaching, I grew to believe in a spirituality of learning that I came to embrace for my own life and that I have tried to model for students. It is an ever-recurring process: a commitment to listen, the courage to state my own convictions, an openness to the views of others, the willingness to change my mind, the refusal to make an idol out of ideas and approaches, and the capacity to hold strong commitments without carving them in stone and without imposing them on others.

I also came to believe that a spirit, indeed a holy spirit, undergirds such communal dialogue—with guidance, with deep regard for a diversity of gifts, with a longing for the weak to flourish, and with the manifold gifts that sustain a community, the greatest of which is love.

2

Teaching as Vocation

Autobiographical Reflections

IT MAY BE HELPFUL to the reader for me to share some reflections and experiences that have come to inform my sense of vocation as a teacher. I have been fortunate to have a career doing what I love to do. I love to learn. I love to share my learning with others. I love to engage students in learning. And I love to learn with them. Early in my career at the seminary, a five-year evaluation committee said to me, "We see some administration in your future." Without hesitation, I immediately responded, "No, you don't!" Of course I did do my share of administrative work over the years. But I personally felt called to teaching. I figured I'd better stick to teaching.

A DEEPLY SATISFYING SENSE OF VOCATION

In the course of writing these reflections, I had a dream. At the time I had the dream, I had been retired for several years and I had not done any teaching during that time. Yet in my dream, I was invited to give an informal lecture in a lounge at some unidentified seminary. I was pleased to be doing it. As I walked down the hallway toward the lounge, I thought to myself: "I am going to enjoy this. When I taught before, that is when I experienced ecstasy." With that brief word, I awoke.

Actually, ecstasy is a word that does indeed make some sense when I think about my experiences as a teacher. Not the kind of ecstatic experiences in which one is overcome with excitement. That kind of ecstasy would overwhelm students and stifle the learning process with an ocean of emotion. Rather, it was a quiet ecstasy that relishes the interaction in meaningful dialogue, insight, laughter, and transformation.

This quiet ecstasy is not a matter of standing "outside oneself." On the contrary, it is a matter of being fully present. It is embodiment in relation to who and what is around—being wholly present in that time and place. It is being centered in relation to all the other persons in the room. I have had moments when I would spontaneously say to the class, "You know, I would not sooner be anywhere else, with any other people, doing any other thing, at any other time, than I am with you, right here, right now."

Meaningful Experiences in the Classroom

Of course, there is an ebb and flow to the experience of teaching. Part of the "flow" comes when there are special moments in the classroom. Sometimes I would begin to share on a subject in a way that transcended my normal conversation in class, and I became aware that the class had also become intensely absorbed in the moment. Being engaged with the students at this kind of level can make it a very meaningful experience. Or sometimes a student would say something that seemed to reach down to a profound matter of human significance. Such comments have the potential to dive down deep with the class and stay there awhile in dialogue. We cannot determine these times, but we can anticipate them. And when they happen and when the issues are addressed and everyone grows from it, even when there is frustration and conflict, there is an intense satisfaction.

Biblical Greek distinguishes two different experiences of time. *Chronos* time is the linear experience of time in hours, days, weeks, and so on. By contrast, *kairos* time is "opportune time" or "occasion time." When a class was going along normally, I considered myself to be on linear *syllabus* time, moving along with the subjects and methods that need to be dealt with. However, when one of these special moments presented itself, I immediately thought of the class as being on kairos time—"opportune time." Then chronological time stopped. I no longer worried about the material to be covered that day or where we were on the schedule; we were in a different zone of awareness.

In those moments, my main goal was to seek to enter into a more profound level of conversation, bring the whole class along, and see how long we could stay at that depth—by listening, sharing, and engaging each other in things that matter in some foundational way.

Trust and Love

Caring about the students has been an important part of my vocation. This conviction was formed in my early years. Growing up in a small Pennsylvania town, I had many teachers who cared deeply about the students. I recall one occasion when I went to my ninth grade history teacher saying that I was afraid I might be having a nervous breakdown—going to school, doing homework, working twenty-five hours a week in a barber shop as an apprentice, being in the school band, and practicing for a school play at night. What Miss Ruck said to me (words I clearly recall) was unbelievably freeing and healing: "For the next few weeks, I want you to sit in the back of the room and look at *TIME* magazines. And you are excused from any assignments for the time being. Do not feel any pressure from me. Just get to feeling better." And I did what she said. And I got over my anxiety. I cannot say how often I have thought of the grace of that moment, and I have sought to pass it forward to students of mine who found themselves in unusual stress or distress.

As I have come to see teaching and learning as meaningful dialogue, I have come to realize that you cannot have dialogue without trust. Transformation comes most often when people are safe enough to be open to change. So I have sought to care about the students with intention. In my latter years of teaching, part of my class preparation was readying my spirit for the time with students in the class. I used the class list to pray for students by name. I prayed that the impending class time might be sacred time and sacred space and prayed for their well-being apart from the classroom. And I told my classes that I loved them. Not often but especially after I had spent a number of meaningful hours with them over the course of a semester and it seemed appropriate, usually as I was ending a class, I would say in a most ordinary way, "I love you." I have found that these sentiments can be expressed in a matter-of-fact way while also maintaining the proper teacher/student relationships with appropriate boundaries.

USING OUR PAST LEARNING EXPERIENCES TO FORM OUR TEACHING

Our vocation in teaching is often shaped by our own experiences of learning. We want students to experience what we found meaningful in *our* educational journey. It is likely that most of us at some level are seeking to replicate for our students the joy of learning that we ourselves discovered as students. We recall a teacher who "turned us on" to learning, a startling insight that left us with wonder and delight, the satisfaction of writing a paper and being acknowledged for it, a course we took in which our fascination just could not be fully satisfied and we found ourselves lost in the library or online digging for more, or a time when we were transformed by what we learned. In my case, such experiences of learning were interwoven with a personal quest for religious meaning.

A Crisis of Faith

I was the child of a pastor. As a youth, I had been very active in church and regional youth groups. I planned to become a Lutheran pastor like my father. Further, when I was fifteen I had a powerful mystical experience of the presence of God that transformed my life and flooded me with love. While I told no one about this experience until many years later, the relationship with God that this experience generated quietly fed my inner life and fostered an intense love for others over many years. Then, when I was a senior in college and studying philosophy, I came to see that the conceptual framework in which I had understood my religious experience and the images I had used to understand the reality of God no longer worked. When the framework for my religious experience crumbled, so did my relationship with God, my peace, and, frankly, the strength of my love. I felt empty and desolate.

I struggled with this death or nonexistence of God for a long time. I did not know if I would again recover faith or ever experience God again. But I did not give up seeking, even though I did not know where it might lead. I had given the study of philosophy a chance in college, so why not give the study of religion a chance in seminary. After college, I went to England to study the Bible. There I not only had the intellectual experience of the absence of God. In addition, I had a profound existential experience of that absence—of there being no god, an empty sky, no deep meaning in the universe, no inherent significance to life whatsoever.

In its own way, this experience of disintegration of meaning was just as profound as the earlier mystical experience of integration. I came to believe that meaning, any meaning, would have to be created by us. I was not agnostic, as if I were uncertain; rather, I was an atheist by belief and life experience—not by a choice. It was just the way it was.

Yet it was my study of the Bible at Oxford that enabled me slowly, bit by bit, to come back to an understanding of God—or rather, I should say, go forward and find new and richer experiences of God. This experience of the dissolution and recovery of faith liberated me to be free to doubt, free to know uncertainty as part of faith, free to embrace ambiguity amid a relationship with God that was ever changing, dissolving, reemerging, and growing. I became comfortable with risk and disbelief, and even loss of faith, as an integral part of the journey—to question my *formulations* of God so that I might leave space for the possibility that the *reality* of God might emerge and surprise me in new ways.

Implications for Teaching

Repeated experiences of losing and gaining faith over the years helped me greatly to understand what might be happening with students I was teaching. When I taught, I never set out to create a crisis of faith for my students. Nevertheless, the material we studied in the Bible and the conversations we had in class often led students into a crisis of some dimension about their faith. The gift from my own experience was that I was comfortable with such crises. And I was comfortable with hard truths about religion and about the Bible. I was not afraid for students in their struggles. And I could often provide some guidance that enabled them not to be afraid but also not to withdraw from their quest for the meaning of life in a way that would block the possible work of God in their lives—even in their disbelief. Nor did I ever make any assumptions about where their quest for truth and meaning might lead them.

My experiences also taught me to think this way about education in general; that is, that education is not just a matter of acquiring knowledge or skills or methods, although it does do that. Rather, learning can be intensely life changing. I am not talking about conversion. I never preached in college classes and did not seek to turn anyone into a Christian. Nor am I speaking of psychological therapy. That has no place in the classroom. Rather, I see learning in any subject as a process of challenge and growth, in which the human person is engaged in a process of change and movement, without knowing what direction it might take or what the outcome might be. Honesty and a search for truth are hallmarks not only of a liberal arts education but also of the human journey toward a meaningful life.

Life-changing experiences can be part of almost every subject in the liberal arts curriculum, whether it be literature, history, political science, or anthropology. Across the spectrum of subjects, we can expect students to engage actively with their learning: to entertain ideas, to embrace possibilities, to imagine new worlds, to experience the lives of people different from themselves, to let their beliefs and values be challenged, to be open to change and difference. I think this is just good education in any field—from the humanities to the social sciences to the sciences. One of the most disheartening moments of my teaching career was when a young student at Carthage said to me, "I don't think anyone is going to change in college. By this age everyone's mind is made up about things." I was not so much discouraged in my role as teacher as I was sad for her and others like her who shut their minds to the adventure of learning—and to the quest of being human.

My role as a teacher was not to decide whether or how a student should be changed or transformed or what views they should hold or what they should become. That was a mystery out of my control and beyond my purview. Carthage is a liberal arts college devoted to an open quest for truth. And, as a seminary, LSTC values open dialogue about matters of faith—even promoting itself at one point as "A place where all your answers are questioned!" How do I know what is true anyhow? Truth and reality are larger than my narrow compass. Students have lives very different from mine. My role was to make the learning as meaningful as I could and to give space and opportunity for serious engagement with the profound issues present in the biblical material. Students may change in some small way over an issue they encounter. Or they may experience a dramatic personal upheaval. Or they may embrace new and different cultural values. Or they may end up affirming who and what they were to start with, even though they will still end up being different for having gone through the process of challenge and discovery.

All of this sounds much too dramatic. And, truth be told, my classes were mostly quite mundane and ordinary. But the ingredients for change were there, the ethos for potential transformation was present, and I was always trying in a variety of ways to light the flame or create conditions for a spontaneous combustion that might result in some illumination. Obviously, transformation is not the only thing going on in a classroom. For example, when I was reviewing Greek verb tenses or giving a time-line for the growth of the early church or recounting the details of the Roman-Jewish War. Nevertheless, these can be ingredients that lead to something that brings some enlightenment. And when we were performing biblical stories or trying to understand the rhetorical impact of Paul's Letter to the Galatians or mulling over the blind hypocrisy addressed in the Sermon on the Mount, the possibilities for transformation were lurking at the edges and pushing up through the cracks, seeking to break open to the center of things as we pondered the human condition. To be honest, I myself was also looking for change and transformation in these classroom conversations.

Cultivating the Love of Learning

Experiences as a student during the two years doing an MA in religion at Oxford in England helped to form some important convictions about teaching and learning. At Oxford, an insatiable appetite for learning was awakened in me. The educational system was so different from what I was used to. There were three eight-week terms with two six-week breaks in between, plus the summer break. During the terms, we went to lectures at the different colleges of the university. However, there were no assignments or tests connected with them nor any grades. We had one essay to prepare each week to read aloud to a tutor in an hour-long session, with one other student present. These essays were not graded and did not count as a class. While some practice exams were administered, there was nothing in the two-year program that counted toward the degree except the two weeks of exams at the very end of the two years. Talk about pressure!

But all through this time, I did not want to stop learning! What hooked me? It was this: everything was based on self-motivation and self-discipline. If you learned, it had to come from *within* you. As I look back on my American college education, it seems almost as if it could easily have been experienced as an assembly-line education: students had certain required courses to take for their program; they chose from a list of courses offered each semester (determined by the faculty); and they followed the syllabus of class times, readings, assignments, tests, papers, and extra credit (set up by the teachers). They worked through their program and got a degree. Unless a student was highly motivated, the structure of the educational program itself did not automatically empower students to take responsibility for their own learning. It was tempting for students to think of learning as taking the tests in order to pass the courses and then getting through the courses in order to complete the program. I know that there were ways to transcend these obstacles so as to take responsibility for one's learning. I know that many of my fellow students at Gettysburg College did just that. But I did so also to a limited extent. I think a lot of US education has changed since that time. How to break through this impasse?

Oxford, on the other hand, virtually required self-discipline. Week after week, I was on my own preparing an essay for my personal tutorial with the teacher as mentor and one other student—to make sure my shame was public! Each week, I was challenged to do better, to figure out how to read and interpret and write. I depended less and less on secondary materials, so that I could decipher the puzzles of the text for myself. It was a struggle for me. One story to illustrate this process. In assigning the very first tutorial, Dr. George Caird gave the handful of new students eight subjects from which to choose. I chose "The Kingdom of God in the Teaching of Jesus." I went to the library and, lo and behold, I found a new volume by Norman Perrin entitled *The Kingdom of God in the Teaching of Jesus*! I was elated. During the week, I studied that book hard and wrote a thorough review of it. At the tutorial with Dr. Caird, I read my essay aloud. I thought I had done a creditable job. However, after a long pause, Dr. Caird said, "Mr. Rhoads [pause], the assignment was not on Norman Perrin's book on the kingdom of God [pause], it was on the kingdom of God *in the teaching of Jesus*." At which point, he slowly opened toward me the Greek text of the New Testament he was holding on his lap and added, "Now, where do we begin?" In some sense, that question was the beginning of my vocation as a learner.

Finally, after ten or so tutorials, I did an essay on the concept of "the son of man" in Ezekiel. I used no secondary sources. I must have read Ezekiel twenty-five times in order to come up with the various ways Ezekiel uses "the son of man." And I had fun doing it. When I finished reading aloud my analysis in the tutorial, Dr. Caird seemed somewhat surprised and said, "That's not bad for a first attempt." This was the first compliment I had received all year! And it was enough. I was beginning to get the idea that I could approach a text and learn something interesting on my own—if I had a set of my own questions and fascination enough to stay with it.

Over the two years at Oxford, I came to have confidence that I could come up with something original about the texts I was studying. So, subsequently, when I went to the secondary sources, I would find things that I had already come up with on my own; and often, based on my own work with the text, I would disagree with certain points and I would know why. I was hooked. By the time I left Oxford, I knew I wanted to teach—partly because it was the best way I could keep on learning!

Enlarging an Appetite for Learning

When I returned to the states to take a final year of seminary at the Lutheran Theological Seminary at Gettysburg, I was excited about everything. Each course I took was a feast. Following that, in the graduate program in New Testament at Duke University, I took classes and formulated seminar papers in "discovery mode." When I wrote my dissertation on the political history of Israel according to Josephus, I spent the entire first year studying only the primary sources so as to formulate my own thinking before I ventured to see what other scholars might be saying about the subject. Every morning I could not wait to get to my carrel in the bowels of the Duke library and begin the day's search.

FUMBLING EFFORTS AT TEACHING

At the end of my program I was hired by telephone interview, sight unseen, to teach at Carthage College. I arrived completely green as a teacher. In graduate school, they did not offer courses on how to teach. I had been a teaching assistant at Duke Divinity School for several outstanding teachers but mostly to observe and assist in grading. As a result, in my first year at Carthage, I did not have a plan. I would have to make things up as I went along.

As might be expected, my initial efforts to teach were quite awkward, actually rather ludicrous. I was trying to pass forward my experience of self-motivated learning to a large group of eighteen-year-olds in a required course on the New Testament. In the very first class, I got the thirty-two people in the class into a circle and began to see if I could replicate my one-on-one experience with a tutor at Oxford. I can still recall the particular room and just where I was sitting. And I vividly remember thinking to myself, "Now, how am I going to do this?" That turned out to be the question I asked pretty much every day of my thirty-seven year career. The answers, when they came, mostly originated from students and from my failures.

I think most teachers want students to have an experience of discovery that is similar to the experiences that motivated them in the course of their own education. It is a noble desire, and recreating how we ourselves discovered the love of learning can be contagious. Ultimately, however, we cannot reproduce the conditions of our own learning. The students we teach are at different levels, they have different interests, and they are a different generation. Besides, people learn differently. So in the end, we have to garner wisdom from our students that will show us how *they* can discover the love of learning—without trying to put them into our mold.

What Am I Teaching For?

From the first day, I was absorbed in the challenges of teaching. From my biblical studies over the years, I have come to see "vocation" as an expression of the gifts and fruits of the Spirit. For me, the vocation of teaching draws upon the combined *gifts* of teaching, administration, and discernment. By "administration" as a gift of the Spirit, I mean the capacity to organize a classroom so as provide conditions for meaningful learning to take place, so that the human spirit of the students might blossom and so that perhaps even the Spirit might show up. By "discernment" as a gift of the Spirit, I mean that there is some intuition about what to do, when to do it, and how to do it so as to respond to student learning in a way that generates kairos moments of transformation that make learning exhilarating. In addition, vocation is a matter of striving in feeble and fumbling ways to model and foster the *fruits* of the Spirit: love, joy, peace, patience, kindness, goodness, faithfulness, humility, self-control. I never explicitly shared any of these thoughts about vocation with students, and I talked about the Spirit only as it related to the subject matter. Nevertheless, these reflections ran deep in what I tried to do.

Thoughts about the Spirit led me to a larger question that connects what we do in the classroom to what is happening in the world. The governing questions became: "What is God doing in the world, and how does this classroom participate in and manifest that activity?" When

I first began to teach, I just wanted to be the best teacher I could be. Then, I had an epiphany one day in the middle of a college class (I recall the room, the students, and where I stood) when I asked myself: "Why am I doing this?" I had been working hard to be the best, most effective teacher I could be. But now I was asking: "Best, most effective teacher *for what*? What am I doing, doing what I am doing?" What were the human values I was seeking to foster? What vision of the world was I hoping to nurture? How could I model the freedom of learning that I valued so highly and also model the care for others, the attention to the vulnerable, the capacity for selflessness, the facilitation of cooperation, the love of justice and peace, the desire to be responsible citizens of the country and the world, and the importance of caring for the earth? And, what might God be doing here in the classroom under the radar? So often, we simply do what we want to do, quite unreflectively, and then ask God to bless it, rather than asking what God is doing, and then seeking to be agents of that work. Now I was asking the latter question. "What in the world is going on?" In this process, I found that my "career vocation" became embedded in a basic and more encompassing "human vocation."

All Teaching and Learning Is Political

From that point on, my teaching was less about me and how well *I* was doing as a teacher. It was more about the students. Duh! This insight became clearer to me as I went along. Years later, when my wife was ill with life-threatening cancer, we met some doctors who arrogantly sought the kind of treatment for her that served their research agenda and not Sandy's well-being. Then we met a doctor who said to her at the first visit, "I have no ego in this. I just want you to get the best treatment for your condition." At which point, he referred her to another hospital for a stem cell transplant, which was the beginning of her (quite miraculous) recovery. Teaching, too, is about the students, what *they* are learning, how *they* are learning, and how *they* are being prepared for citizenship in the human community. And I struggled to "have no ego in this."

When I had the epiphany about what I was teaching *for*, that was the moment when I also realized that all learning is political—not in terms of political parties and political ambitions but in terms of the ways we live together as a society. I had recognized that all learning was personal as we seek transformation in encounters with the subject matter. Now, I also saw how irrelevant so much of our learning is if it is not connected to the issues we face in the world and the realities we face as humans. In other words, the *content* of the learning and the *process* of the learning have to be part of addressing our world and of participating in the creation of alternative worlds—a classroom that not only engages the world as it is but that also empowers us to imagine and create the world in new ways. To do this is to think of the classroom as a laboratory of life. This may be the only approach to teaching and learning that is viable.

Now at one level, again, as an actual description of my classrooms, this is grandiose at best and dishonest at worst. I doubt if my students would even recognize that I was doing any of this or that they would see these ruminations as reflective of what they actually experienced in my classes. Except in relation to some things on some days, I have been depicting my persistent ideal and my desire, not what actually happened every day.

Freeing Students from My Need to Succeed

Shortly after I had this insight about why I teach, I also had another epiphany—that I should not make my motivation and my energy for teaching dependent on student responses. After three years of teaching first-year students in required courses in New Testament, I was becoming somewhat frustrated and resentful that the students were not fully responding with the enthusiasm and dedication I had hoped. I was taking their attitudes and the level of their efforts personally. I was tempted to express my frustration at them as a means to motivate them to respond in a certain way so as to make me look good or feel good about myself as a teacher. To do this meant that their own motivation might be even further eroded or, worse yet, that they would do their studies out of guilt or shame or due to a need to please me or not to disappoint me. Now that couldn't be good!

At the time, I happened to be reading *Franny and Zooey* by J. D. Salinger. In the novel set in the forties, the oldest brother Seymour was part of a family of brilliant children who did a radio show, *It's a Wise Child*, in which they entertained radio audiences by answering questions posed to them. Seymour's name ("see more") reflected his wisdom. His younger brothers on the show looked up to Seymour, but they were mystified that Seymour always shined his shoes before every show, despite the fact that, since this was a radio show, no one would see his shoes. After Seymour died at an early age, the brothers recalled Seymour saying that he shined his shoes "for the f–t lady"—an imaginary listener as a poor woman living out in the sticks sitting on her porch in the heat listening to this "wise kids" program while she swatted flies from her face. In other words, Seymour was doing it for folks who could give him no accolades and bring him no prestige. He was doing it for people simply because they were human beings. He was doing it as an expression of who he was and not because of what he could get out of it or how people would respond.

After reading this novel, I saw the correlation between this story and my need to use my students to make me look like a successful teacher. So, as a means to help myself get over any need I had to have the students respond a certain way, I shined my shoes regularly for the rest of the year! I did it just to remind myself that I was doing this teaching out of my vocation and out of grace. I can only do what I do and then seek to learn and improve from my mistakes. The rest is not up to me. And if I tried to manipulate it, I would ruin the whole experience of the love of learning—for them and for me. So I sought to "detach myself from the fruits of my labor" so that my value and effort as a teacher would not be determined by how students might or might not respond. Of course, it is relevant how they respond, but it should not be determinative of my well-being or commitment. Nor should it rob my joy in teaching. As my predecessor at Carthage was wont to say: "You can sow the seeds, but you can't guarantee the harvest." So, let it be. In some sense, then, the spirituality of teaching became for me the capacity to relinquish control of the outcome. As one student wrote in her evaluation of a class at LSTC, "Teaching is a dying to self in the trust that the Spirit will work in the dialogue of the community of learners." Indeed!

Unfortunately, despite my best efforts to free them, students would sometimes treat me as if I would be taking their failures personally, by apologizing to me for a bad grade they made or by telling me how they had let me down with poor effort. After I learned to detach, I always responded, "You are free to do what you do. You don't owe me anything. You will succeed at some things and fail at others. You will give greater or lesser effort for a whole variety of reasons. I respect that. So you certainly don't need to add on the burden of pleasing me."

A VOCATION OF LEARNING TO COMPLEMENT THE VOCATION OF TEACHING

My sense of vocation as a teacher and as a person continued to grow throughout my years of teaching. It can be added that if teaching is my vocation, then the student's vocation is the pursuit of learning. Often students think that learning is simply preparation for a vocation they will pursue after they graduate. Indeed, part of my teaching vocation is to provide the best preparation for that future. Yet when they have this approach, they think of their vocation as something that will happen only later, when they get a job or a career. They think of the classroom as a penultimate experience rather than also as an ultimate experience in itself. This is a kind of deferred satisfaction. By contrast, I have tried to inculcate in students a love of the experience of learning that gives them a sense of vocation *now, as students*, so that they take responsibility for their learning, so that they enjoy learning for its own sake, and so that they cultivate learning as part of the *human vocation* they will pursue throughout their lives.

3

What Are We Teaching?

And How Are We Teaching It?

College and graduate school teachers have an advanced degree in a specialized field, but likely they have not had a course on teaching and have had only limited opportunities to be teaching assistants. Historically, the assumption of most graduate programs has been that they will teach you the subject matter, but it will be up to *you* to learn *how* to teach it. What follows is pretty mundane and obvious, but it reflects the ways I tried to accommodate to different subjects and different learning styles.

AWARENESS OF DIVERSE LEARNING STYLES

Likely, when we start to teach, most of us tend to imagine teaching basically as a matter of imparting information. We know more than the students do, and we seek to convey what we know. This idea is reinforced by the canon of information about different subjects that we need to cover in various courses. We assign students books and articles. We give lectures that review their reading or supplement it. And we give tests or assign papers designed for students to show what they have learned. Even when we are teaching about methods, we often do so more as a matter of describing the method than of practicing it. The primary model is conveying information. To be sure, when this process is done well it is clearly an effective way to teach.

But it doesn't take long for us to question the limitations of using one approach in relation to how students learn. We know, for example, that some people do better by hearing information in a lecture, while others do better by reading about it, and still others benefit most from visual charts and pictures. There are programs and books that outline diverse learning styles and identify teaching techniques to address them. Even though I did not adopt any of these learning schemes, it proved important for me to be aware of various styles of learning and to provide a range of learning strategies to address them. On occasion, I surveyed a class to find out from them the ways they learned best and what teaching-learning approaches would be most helpful to meet those needs.

DIFFERENT STRATEGIES FOR TEACHING DIFFERENT THINGS

My own efforts to address diverse approaches to teaching and learning focused not so much on styles of learning as on the different things I was teaching. I was asking: What if we are not just imparting knowledge? What if we are teaching skills and techniques? What if we are teaching methods of interpretation? What if we are teaching students to raise critical questions and weigh evidence? What about teaching to foster certain values? What if we are seeking to engender in students capacities such as curiosity or wonder or love? I could not adequately teach any of these simply by imparting knowledge *about* them. Each of these categories involves different teaching strategies and diverse learning tasks for the students. Depending on what was being taught, we should perhaps make distinctive classroom exercises and different means of evaluation.

What follows is a brief profile of diverse pedagogical strategies for teaching different things; namely, conveying information, developing skills, teaching methods, modeling values, expanding consciousness, and fostering human capacities. This reflection provides a very basic framework for issues that I will return to in more detail in other reflections.

EXAMPLE ONE: THE TREASURE OF KNOWLEDGE

Learning information is critical. It is the foundation for understanding and wisdom. It orients students to every subject. The challenging question for me was: How could I teach knowledge in ways that most engaged students so that they could best understand and remember?

Lecturing is the most common form of conveying information in the classroom. Students want lectures, partly because it is a straightforward way to learn and partly because students want to know what a teacher thinks about a particular subject.

At first I thought of lectures mainly as imparting information. Yet there is an art to imparting information that could not only be engaging but even potentially transforming. The art of lecturing cannot simply be reading an essay or talking from notes. Oral communication involves engagement, a sense of flow, and the development of an argument that ideally changes pace, builds to a climax, and leaves the hearers both satisfied and eager for more. Rhetorically speaking, a lecture can lead a class to be changed by the experience. I preferred to give ten- to twenty-minute lectures, long enough to have a focused impact and brief enough so that there was time afterward to assess the impact and to facilitate conversations among class members.

Regarding the conveying of information as an overall educational concept, there were at least four principles I found helpful for empowering students to learn and retain information: repetition, context, engagement, and enjoyment.

First Principle: Repetition

Repetition is the lifeblood of understanding and memory. If something is repeated often enough in a variety of ways, students have a much better chance of grasping it and retaining it in memory. If a student can read about it, write about it, hear about it, talk about it, and recall it for an exam or a paper (i.e., making use of different senses), the chances for short-term and long-term retention are increased significantly.

When it was important for students to learn certain complex and vital information, the process of repetition usually involved several of the following elements: 1) an assigned reading with directions to write a summary paragraph; 2) asking students to read their summaries and discuss the reading in small groups in class; 3) a brief lecture on the material; 4) a brief not-for-credit quiz, which we reviewed afterward together as a class with commentary; 5) sometimes an out-of-class assignment instructing students to repeat the information to someone who was not in the class and to encourage the listener to ask questions to draw out the student's knowledge of the subject. These experiences gave the students several opportunities to recall and repeat the information they were learning.

Giving students for-credit exams on information also focused on repetition. I was straightforward about what they needed to know. Essay exams are of course the best way to measure understanding. To test their understanding in an objective-style exam (true/false questions, matching, multiple choice, fill-in-the-blank), I included space for one sentence after each question for the student to explain their objective-style answer.

Regarding recall, some guidance I gave students before exams was this: "Don't be satisfied with simply *reviewing* the material; you must also practice *recalling* it without benefit of looking at the notes or book *before* you get to the test." Many students would say, "I reviewed all this material last night. I knew it then, but I couldn't remember it when I got into the exam." The key is for students to replicate recalling the information ahead of time while they are studying. In the case of essay exams, students were encouraged to prepare by writing outlines of answers to potential essay questions and then to memorize the outlines. These practices gave students better short-term as well as long-term retention of the material.

Second Principle: Conveying Knowledge in a Context of Coherence

Expecting students to learn isolated facts can be counterproductive if they do not see those facts in context. So, in a study guide or on an exam, students were encouraged to use journalistic questions about who, what, when, where, how, and why.

We can also encourage students to understand specific facts in terms of how they fit into a larger historical or literary context. After we had studied a Gospel, I would show students how to take one detail about that Gospel and see how they could recall, by association, many other details and themes of that Gospel as a whole. For example, the misunderstanding of the disciples in Mark can trigger recall of many episodes as well as the theme of fear as the source of misunderstanding. When the process is done around several key themes particular to each of the four Gospels, students can more easily grasp the distinctiveness of each Gospel. Using a chart that compared and contrasted the different beginnings, endings, plotline, character traits, and main themes of the four Gospels also helped students grasp and retain information about the Gospels within a framework of understanding.

Testing for context can also enhance comprehension. For example, after having taught about all four Gospels, I gave an exam with forty or so different quotations (listed randomly) from the four Gospels. Based on their coherent and comprehensive understanding of each Gospel, the students would identify which Gospel each quotation came from and then give one sentence explaining how they connected that quotation to the Gospel in question. Studying for the exam was not only a matter of learning details from the different Gospels but also of understanding them in the context of distinctive themes, characters, plot, settings, and structure of each Gospel.

Third Principle: Engagement

Students understand better when they have a purpose for reading an assignment. I found it helpful to assign students a paragraph that restated the thesis of an assigned reading and that identified the key supporting evidence. When they understood the reading well, they were able to interact with it with questions and critique—and be more engaged in class discussion.

Students were also engaged when all of them had a chance to talk about a lecture with each other. Immediately after a lecture, I would ask students to pair up briefly and to have one explain to the other what they had heard, have the other confirm or correct, and then together come up with questions or challenges to the lecture. Just because students heard and could follow a lecture as they heard it did not mean that they had understood it or would remember it. If they were able to explain it to someone else, they discovered what they understood and what they did not understand, and they had better recall.

Fourth Principle: Engagement by Making It Fun

It made sense to me that students would understand and recall information better by learning it in an entertaining way. I tried this with a course on daily life in the time of Jesus, which involved a lot of information about houses, clothes, roads, taxes, people and groups, the temple, and much more. I took the book they were reading and turned the details into cards with questions for a game. We got several boards of the popular game Trivial Pursuit, divided up into teams, and played the game with questions from first-century Israel. Because they knew they were going to play the game each day, their motivation was very high to learn this information!

EXAMPLE TWO: TEACHING A SKILL

Teaching a skill involves a very different strategy. The key is to provide a step-by-step process and then offer opportunities to practice the skill.

The Skill of Reading a Book

For a simple example, students found it helpful to learn some steps in how to read a book. I was surprised that many students did not have a method. I suggested the following: 1) Read the title and all cover information about the book. 2) Study the table of contents. 3) Scan the introduction, the first and last paragraph of every chapter, and the conclusion. 4) Now go back and read through each chapter, carefully noting the subtitles and subsections. And 5) as you go, highlight or underline key points, take notes in the margins on agreements and disagreements, and at the end of each chapter write the main point of the chapter and the key points explaining it. 6) When the book is done, list your main learnings and your main critiques. This process also made it much easier for students to review the same book later, because they could read the highlights and notes.

The obstacle to careful reading among upper class and graduate students was often this: they were so eager to critique what they had read and to offer their own distinctive point of view that they tended to skew their understanding of what they had read—in essence setting up a paper tiger so they could make a critical point about it. In that context, an assignment I gave was for students (following the steps outlined above) to write a faithful review of an assigned book *before* they offered any critique. This turned out to be especially helpful for doctoral students, since they would later be expected to summarize accurately the relevant secondary literature as part of their dissertation.

The Skill of Translating a Language

As another example, a step-by-step process for the skill of reading Greek in intermediate classes illustrates the kind of process that could be adapted to many disciplines. Generally speaking, students had strategies for translating that were scattershot and inconsistent. Regularizing their approach took the form of a step-by-step process: 1) Read the Greek several times to pick up as much as you can about the sentence. 2) Identify in English (or the translation language) the basic meaning of the Greek words that you do not know. 3) Note prefixes and suffixes that further identify tenses of verbs and cases of nouns. This involved providing single-page charts of all the grammatical choices *in a standard order*, one for verbs (mood, voice, tense, person, number, dictionary form of the word, and translation) and one for nouns (case, number, gender, dictionary form of the word, and translation). Identifying words in a standard order of identification became almost like a mantra.

More advanced steps followed: 4) Identify syntax by naming what each word is (noun, verb, connective, etc.) and what function it might perform in the clause or sentence. Unless students could identify a noun in the nominative case as the *subject* and an adjective in the accusative case as the *modifier of an object* of the verb and a verb in the subjunctive mood as expressive of a *purpose clause*, they missed the meaning. Again, a chart served to provide the main syntactical options they were likely to encounter. 5) Look up words in a Greek dictionary to determine more sophisticated semantic meanings. Doing these steps slows down the process at first; but after a while, it speeds the process up, as students are readily able to identify fully most words and to concentrate on the unfamiliar or difficult ones.

Whatever the skill being taught, it helped students when we made the approach explicit by setting out steps for the process and working with students to practice them.

EXAMPLE THREE: TEACHING A METHOD

Methods are more involved than skills. Methods are comprehensive and creative; they address complex subjects and situations; and they involve evaluation and imagination. They are the basis for critical thinking. Most innovations in biblical scholarship have come from posing new questions to the biblical texts and history. Biblical study involves such methods as textual criticism, redaction criticism, historical criticism, linguistic criticism, discourse analysis, performance criticism, empire studies, and many more. Laying out the method as a set of assumptions, a clear purpose, a set of goals, and probing questions helps to make clear the way forward. Unlike skills, methods are used in a tentative, heuristic manner—all the while honoring the text and the historical evidence as the final arbiter of meanings. Insights multiply when several methods were combined or used in tandem.

It is important for students not just to learn *about* a method but also to have the experience of *using* the method; for example, by analyzing a narrative, reconstructing historical events, exploring cultural dynamics, and discerning the rhetorical impact of a letter. Students first learned a method and then applied it to a case study.

Steps for teaching a method involve a process of weaning students from dependence on a teacher to the point where they can use the method on their own. 1) Model the method for students. Take them through the process from beginning to end. 2) Next, lead students through the process under guidance in class (perhaps in small groups and on the same text/problem), directing the process and answering questions. 3) Then give students a new assignment to do on their own, asking them to turn in both their notes and their outcomes—and give them extensive feedback. It helps to give this assignment on an identical text/problem for all students, so that they can evaluate each other's work, compare notes, and learn from each other. 4) Finally, choose another text or problem they have not studied in class as a basis to do a final project. In the final project, they are to be as clear and as explicit as possible about each step of the method and the outcome. Students can be graded on their use of the method as well as on the outcome they achieved at the end.

EXAMPLE FOUR: TEACHING VALUES: THE ETHICS OF TEACHING AND LEARNING

There are many values integral to and implicit in the educational process: love of learning; pursuing truth where the evidence leads; respect for the personal boundaries and the opinions of others; respect for academic standards, honesty, and responsibility in academic work; the ability to cooperate and partner in learning; the capacity for active listening and respectful speaking; openness to being challenged and to changing one's mind and behavior; and concern for those most at risk. Add to these the commitment of teachers in regard to knowledge of the subject matter, excellence in pedagogy, respect and affection for students, constructive rather than shaming feedback, fairness in grading, and the willingness to admit mistakes.

There are also more-encompassing social values that we seek to engender: passion for peace and nonviolence; pursuit of justice; respect for personal freedom; commitment to the common good; care for one another, especially the vulnerable; inclusiveness; responsible citizenship in society; sense of global concern; and reverence for the rest of nature. The things we do in planning and carrying out a class—both in terms of content and process—are always ethical choices that manifest such values or go against them. Nothing we do is ethically neutral.

No doubt we do foster these positive values in the course of teaching. However, we seldom make them explicit. I learned a great deal about myself and my teaching by naming these values and by asking myself and occasionally asking students specifically in what ways I did in fact model them, incorporate them into my syllabus and assignments, promote them among students, and evaluate my success or failure in doing so. Being explicit led me to be more intentional about the ethical dynamics of teaching and to make changes accordingly. If I had it to do over, I would set aside time in each course to list a set of such values and ask the students in what ways the course was succeeding in promoting them. Such a conversation would have helped me in subsequent course planning and also made students aware of the values they themselves could manifest in their learning process.

EXAMPLE FIVE: TEACHING TO EXPAND CONSCIOUSNESS

The key to expanding our consciousness is the imagination: the ability to enter and imagine the world a different way; the capacity to embrace a worldview all the while being respectful of and open to the worldviews of others; being able to embrace more than one worldview; the possibility of conceiving of new worlds; and the ability to tolerate the ambiguity involved in each of these experiences.

Many people discover expanded consciousness when they have spent time in another culture or subculture. By immersion in another society, we see our own native place from the outside. By expanding our awareness of "otherness," we are changed. We also experience the shaking of our foundations in social movements like the civil rights movement and the women's movement. Literature and film introduce students in imaginative ways to people, places, and situations different from themselves. There are ample opportunities to bring these consciousness-raising experiences into the dynamics of the classroom.

Expanding consciousness also happens with the study of the Bible. Students with a religious background often come to the study of the Bible with the idea that there is one truthful theology and one interpretation of the Bible. It can be a crisis that leads to transformation when students realize that there is not one theology, that there is not one correct interpretation of the Bible, and that the Bible itself is a collection of writings that are remarkably diverse in their worldviews.

I have used four progressive pedagogical approaches in an effort to expand consciousness and to relativize the worldviews of students in the study of the Bible.

Historical Context

First, when we look at the New Testament from a historical point of view, it is astounding how little we know with any certainty about so many things: the dates, places, and authors of different writings; the testimonies about the historical Jesus, given the differences and contradictions in the four Gospels; how the writings began as stories and letters and only many years later became accepted as Scripture; the meaning and impact of the writings in their original contexts; and so on. Simply acknowledging these uncertainties often results in a loss of certitude that the students might have entertained about these matters and challenges the worldview with which they come to the study of the Bible. Uncertainty and ambiguity about the Bible can open up opportunities for students to experience other ways of thinking.

Narrative Worlds

Second, approaching the Gospels as narratives enables one to treat the Gospels as worlds for students to enter and experience in imagination—much as one would enter the imaginative world of a short story or a film.

Narrative criticism moves away from looking *through* the narrative to the historical Jesus and instead looks at a Gospel *as a story in its own right* with characters, settings, and plot, all configuring a world with an impact on its hearers. Add to this the use of cultural anthropology to show how strange these narrative worlds are in contrast to our own. Entering these first-century stories is like walking through a door into a strange culture or crossing a border into another country.

Performance

Third, to enter the world of a Gospel or other writing of the New Testament even more deeply, I would invite students to perform passages of the New Testament from memory, while other students were audiences for the performances. When students *perform* a passage, they not only enter the world of a Gospel or a letter, they also assume the voice and the perspective of the author, and they become aware that the biblical work is designed to have a distinct rhetorical impact on hearers. All of this represents an experience of the Bible *in a different medium*. When students subsequently say, "I feel like I am encountering the Bible for the first time" or "I will never be able to read the Bible in the same way again," I know that their consciousness has indeed been changed and expanded.

The Relativity and Particularity of the New Testament Writings

Finally, when students imagine the worlds of several of the writings in the New Testament, they become aware of the relative and particular nature of each of these worlds. They discover that each New Testament writing has a somewhat different view of God, understanding of the life and work of Jesus, configuration of community, set of values and behaviors, and view of the future. Each writing expresses the creativity of a particular author and addresses the needs of a particular community. In recognizing that the writings were not addressed universally to all people in all times and in all places, students are challenged to expand their awareness of the particularity of each of the writings in the collection of the biblical canon. Becoming aware of these differences helps students to recognize that their own worldviews are also situated in time and place—and thus they can better see and evaluate the values, beliefs, and relationships of their own world as seen through the lens of the diverse perspectives of biblical writings.

EXAMPLE SIX: TEACHING TO AWAKEN AND STRENGTHEN HUMAN CAPACITIES

Here we may be moving into uncharted pedagogical territory. We can develop strategies to teach information, skills, and methods, but what about teaching human capacities and aptitudes? How do we teach curiosity? How do we open up wonder and a sense of awe? What about encouraging compassion and tolerance? What about being open to mystical experiences? What about the sheer joy of learning?

Of course, this is audacious. We don't "teach" these things. Perhaps we can engender them. Perhaps students acquire them by osmosis or contagion. Or they are awakened to them. It may be something they discover and are surprised to find. Perhaps we can model them and provide conditions for them to happen. Then together we can be open to them and linger with them and celebrate them if and when they happen.

Developing capacities like these is related to something deeper than academic studies. Such capacities have to do with our basic humanity. And isn't education about seeking to draw out the full humanity of the learners? So why not be self-conscious about fostering these capacities as part of the educational experience? Should we not work for our humanity to unfold and blossom by cultivating, where appropriate, experiences of joy and grief and fascination and compassion?

We can begin by lifting up such human qualities and experiences. We can describe our own experiences and invite students to do the same. We can reflect on them when they occur as a motif or an event in a biblical text we are studying. The New Testament manifests a wide range of human emotions, relationships, and transformations, both individual and communal, including life-changing religious experiences.

Clearly any kind of manipulation or controlling activity on our part will not be appropriate. Nor would such approaches be effective. There has to be freedom for the unexpected to happen. Such experiences often happen by indirection in the course of doing other things. And, of course, such capacities are not something that can be evaluated and graded. Nevertheless, affirmation and encouragement may be essential. I often tell students at the beginning of the course: "You will be studying the New Testament, reading books, discussing the subject matter, and writing papers. Nevertheless, some of the most important dynamics in the course may be deeper human experiences that happen because of your personal or group encounter with these astounding writings. I encourage you to be open." Do the students expect a class to change their minds and hearts? Why not? If we do not expect the unexpected we will likely not encounter it.

In fostering the last three approaches—learning values, expanding consciousness, and awakening capacities—I occasionally asked students to keep a journal of their personal experiences in relation to the class, not to be graded or even read but as a means of tapping into these deeper strains of learning.

EXPANDING THE POSSIBILITIES

No one teaches everything at once. And no one teaches everything the same way. Laying out the diverse approaches to teaching may help to sort out just what it is we want the students to learn at any given time, enabling us to make use of the distinct modes of pedagogical interactions that need to happen for one goal or another to be achieved. Clarifying the possibilities of what we are teaching and what it is that students are learning can engender opportunities for greater effectiveness in the classroom than might otherwise have been the case.

4

Hospitality in the Classroom

THERE IS LITTLE MEANINGFUL and critical dialogue in a classroom unless it is a safe and friendly place for students to be engaged with others in the pursuit of learning. An ethos of hospitality contributes significantly to such an atmosphere.

I learned about a teacher's hospitality from the most loved teacher and chaplain at Carthage College, Dudley Riggle. Dudley has a profound theology of grace, an unconditional acceptance and appreciation of everyone; and everything he does is informed by it. Dudley carried that gracious care into the classroom by anticipating what students might be thinking and feeling, and then putting them at ease.

Here's how Dudley described his philosophy and practices of teaching to me in my early years of teaching: "Much of my approach to teaching has to do with hospitality. I arrive early and welcome the students as they come in. I put on the chalkboard the list of things we will cover during that class period. I learn their names at the beginning of the course. I get their papers back on time. I see routines as matters of hospitality. . . . I find," Dudley concluded, "that if I take them seriously as students, they will take *themselves* seriously and do their best work."

I was so taken with this image of hospitality that it reoriented my approach to the classroom. I saw that hospitality is not just some spice added onto a recipe for good learning. Rather, hospitality is a key ingredient to the experience of good learning.

HOSPITALITY AS SACRED TRUST

The image of hospitality is often associated with our homes. If we imagine the classroom to be our home, how would we treat our guests? Hospitality can be a sacred art meant to give the invited guests—friend, acquaintance, or stranger—the most meaningful and welcoming experience we can offer. Just so, students should feel at ease and be glad they came, not because of patronizing gestures but through genuine openness.

In ancient Israel, hospitality was a sacred trust of caring for and protecting strangers and aliens. Hospitality was not just for neighbors or for "people like us" but also for strangers. There was a solidarity with the guest that required their needs be met and that they be treated with kindness. Israelites were told to recall that, at one time, *they* had been strangers and that they should learn from their experience. So too, we teachers were students once. Could we not treat these student-strangers who are in our classes as we once had wished to be treated?

Hospitality was also central to the early Christian movement. Proclaimers and healers went from place to place depending upon the hospitality of others to welcome them in their homes. Hospitality was a profound expression of solidarity, a covenant of peace and protection. To give and to receive hospitality was to acquire "brothers" and "sisters." Some New Testament writers portrayed hospitality as a metaphor for all Christian relationships. Paul writes the admonition to "welcome one another" (Rom 15:7). This places hospitality as a holy act that imitates the way we have been treated as part of the Christian community, as Paul adds, "just as Christ has welcomed you." This is an invitation to make any place a sacred space of hospitality.

HOSPITALITY IN PRACTICE

So how do we enable students to feel welcome? How do we create an atmosphere where people are free to speak and learn without being anxious or fearful? How do we facilitate for them the most meaningful classroom experiences—whether the class is ten or forty people? If dialogue is to be honest and if students are to be open to transformation, then students need to know that they are in a place where they and their opinions will be valued. Here are some things I tried.

Arriving Early

First, I arrived before the students. Often, I would arrange the chairs and tables for that particular class. I got my papers out and ready for teaching. Then I just walked among the students as they arrived, greeting them, talking with them, and asking how they were doing. On the first day of class, I shook hands with them as they entered the classroom. I thanked them for taking the class and told them that I looked forward to being with them. I was indeed genuinely grateful that they were there, and I wanted them to know that.

If on the first day I had not met them before, I would learn something about the students—where they were from or what program they were in. After the class had been going for some weeks, I used this time before class to ask someone how they were feeling or how their family was doing. Sometimes I would take a student aside before class to forewarn them confidentially that they did not do so well on a paper I was about to return to them, and I invited them to talk with me about it later. I also lingered after each class as a means to make myself available. From the beginning of the course, I assumed that my relationship with individual students would last through the semester and beyond. I tried to welcome people to the classroom as I would welcome them to my home.

It's a Matter of Timing

Second, I began on time and ended on time. This seemed to be a matter of basic respect. If some students were late, I did not wait for them. This would penalize students who came on time, and it would be teaching people that if they came late they would not miss anything. At the same time, I was glad to see students even when they arrived late—and I assumed that there were good reasons people were late. Many of the students made great sacrifices to be in school. And there were always some who had traveled a good distance on that day to be there. So I felt that I owed it to the students to fill the class time with good learning experiences.

And I ended the class on time. Despite my best efforts, I sometimes found in myself an urge to keep on making that important point at the end of class, even if it meant that the students had to stay a few minutes longer. But this was not respectful of them. Besides, at this point, they were giving signals by putting away notebooks and zipping up backpacks. So what were they learning at that point?

Also, in the early years I usually waited until the last few minutes of the class period to go over the assignment for the next class. That did not work well. Invariably, there was not time to explain it well and not time to field questions for clarification. I would end up going past the end of the class time. So I decided to give the assignment for the next class period at the beginning of the class or midway through the class. This way I could be sure that the assignment was clear, that the students had time to ask questions about it, and that I would not go past the ending time of the class. Going beyond the end of class is either poor planning or a matter of taking myself and my subject too seriously. There is seldom anything so important that it cannot be interrupted or wait until the next time.

Where Everybody Knows Your Name

Third, as an expression of hospitality, I got to know my students' names. Especially with large classes, there was a need to be intentional about learning student names. And it was well worth the effort. Right after registration, before the course began, I requested the class list from the registrar and I began to memorize it. If there was a campus photo directory, I connected the names to the pictures and practiced them. Then when I arrived at the first class period, I already knew the names, and I would begin to correlate the names and photos with the actual students. I repeated their names in my mind as I met them. I usually found some reason for them to talk in pairs during the first class; and while they were talking with each other, I would take the list and practice the names in my head. Even with a class of forty or forty-five, I knew their names before the end of the first class period. Of course, I quickly forgot. But I practiced again, and by the second or third class, I could address everyone by name. This effort paid dividends in fostering the personal nature of learning.

I also led students through a process that would enable them to know each other's names as well. Knowledge is power, and if the teacher is the only one who has a class list, then students are placed at a decided disadvantage. So, all students got a class list with the names of all the students. In the first class, I would invite each student to introduce herself or himself to the class. I would stop every few minutes and see if the students could recall the names of the last six or so students who had introduced themselves—without first consulting their class list. I did this by having the students work briefly in pairs to recall the names; and, of course, they would also get to know their conversation partner in the process.

Having students learn each other's names served to generate an ethos of dialogical learning in the class. The students were going to work together in small and large groups throughout the course—both inside and outside of class time—so they would be learning from each other. I reminded them that "this semester, we'll spend forty hours together in class. It would be very helpful if we knew each other's names!"

I came to see the classroom as an important opportunity to build community. In this way, learning became a significant social event for the students. They came to class to be with their friends and to talk about things that mattered to them. So I became intentional about helping students to get to know each other better and to make new friends. I made sure that students regularly got in small groups with different people so they could learn from everyone. I frequently had students say on their evaluation of a class: "I learned as much from other students as I learned from the teacher." Learning each other's names in the very first class period gave the message that they would become partners in learning.

Let Them Know That the Course Matters to You

Another thing I did as a matter of hospitality was to communicate with students between classes. Of course, when I saw them outside of class, I greeted them, and I often asked how the class was going for them. When I asked them how the class was working for them, I did not do this in a perfunctory way. I gave them my full attention to let them know that I was serious about wanting to know how they were doing and if there were any blocks to their learning.

But I also learned to communicate regularly by e-mail (well before digital learning!). As soon as I got the class list, I prepared a distribution list of the students and sent an e-mail to them before the course began—welcoming them and saying how I looked forward to the class. After each of the weekly classes, I sent an e-mail message telling them how much I appreciated the class and their enthusiastic participation, often noting some conversation that was especially meaningful or naming something else that I enjoyed about the last class. I usually also included a copy of the assignments for the next class as a reminder and to provide information for those who could not attend. The message was brief. But it made it clear to the students that we were a community and that each of them was an important part of it. For some students, this proactive communication was an important connection with me, with the class, and with the subject matter. It also made it clear that I was accessible to them.

DON'T LEAVE THEM IN THE DARK

One of the first things we learn as teachers is that students need a syllabus. Most teachers prepare rather thorough syllabi. Unfortunately, it took me a while to appreciate this practice. For years, I gave out a syllabus for each course but only with minimal information: a list of class dates, the subjects to be dealt with, and some projected assignments. I gave the detailed directions for assignments, class period by class period. And I distributed in-class handouts class by class. *I myself* knew what I was planning to do, but the *students* did not know in detail what would happen next until they got the assignments for the next class.

Then, my wife got cancer and endured a three-year siege of illness before she got a stem cell transplant that saved her life and restored her health. Also, at that time we were raising two young grandchildren in our home. In addition, we lived ninety miles from LSTC. During that time, I could not be sure I would be able to arrive ahead of any given class to prepare and photocopy the handouts. Nor could I be sure I would not need, on any given day, to turn the class over to one of my colleagues who had so graciously volunteered to substitute for me when I could not be there. So during the first summer of my wife's illness, I developed a comprehensive syllabus for the whole semester—not only class dates and subjects to be covered but also assignments for each class in complete detail, every handout for every class, and extensive directions for writing papers. I gave the entire syllabus out the first class period, almost ninety pages!

I was delighted by the difference it made (but not for the tree!). To begin with, it made a great difference for me. I did not have to formulate the assignments and class exercises before each class. I did not have to rush around to get handouts copied and ready. I could concentrate on planning the flow of the class period itself, developing the subject matter, and preparing my spirit for interaction with the students. And such a complete syllabus made a significant difference for students. All their handouts and assignments were organized in one place. They could plan ahead for weekly work and term papers. They could consult ahead on just what would be involved in the writing of the papers and the basis upon which they would be evaluated. And anyone who substituted for me had everything they needed to carry on without confusion.

Students already have enough reasons for anxiety built into the educational experience. They did not need *unnecessary* anxiety due to a lack of information or due to obstacles that prevented them from planning ahead. So, part of the hospitality I learned to show was to give them all the information they needed about the course at the start so as to alleviate any unwarranted apprehensions. Then they could focus better on the learning itself.

Timely Feedback

Along with this process of letting people know ahead of time what to expect in the course came the importance of giving timely feedback to the students' work. First, there was feedback *in class* for daily assignments. When students did an assignment for a particular class and then did not have a chance to discuss it or deal with it in that class, this was often discouraging. Why prepare for class when the assignment is not relevant to what happens in the class for which they have prepared? So I tried always to have the students discuss or do a cooperative exercise using their preparations for *that* class.

Then there were the assignments they turned in for grading or credit. Here, I tried to return their work on the next class period. For some students, there is a psychological block to moving on to new material until they know how well or how poorly they might have done in previous work. So I was committed (even though I sometimes did not succeed) to return their work by the very next class period. And it was clear to the students that I had indeed read their work, because I gave extensive reflections and evaluation. Following Dudley's lead, it seemed to me to be a matter of hospitality to take students seriously by taking their work seriously.

Food and Hospitality

Finally, food is an important aspect of hospitality. Sharing food and drink is an important form of community building. Obviously, students cannot share meals together unless the class agrees to go to a local restaurant before or after class. Sometimes one of my students would bring cookies they baked. It created a festive atmosphere and it took seriously the fact that students need a break and some sustenance to get through a three-hour seminar—or whatever length it may be.

One LSTC colleague began her courses by inviting students to sign up to take turns bringing snacks for the class. Each week the students looked forward to sharing these goodies at break time. Such a practice increased the social relationships among members of the class. Instead of scattering at break time to find coffee machines or student lounges, they stayed in the vicinity and talked with each other. Such an arrangement also made it easier to reconvene the class after the break.

Be at Home Here

In the end, the ultimate goal of hospitality is, in some sense, to transcend just hospitality. It would be limiting to think of the class as *my* classroom and the students as guests only. The purpose of hospitality is to make people feel at home. "My classroom is your classroom." In the most basic sense, all class participants are part of the hospitality that contributes to the meaningfulness and effectiveness of a course. On occasion I heard complaints from students about another course they were taking. I would say to the students: "Why do you think that you are helpless about this? As a member of that class, you have power. You have every right to speak with the teacher about the problems as you see them and to suggest ways that would facilitate learning in a more constructive way." And I hoped such an attitude would pervade my classes; namely, that students had a sense of co-ownership of the class—a sense that the commitment of everyone, the participation of everyone, and the evaluation of the class by everyone were critical to the success of the course in meeting its objectives. I often said to one student or another, "Thanks for what you contribute to the effectiveness of our class."

A colleague in pastoral care developed a "covenant" with students at the beginning of her courses. Together, they outlined the goals of the course and what they would expect of themselves and each other—teacher with students, students with teacher, and students with each other. Then they agreed to the covenant. This process created an atmosphere that it is "our" class and that all of us contribute to making it work well. I learned about this approach too late to try it myself. But I recognized that such a covenant expressed what I had been seeking to engender. That is, we work together to become a community of learners with relationships that allow us to be open and honest with each other in meaningful dialogue.

AN ATMOSPHERE OF HOSPITALITY IN THE INSTITUTION AS A WHOLE

In any academic setting, hospitality is not just for the classroom. It is for the places of entrance, the library, the cafeteria, the president's office, the dean's office, the business office, the registrar's office, the community life office, the admissions office. Hospitality belongs to everyone, from the maintenance staff to the president's secretary. As one maintenance person said to me, "I want everyone who comes here to know that we are glad to see them."

An especially exemplary place of the hospitality at our seminary was the Language Resource and Writing Center. It was abuzz with activity. When you entered, you saw people from domestic and international places of origin conversing with each other in many accents and languages. Here students gathered to mentor each other in writing, do group assignments for class, use the computers, take classes on how to study, and get tutoring in English as a second language. Because many of those who came to the center were seeking academic assistance, they often entered feeling vulnerable. But the atmosphere of friendliness overcame their apprehensions—with someone at the desk to welcome people, the availability of inexpensive snacks and often some free food, tables with chairs in small rooms for mentoring, colorful artwork, photographs of those who made use of the center, and a director whose door was always open. It was a very hospitable place—a model of mutual teaching and learning, the ingredients of which could be adapted to many classrooms.

SO WHAT?

All of these elements of hospitality are important ingredients to good learning. They not only create a safe space for learning; they foster an *ethos* of trust and openness. They generate an atmosphere where students and their ideas will be taken seriously—honored and engaged constructively. They enable deep and honest conversations to take place. They provide space for learning that can involve challenge and growth. They create community where, at any given time, all can be teachers and learners. In the end, hospitality does not have to do with a series of activities or pedagogical strategies or contextual mechanics. Rather, hospitality has to do with relationships. There can be no productive dialogue without good relationships. And hospitality clearly fosters good relationships.

5

Radical Hospitality

THE GOAL OF MY EFFORTS to show hospitality as a teacher was to engender an *ethos* of profound respect. My role was to model such respect. I did not always succeed in doing that.

There was a question on the LSTC course evaluation form that students filled out for each class at the end of the semester: *Did the professor respect the views of those in the class?* The answer was on a scale of one to ten, ten being the highest. Occasionally there would be a three or four from someone, and I knew that something had gone terribly wrong. I looked to see if others had also given low marks on their evaluations for the same course—to see if there was a pattern of negative responses. If there was only one person who gave a low mark, I tried to think back over what I might have said to someone that led that person to feel disrespected. And I considered that this person might have discerned a general problem in communication in the class as a whole, of which I and other students were unaware. Evaluations were generally anonymous (signing it was a choice). I wished I had been able to ask the person and learn from them, so I could have avoided the problem in the future. And I wished there had been a space below the question on the form that gave the student an opportunity to explain their numerical evaluation.

VALUE OTHERS DEEPLY AND DO NOT DISPARAGE THEIR VIEWS

But the issue of respect had to go beyond the modeling by the teacher, especially in religion classes. The question of respect toward each other was so important in New Testament classes because we were dealing with things of ultimate value to people. We were dealing with their self-conception as a person, their experience of God, their longing for a just world, the values to which they have committed their lives, as well as the hopes they have for the future—for themselves, for their families, for friends, for the world. The New Testament writings deal with the most profound human issues. They were written by people who expected the end of their world to occur imminently and who were being persecuted for their beliefs and actions. In that context, everything was incisive and acute. Everything had to do with life and death. The matters they dealt with were and are matters that matter.

If the students in my seminary classes were not themselves dealing with significant issues in this very class they were taking, then it was my job to remind them that the folks in the parishes they would later serve *would* be dealing with them—in spades. So if the class experience was to be more profound than perfunctory, more personal than simply intellectual, then it was important that we learned how to talk about these critical issues with each other in the most thoughtful and respectful ways.

Ultimately, then, the question of hospitality was about the respect that all of us were giving to each other in the classroom. I say "to each other" because it was my task to see that respect pervaded the whole learning process, not just my own actions and attitudes as the teacher. I use the word "hospitality" because that term is fundamentally about how we value and respect others, how we receive each other, and how we talk about groups or individuals who are not represented in the class, including people with whom we may strongly disagree.

My colleague at LSTC, Linda Thomas, provided our faculty with a set of guidelines for respectful discussion that lays out the features of communal hospitality.

GUIDELINES FOR CIVILITY IN THE CLASSROOM

- Respect the personhood of others, while engaging their ideas.
- Carefully represent the views of those with whom we are in disagreement.
- Be careful in defining terms, avoiding needless use of inflammatory words.
- Be careful in the use of generalizations; where appropriate, offer specific evidence.
- Seek to understand the experiences out of which others have arrived at their view. Hear the stories of others, as we share our own.
- Exercise care that expressions of personal offense at the differing opinion of others not be used as means of inhibiting dialogue.
- Be a patient listener before formulating responses.
- Be open to change in our own position and patient with the process of change in the thinking and behavior of others.
- Make use of facilitators and mediators where communication can be served by it.
- Always remember that people are defined, ultimately, by their relationship with God—not by the flaws we discover or think we discover in their views and actions.

Stated in a negative way, the basic principle of these excellent guidelines is: do no harm. Stated in a positive way, the main principle is: receive the ideas and values of other individuals and groups, even and especially those who disagree with you, with the respect with which you would want yourself and your ideas to be received.

A DISTURBING EXAMPLE

When I read the evaluations for one seminary course, I came across a comment that deeply troubled me. On the evaluation form, the student was registering her experience of being put down and marginalized. Fortunately, the student had signed her name on the evaluation and I was able to follow up with her. She was a Roman Catholic laywoman who was taking a degree program at a sister institution in Hyde Park, the Catholic

Theological Union. She had signed up for an LSTC class as part of her program. So I e-mailed her a note saying that "it would be very helpful to me if you would be willing to give some specific examples of comments and tangible kinds of behavior that made you feel this way. I am eager for this not to happen again, and I want to know the nature of it so I can head it off."

In order for you to appreciate all the dynamics of the situation, I have included her recounting (with her permission) of her experience in full.

> Dear Dave,
>
> Thank you for your e-mail.
>
> The first incident occurred on the very first day of class. This student had just met me, and remarked vehemently on the thick-headedness of the Roman Catholic Church in its stance on the ordination of women. Now, while I happen to disagree with Rome's current stance, I was somewhat surprised and not sure how to react. When I first meet someone of another faith tradition, I do not remark on what I perceive as a negative aspect of that person's faith tradition. Pastorally, I would think to do so could be a bit off-putting. When I am engaged in any interfaith/inter-religious dialogue, I think it is important to establish a personal relationship with the person, and then respectfully question issues about their faith tradition, so it is clear that the other's faith tradition is honored, but an aspect is puzzling. Had that been the only incident, I would have written it off as my being sensitive.
>
> For me the most egregious incident came when we were in small groups. We were to discuss the "social location" that we bring when we read Scripture. A student at the table in front of mine said—loud enough for his table and mine to hear—"now that he's not Catholic, he actually reads the Bible." The remark was hurtful and insulting enough, but what compounded it was that the student's entire table laughed, as well as two students at my table, with one student at my table chiming in "that's the truth." Essentially, about 1/3 of the class thought nothing about such a remark, and thought it was humorous. Their complicit cooperation in this prejudicial remark was equally disturbing. Dave, I am a Catholic who does read Scripture regularly, who treasures reading Scripture. The Word of God, as Heb 4:12 states, is "alive" for me. Apparently, another student must have seen the shocked/stunned expression on my face, because the student who made the original remark apologized by explaining he

"didn't mean anything by it." I have no doubt that if a Catholic was not in the class, the remark would have been laughed at, and that would have been the end of it. But the remark was a derogatory, discriminatory remark (I felt), aimed at putting down one group (Catholics) while exalting one's own group—which struck me as extremely counter-[the Gospel of]Mark. That aspect concerns me, because these students are future pastors who will be endowed with the privilege and responsibility of preaching and forming a congregation; I worry that prejudice or prejudicial attitudes might be spread to these good people's congregations.

In another small group session, a different LSTC student remarked that the religion of Islam is all based on fear and punishment. When I said that I respectfully disagree with that student's point on Islam, I was told I was wrong, that this student even argues with professors regarding Islam and that since 9/11, people have just been "nice" to Muslims—resulting in bad teaching about Islam. This was an incident where I knew to say anything further would fall on "deaf ears." While I have taken a class on Islam, have Muslim friends, participated in an interfaith dialogue trip and various activities, if this student argues and still disagrees with everything a professor on Islam says . . . I don't have the Islamic training of a scholar, I could only witness to my personal experience, which I tried to do. Again, it was the prejudice that concerned me—for that student's future congregation.

Another student in a different small group session remarked about the fundamentalist Christians and "their" beliefs, with references to "those" people. This same student also remarked about "those" superstitious Catholics who saw the Virgin Mary in the underpass, and who look for visions of Mary in cornflakes. And while I personally don't look for Mary in salt stains or cereal, there is probably a way to respect the faith of those who might without being contemptuous. Perhaps by respecting their search for God, we could journey together, while disengaging ourselves from superstitions, and other things that keep us from full union with God. (And I write this knowing that I can just as easily judge others!)

Truthfully, after a while, I became accustomed to hearing remarks about "those people," whether "those people" were Catholics, Muslims, fundamentalists, and—one night—the poor and what "they" (inappropriately) choose to want for Christmas. (That discussion was I believe, the first time I had the courage to

> speak up in a plenary session, the numerous remarks about the poor and their erroneous judgment [were] too bothersome for me to remain silent.)
>
> Dave, please understand that I only wrote the concerns about my classmates in the evaluations (both final, and half way through the semester) so that these attitudes can be addressed and prevented. It was not to malign anybody, or even because my feelings were hurt. I especially did not do so to hurt your feelings. It was difficult for me to do so; I only articulated the concerns because I believe I have a moral/ethical duty to do so—in the hopes of building up future pastors who will, in turn, help build the Reign of God.
>
> Again, Dave, I hope that my elaborating on these incidents is not hurtful to you. You were always and consistently gracious and a welcoming presence to me. Your greeting and welcoming me every week meant a great deal to me. Thank you for sharing so much of your knowledge and of yourself—your personal struggles (i.e. with Jairus' daughter pericope). You gave very generously of yourself to the class. I am grateful to have taken a course with you, and would eagerly do so again.
>
> I wish you and your family all the best and many continued blessings from God.
>
> Peace and joy,

You can imagine how I felt receiving this report of her experiences. I had such compassion for her and such regret and anger that this had occurred. How could these things happen in a seminary where we proactively encourage regard for one another and profess to honor diversity? I had to acknowledge that there might have been less hospitality and less respect practiced in many more situations than I had been aware of. If I had been unaware of it in my classes, I had most likely also been unaware of it elsewhere in our seminary life.

ADDRESSING THE ISSUES

In response to this situation, I had a lot of questions. How can I understand the dynamics of these events? And how can I prevent them from happening again? How can I become aware of it when it happens? How can I address it when it occurs? What can the seminary do as an institution to foster a greater ethos of respect? What should I do?

Being Explicit About What Is Expected

There is every good reason to speak about these kinds of situations at the beginning of a class, sharing the guidelines for civility and giving examples of offenses and examples of how to deal with them when they occur. This alerts everyone and anticipates what may happen when an incident occurs. Such explicit guidelines would be especially helpful in classes where students are together a lot in small groups. There is no way for the teacher to monitor all that may happen; therefore, training and trusting the students become essential.

Modeling Respect for Everyone

The comments by students were crass stereotypes made about other individuals and groups. Yet, at one level, why should I be surprised at all? I should know from my own inner dialogues and unguarded private conversations how much it reflects our human nature. It seems to be built into our human genes that we tend to define ourselves over against other groups by an "us and them" mentality at various levels. When that happens, the other groups become foils for our superiority and the superiority of our traditions. We put others down as a way to lift ourselves up. When Jesus tells us to love our enemies and to consider the hated Samaritan as a model of ethical behavior and when Paul admonishes people to "consider others better than yourself" (Phil 2:3), they were promoting attitudes and actions that were counterintuitive to our basic human instincts.

So I needed to be careful here. Given my compassion for the victim, I might be so incensed at the offenders that I would just end up drawing the line between "us and them" in a different place—between those who do and those who do not show respect to others. So I had to think of this as a common human trait in *all* of us that we needed to address as such. We will not transform people to resist their human nature by lecturing and shaming. Though the behavior of the students violated a deeply held value of mine, I needed to treat the offending students as I wished them to treat others. The behavior represented an issue deeper than a matter of discipline. Issues such as this may give us a rare opportunity to talk together about this problem at a profound level.

Sharing Critique in the Context of a Relationship of Respect

Students showed disregard for their classmate without even knowing her. She was subjected to disparaging remarks about her Roman Catholic community. And she had it absolutely right: if you disagree with another's traditions, first establish a relationship of openness and respect, and then you can share your puzzlement or concern about certain aspects of their tradition out of a sense of solidarity with that person.

We Are All Implicated

Apart from our Roman Catholic student, we were all implicated. The students who made the remarks were surely complicit. The students who laughed and joined in were complicit. The students who overheard the remarks without challenging them were implicated. I was responsible because I did not set clear guidelines or monitor the small groups adequately. And the seminary as a whole might have done a better job of promoting guidelines for conversations in all classes to be included in every syllabus. Perhaps our course evaluations should include the question: *Did the students in this class show respect for each other?*

Beware of Unanticipated Consequences

Some of the disparaging remarks reported above were made about people who were not part of our group as a class or as a seminary or as a denomination. This made it all the more important that I as a teacher model respectful talk about *every* person and group. I became acutely aware that if I disparaged a group not represented in the class, say fundamentalists, three things would happen. First, if it turned out that there were students in the room who shared a literalist approach to the Bible, they would be hurt and shut down. Second, such talk would destroy all of the students' trust in me as a teacher. If I were a student and heard a teacher talk that way about *other* people, I would wonder if he or she might not also talk about *me* and my views that way when I was not present. Third, such talk creates a climate of intolerance. It would therefore be giving others permission to do the same. So we might add to the guidelines listed above: *Speak about all people outside the classroom with respect.*

Be Aware of the Power Dynamics

The groups that were attacked in this class seemed to run the gamut from Catholics to fundamentalists to Muslims to the poor. As long as we are part of a majority in a group comprised of like-minded people (Lutherans) and on our own turf (in a class at LSTC) and predominantly from the same economic class (middle), we will be in danger of exerting our power by talking about other groups. As long as the group is predominantly like minded, then the group may think it can get away with making disparaging remarks about other groups or even making comments that disrespect one or two people in the class. And no one (at least no one in a like-minded group) will think the less of us for it.

We can learn from the power dynamics of this situation when we imagine a reversal of the situation. How would I speak if I were the guest? If I were the only LSTC student in a class at the Catholic Theological Union, would I have said the same things? Or how would I talk about Muslims if there were Muslim students in this class who presented matters from their point of view? And how would I feel if others disparaged my tradition?

Providing a Safe Atmosphere to in Which Name Offenses

Usually people who are victimized by disparagement or who are defending groups that have been disparaged are a minority in a class. It takes courage to speak up. Ideally, it would be helpful if students felt confident enough in a safe context to share their objections with each other so that the hurt or the injustice could be addressed. Maybe I as a teacher could have provided some protocols at the beginning of the course regarding what people might say in such circumstances. Hopefully, what followed would be an interaction that rectified the situation, all the while treating the offender and the one speaking up with respect. Under any circumstances, I as a teacher could make myself accessible for students to share their experiences with me in confidence. And unless I explicitly invite students to do so, I doubt if they would be likely to do it.

What Can Be Learned?

Maybe every institution should require all students to participate in a diversity workshop. After all, many corporations have regular diversity training sessions for their employees. At a minimum, open discussions would be essential. Seminary students preparing to preach can take note and apply this to their future ministries. Can they prepare sermons in such a way as to anticipate how people from very diverse social locations would respond were they present—Jews, poor people, those of differing gender or sexual orientation, rich people, or people of another denomination? Do they prepare sermons to speak only to the in-crowd, or do they preach in such a way that they could preach those same words also in a very different venue—say in a homeless shelter or at a synagogue or in a jail. Understanding the power dynamics *now*, in seminary, is critical for ministry *later*. The classroom atmosphere can provide teachable moments that may have significant implications for the future vocation of the students.

The same can be true for college students entering their vocation as citizens who will contribute to the well-being of society. Why not make it part of a student's educational preparation to receive diversity training in college and to reinforce it in every class—whether they be college students entering careers in the larger work world or seminary students entering ministry.

ENGENDERING RESPECT IN THE CLASSROOM

How can we positively generate respect in students, and how can we create an ethos in the classroom so that this kind of talk is less likely to happen? As I argued above, one step is to set guidelines and to go over them in the class. A second step is for me to model these guidelines. A third step is for me to encourage all of us in the class respectfully to challenge each other when we perceive that the guidelines are not being met. Perhaps the most important step is to consider that we may indeed learn from those with whom we disagree. What else?

Openness

More important than guidelines and modeling may be the intangible ethos of openness. The respect I am talking about here is about so much more than the mechanics of conversation. It is about a root-deep posture of openness toward other human beings.

A fundamental aspect of that openness is a profound desire to want to know what another person thinks—to ask questions, to be silent in the presence of another person, to listen intently without judgment, to explore another's world with imagination, and to enter with empathy into the life of another. This takes an un-self-centered act of letting go of one's self, of putting our responses on hold, of not trying to think of a retort or a creative answer or to "fix" a problem.

Now, class discussion is not therapy. And I do not think it is wise for students to delve deeply into each other's personal lives in a classroom setting. Nor do I mean to suggest that people are so fragile that we have to handle each other with kid gloves. Nor does it mean we cannot express strong feelings and entertain vigorous debate. Challenging others can be a matter of respect. *How* we do it is critical. The older I get, the more I have come to think that it is a rare occurrence to find people who are genuinely interested in what others have to say. It is quite uncommon to find people who listen actively without judgment or advice. Still, this is what I wanted to foster in my classes in ordinary conversation about the interpretation of the Bible—people who are deeply interested in probing what the Bible says and what other students think about what the Bible says.

The Art of Listening

Here are two suggestions for practicing the art of listening in the classroom. Both can be done as exercises in pairs. The first exercise can perhaps be done in response to something controversial that has come up in class. Let one of the pair begin on a subject. Let that person say all they want to say. The other person can listen and ask questions for clarity but not for the purpose of challenging or making points. Then, when the one person has finished speaking, it is up to the listener to repeat or summarize faithfully what that person has said, to the satisfaction of the person who was speaking. The listener then asks if they got it right in echoing what she or he said, and the original speaker can confirm or correct. The original speaker can then add anything they would like to add, and again the listener is to summarize. At that point, then, the roles are reversed, and they go through the same procedure. The second person speaks until they feel as if they have been fully heard and understood. When this is complete, they begin to respond to what the other has said, pro and con, with the same process. This may lead to some sharp differences, but the process keeps going. Again they take turns listening and summarizing. Eventually, some measure of agreement is discovered or the conversation partners agree to disagree, but they have at least understood why the other person takes the position they take and how each has appreciated the other.

The second practice is simply to explore what another person thinks. Imagine you were interviewing someone, say for a talk show or as a journalist. They are the guest, the focus of attention, and you are the interviewer. You focus on the matters at issue in the classroom for that day. You begin with some general questions. Then you may have questions suggested to you by what that person has said. This may lead to even more probing questions. You are engaged in drawing this person out. Maybe you have questions that get to the heart of the experiences that have led the person to think as they do. Maybe you have questions that lead them to think about things they have not yet formulated. You may ask the person to explain certain things you do not understand or agree with. You may state your own opinion about something as part of the conversation, but then the focus quickly moves back to the interviewee, and what their response might be. After this process, the places are exchanged, and the interview moves to the other person. When this exercise is first attempted, the person being interviewed may feel as if they are being grilled. It is therefore important to agree that at any point, the person may respectfully decline to answer a question or pursue a line of thinking. Again, the idea is to get past a wooden use of this "mutual exploration" process and incorporate it into the ordinary classroom discussions that take place in pairs or small groups or even with the class as a whole.

Both of these practices can be done in pairs by everyone in the class at the same time. Or they can be done by two people with the rest of the class observing the process—a sort of fishbowl setup. However, the point is that people treat each other with an open hospitality and genuine interest, identifying and honoring similarities and differences. The idea is to understand empathetically what has led another to take a certain point of view.

We have given each other a voice and treated each other with respect. We have empowered others to speak because they know they will be heard and understood. This is a fundamental goal of any educational experience, and it is an outcome that students can bring about for each other.

THE OPPRESSION OF THE BIBLE AND THE USE OF THE BIBLE TO OPPRESS

In studying the Bible, there is an additional dimension of hospitality, namely, the respectful hospitality shown (or not shown) by the New Testament writings themselves. How can we say "do no harm" when various biblical writers discriminate against Jews, women, and slaves, foster racism and homophobia, and advise people to submit to an oppressive government? This is an aspect of the Bible we must face honestly if the Bible is to be part of a respectful dialogue. I like to think that we are in dialogue with the Bible, eager to let it say what it has to say without twisting it or making it say what we think it *should* say. As with our contemporary conversation partners, we may want to give it the benefit of the doubt by putting it in historical context, aware that these writings are from six thousand to two thousand years old. But we also need to be aware that the Bible has power in our society. Our dialogue with the Bible should acknowledge its power—such that we seek to further its power for good and at the same time stand against its use for oppression, discrimination, and marginalization. Fortunately, much of the Bible does stand in opposition to these things, and we can use life-giving and liberating parts of the Bible to counter those parts that have been used destructively.

Either way, the key principle is this: never use the Bible to oppress. In that regard, Christians have a terrifying history of harm to so many groups and individuals. I never encountered it as starkly as in Neil Elliott's book *Liberating Paul*. The title is a double entendre meant to suggest that the author wanted to liberate Paul from those who would use Paul to do great harm. And he also wanted to show that Paul was actually in fact a very liberating figure. His first chapter blew me away. He cites example after historical example of the ways in which the letters attributed to Paul (some letters attributed to Paul were really written by others after his death) have been used to devastating effect against groups of people. He goes into great detail about the horrors perpetrated upon women in early American life, especially in relation to the Salem witch trials. He talks about the way Paul's letters were employed by slave owners to justify the ownership and brutal treatment of slaves in pre–Civil War America. Then he catalogues the atrocities upon Jews in the Holocaust and the ways Paul's letters were so fully misused in that tragedy. He recounts the ways in which the US government supported tyrants in Central America and the ways they not only approved but even trained Central American people to kill any who stood in opposition, citing the Pauline admonition to "let every person be subject to the governing authorities" (Rom 13:1) as justification for their actions. And he recounts the suppression of homosexuals as deviants who deserve nothing but shunning and death.

It took me a long time to get over that chapter when I first read it. Even now, every time I read it, I am deeply chagrined. And I reread it every semester with my class. In classes on Paul, it was one of the first readings I required. Students were to state the thesis or main point of the chapter and then enumerate the examples Elliott gives to support his point. The discussions about this assignment were often among the best in the entire course. Students were open to doing some meaningful soul searching. Some students attested to the harm that the letters attributed to Paul had done in their own lives and communities—a pastor advising a wife to stay in an abusive relationship or the grandmother of a black student refusing to read anything written by Paul to her children or grandchildren. Only as we were able face up to this harm from Paul's letters could we be in genuine dialogue with Paul.

To be sure, Elliott exonerates Paul from much of this harm. He explains what most scholars agree upon, namely, that Paul did not write the letters with the household codes that subordinate women and slaves. These household codes appear only in Colossians, Ephesians, and the Pastoral Epistles—letters attributed to Paul but most likely written pseudonymously in Paul's name after Paul's death. He also points out that some of the harmful passages in the genuine letters of Paul were probably interpolations added by later scribes in the course of copying the letters. Some of the genuine passages that are harmful have been misinterpreted and misused. When we see the person of Paul only though the genuine letters that Paul did in fact write and apart from those he did not, we are able to see Paul as a genuinely liberating figure in the context of the first-century Mediterranean world, for whom "in Christ there is neither Jew nor Greek, neither slave nor free, no male and female" (Gal 3:28)—a statement that counters the major power dynamics of the ancient world.

Nevertheless, those pseudonymous writings attributed to Paul, which Paul did not write, are indeed in the Bible. And we have to deal with that. And we have to deal openly and forthrightly with things that have had harmful consequences from Paul's genuine letters. This honesty makes it easier for us in class to be hospitable to Paul. This honesty frees us to be in a dialogue of respect with the Bible, without compromising our commitment to stand against oppression. We can listen closely to the Bible and let it say what it says without covering for it. We can say what we honestly need to say in critique of the Bible. The result of such a dialogue is that, usually, people who come into the class with a very negative view of Paul actually come to respect Paul and sometimes even to love him, problematic issues and all.

MUTUAL REVERENCE

In his book on mission, *Bread for the Journey*, Anthony Gittins, a professor at the Catholic Theological Union, puts forth a view of mission in a framework of profound hospitality. He portrays the missionary as a *guest*, aware of being in another's space, aware of needing to respect another's culture, eager not to violate certain customs or habits, open to learning from that culture, open to being changed by the encounter with that culture, and, in the process, where appropriate, also open to sharing. We need such a view of hospitality in everyday life, in which each of us is eager to give as well as to receive hospitality as a guest of others. This is mutual hospitality of the most respectful kind.

And at the heart of the relationships of such hospitality there is a dimension even deeper than respect. Theologically, it is a matter of *reverence*, reverence for other people as children of God, as Linda Thomas's guidelines remind us. We have lost a sense of reverence in our culture. But we can recover it by experiencing again the awe and wonder of human life. Deeper than our agreements, deeper than our profound disagreements, beneath the need at times even to work against one another, there can exist a profound regard for the life of other persons. Teachers and students can model such reverence. It can serve as the basis for some of the most profound learning that can take place in any classroom. And it can work out from there to influence and shape our common life together in the world.

6

Generating Student Questions

What follows may seem like way too much to say about the simple act of asking questions. But undergraduates struggle and need help. Graduate students do better, but they still need to become self-aware and intentional. And we teachers may need to learn better how to evoke curiosity and how to model the practice of posing questions that probe and provoke. Curiosity is the heartbeat of learning. And learning begins with a good question.

So, what is it about a good question? What happens when the question itself becomes a fascination? It may be a question that names a puzzle to be solved or a conundrum to be contemplated. It may put a finger on a piece of evidence necessary for understanding. It may point to a contradiction that problematizes or complexifies our thinking. It may challenge our fundamental assumptions. It may be a question to which there will be no certain answer. It will probably be a question that leads to other questions. But when you get a good one, it is often better to have a good question than an answer!

WHAT'S SO IMPORTANT ABOUT A GOOD QUESTION?

A rabbinic story is told about a distraught man in a rural community who ran desperately through the town in the middle of the night screaming, "I have to find an answer to my question, 'What is the meaning of life?'" After considerable disturbance of the peace from the incessant repetition of his question, someone suggested he wake the rabbi and ask him. He went to the rabbi's home, pounding on the door and calling out, "I have to find an answer to my question!" The rabbi came to the door and invited him into his study and asked him what his question was. He said, "What is the meaning of life? Tell me!" The rabbi replied, "I can't help you. I won't help you." "Why?" the man answered, "I am desperate to know." "Because," the rabbi said firmly, "You have a great question, and I refuse to ruin it with an answer!"

Joseph Sittler, a wonderfully creative theologian, recounted an event that happened years ago when he was invited to preach at Yale Divinity School. He preached on that difficult parable about an unjust steward (Luke 16:1–8). He reflected on the contours of the parable: when the steward was dismissed for treating clients unjustly, the steward compounded his immoral activity by going around and making friends with the clients by lowering their obligations to his master in order to assure favors for himself after he left his position. Sittler then observed that Jesus told the parable as a model for behavior. Without further explanation, Sittler posed this question: "Now what was it that our Lord found so commendable about this crook?" With that, he said "Amen!" and sat down!

The faculty and students held a forum with Sittler after the service. At that forum, one of the Yale professors said, "I did not hear a sermon today. There was no discussion of the human condition. There was no gospel announcement. There was no application of the text to our time." This was followed by a long silence. Finally, a woman in the back raised her hand and said, "You may be right, but I can't get that question out of my mind!"

Now there was a question! There was a question that named an enigma, that opened up the text to multiple explorations, that had no definitive answer, that surely would lead to other questions, and that, perhaps most important of all, stuck in the craw! It just makes you want to go back and reread that parable and turn it over in your mind and find out what others think and try out some ideas. The discussion might change your view of the parable. The exploration of the question might change your way of reading all the parables. It might even change your view of Jesus. What a great question to start a discussion. And what a wonderful way to evoke curiosity.

CURIOSITY AND QUESTIONS

Asking questions is related to a sense of curiosity. It demonstrates the desire to probe into the meaning and dynamics of something. It signals an appetite for learning, a love of adventure and exploration. It marks a tolerance for uncertainty and ambiguity, a trait that is basic for creativity and innovation. Learning begins with a question. But how do we teach curiosity? Perhaps curiosity is a character trait that cannot be taught. Maybe it can be picked up by example or contagion or osmosis. We see people who are fascinated with things and who love to investigate them, and we are drawn to imitate them.

That possibility may be reason enough for a teacher to model curiosity and the practice of asking questions. When I was a student, I always wished the lecturers would share the questions that got them into their discipline or that lay behind their ideas. They just gave the statement of a problem, the evidence, and the outcomes but not the underlying questions that drove them to investigate the problem in the first place. As a teacher, if I wanted students to ask provocative questions, *I* had to pose provocative questions as well. And I had to show a willingness to be open to students who were ready to pose question about my views.

When I first started teaching, most of my questions were a cat-and-mouse game of "guess what's in my mind." I had the answer, and I was trying to get students to come up with the same thing I was thinking. Nobody wins this game. I learned from *Teaching as a Subversive Activity* by Postman and Weingarten that teachers should never ask a question to which they already had the answer. In their view, a question that was appropriate for learning may be a "factual-type" question of uncertainty to which there are several possible answers. Or it may be a question for which the teacher surely does not have an answer, such as "What do you (students) think about this?" Or the question may be an opinion question to which the teacher has an opinion but not *the* answer. In this last case, so as not to close down discussion, teachers may want to avoid or delay offering their opinion. In any case, all of it can evoke curiosity.

WHY SO LITTLE CURIOSITY?

It is astounding at times how little curiosity human beings can exhibit. This is the dilemma I faced from my first year of teaching in college. Students showed little initiative in asking about something, even when they were invited to do so. Why was this so? It could be because of a lack of interest or because they were satisfied with a surface explanation or maybe even because it might involve more effort. Perhaps they were afraid of embarrassing themselves by exposing their ignorance. So they would just wait for me to explain things. It was not just young students who had this hesitation. Second-career students and graduate students were also reticent to pose constructive questions, questions that would clearly advance their learning along with that of the whole class, including mine.

It was always strange to me how students would skirt some of the most important questions, often personal questions, because they did not feel free to ask the teacher or one another about their view of things, why they think a certain way, or what drives them. Sometimes when I gave a guest lecture in a class, the students were emboldened to ask me a lot about my views. Maybe it was because I was novel to them or because they would not be graded by me. I don't know. But I wish that my own classes had been more proactive in this regard. It was amazing how students who asked questions out of a great desire to know what I knew or what others thought about something were able to draw things out of me and one another—things we did not even know were in there!

The failure to ask questions may, in part, be related to anxiety. This anxiety has to be addressed before students feel free to exercise their curiosity. After all, "curiosity killed the cat"—so what might it do to a student in a classroom? We do not know something, and so we would like to ask about it. Yet what if everyone else already knows the answer? What if the teacher makes it appear foolish that I asked about this? At all costs, as a student, I don't want to do anything to embarrass myself in front of my fellow students. So, it often takes courage to pose questions. I remember asking a question and getting a humiliating response from the teacher that made me feel like I wanted to die. It took me some time to get over that. Eventually, I had to accept the fact that the whole idea of a question is that it exposes our ignorance. And if I wanted to learn, I was going to have to ask questions. Questions are challenging. As a teacher, my goal was not to make the students comfortable by avoiding disconcerting questions. Rather, my goal was to create a place safe enough for students to be comfortable with being uncomfortable! How else could students learn a tolerance for ambiguity?

FOSTERING AN ATMOSPHERE HOSPITABLE FOR QUESTIONS

Perhaps one step is to create an atmosphere in the classroom that welcomes questions, that is, to create a hospitable atmosphere in which question-asking is an integral and valued part of the classroom experience for students and teachers alike? Above all, we may need to be absolutely clear that we actually, really, honestly do want questions. Sometimes I would say, "You might have had a bad experience in the past asking questions in class. But I want you to know that I welcome questions. I know you may feel they expose what you do not know. But that's the whole point of learning. I am depending on that. Questions enable me to teach better and you to learn better." Then I needed to act in such a way that fostered and maintained that atmosphere.

Here are eight principles I learned—through trial and mostly error—as I struggled to avoid things that hindered questions and tried to do things that would foster questions.

1. Do Not Belittle the Question or the Person Asking It

This seems pretty obvious. If someone asks a question, we can in no way put down the question. We honor the question, no matter what it is. Indeed, we take it seriously! The question represents where the student is—and it is critical to respect that, because this is where teaching/learning begins.

If we give any indication that we think the question is stupid or inappropriate, then not just this student but the whole class is doomed. If we indicate or imply that a question is dumb, then we are suggesting the student is not too smart or should have understood or was not listening. I was aware of this when I first started teaching, but I felt as a teacher that I had to correct students at every point. So I would try to rephrase the question or suggest that a different question would be more appropriate. Then, several times when this approach resulted in a nonresponsive class, I found myself apologizing. But it would not work to apologize *privately* to the student because I had put down their question. I needed to apologize before the whole class, because it was a *public* put-down and because the whole class had been affected by it.

I didn't initially understand the impact my words had on *other* students who did not ask the question. By putting down one student's question, however subtle I tried to be, I might have thought I encouraged other students to ask smarter questions. No. All I did was to lead other students to say to themselves: "If you think I'm going to ask a question like she did and risk looking like an ass in front of the teacher and my classmates, you're nuts. And even if I ask a question that the teacher likes, I would still look like an ass to my classmates. I'm not saying anything." I needed to make only one mistake, one time, to get frustrated or blow up or act indignant at a question, and it could poison the atmosphere for that class and that semester. Besides, it helps to remember that if a student asks a question, there is a 99 percent likelihood that other students have the same question—however obvious or simple the question may be. So, if that is the case, then more than one student is feeling stupid and humiliated by my response.

2. Honor the Question and Give a Good Answer

If the question is repetitious or rather inane, it may be best to give a serious, straightforward answer and move on without letting our chagrin be apparent. But most of the time, we can give an interesting and informative answer for the whole class, no matter what the question. In so answering, we may be making a silk purse out of a sow's ear, but so be it. The point is this: if we give an informed answer, we make the student who asked the question look good. We may even say, "I'm glad you asked that question"; or "I'll bet others are wondering the same thing"; or "What I said was complicated, and I'm glad you gave me the chance to explain it again." No need to make it seem as if we are compensating for a poor question. We just need to provide a helpful answer that makes it worthwhile for the whole class that someone asked it. And all of this must be naturally genuine and not condescending in any way.

3. Listen Carefully So as to Get the Question Right

There is nothing more frustrating for a student than to have a teacher misunderstand their question and end up not answering it, all the while providing an answer to a question they did not ask. This may seem obvious, but it happens a lot. Giving full attention to the person asking the question will not only convey the fact that we are taking the question seriously, it will also help us understand what is being asked. If there is uncertainty on our part, we can repeat the question as we understood it and then confirm this with the questioner. Or ask them to clarify the question. Not a big deal, just making sure the communication is clear. Listening well is a lost art. We need to model it.

4. Do Not Give Long Answers

One of the worst things a teacher can do is to give long answers. I used to introduce the time after a brief lecture as time for class discussion. When one student asked a question, I would launch into a five- or ten-minute answer. In effect, I gave another lecture! The students had already been listening passively to the first lecture, and now they got another. By this time, they were surely saying to themselves, "Is this discussion time or another lecture? If he's going to take that long to answer one question, I'm not going to ask *another* one." So, it is best just to answer the question as succinctly as possible and move on. That way, we also give others a chance to ask questions.

5. Do Not Wait Until the End of Class to Ask for Questions

Another thing I learned the hard way is this: don't wait until near the end of the class to invite questions. This is a no-brainer. If we wait to the end of the class to invite questions, everyone is thinking, "If nobody asks a question, maybe we'll get out early" or "If someone asks a question, he'll probably end up going beyond the class time."

6. Be Comfortable with Silence

When we become impatient with silence, we usually cut questions off. We give a lecture and ask for questions. When no one speaks up in the first eight or ten seconds, we either assume people get it and we move on to the next subject, or we start asking our own questions and answering them, or we just repeat what we have said and ask if they are sure they do not have any questions. Unless we are ready to give the students some time to think so as to formulate their questions, many of them will not be ready to ask anything. Unless we have the patience to wait, even if there is a long, seemingly awkward silence, the questions may not be forthcoming.

7. Do Not Be Defensive

If a student asked a provocative question that challenged my lecture or my point of view, my immediate instinct was to defend myself. But this turned out to be the quickest way to stifle such challenges. There may be several ways we can respond to challenges. Maybe just say that we need to think about it. Or ask the student to unpack their point of view more fully. Or suggest an answer that leads to further conversation. We may want to affirm the question as expressive of another legitimate point of view, and then even elaborate further some points that support the student's point of view. We can also answer the question matter-of-factly in a non-defensive way and ask if that addresses their concern. Or we could always rethink our point of view and change our mind! The main idea is for us to be comfortable and stimulated with being challenged. Maybe best of all, we might say: "I don't know what I think about that. It's a great question. What do you [the class] think?" Or, "That's a great question; let me think this through out loud with you." Or when appropriate, "I don't know." In these ways, we leave the conversation open rather than shutting it down.

8. Be Careful About Challenging the Student in Return

Finally, we can be cautious about asking a student a question back. This may be another thing that puts the student on the spot. Even a question back that asks the student to clarify their question or explain why they asked it can be intimidating. Maybe we could repeat the question in other words and then ask the student, "Did I understand the question correctly?" But even this has to be done carefully. Again, even if we are dealing with a student who can handle the challenge well, we cannot forget the fact that every other student is watching—and thinking, "If he is going to challenge back, I think I'll just keep my mouth shut." The goal is to create a safe and respectful atmosphere where we are able to challenge students but perhaps not when they are asking us a question.

Of course, once trust has been established and there is an ethos of respectful interaction, then the teacher and students can offer challenging and exploratory questions of each other. Surely that is the main goal of all of this effort to provide a safe atmosphere.

STRUCTURE: LECTURE FOLLOWED BY QUESTIONS

Often we may give a stirring lecture, ask for questions, and then become frustrated when none are posed. To address this situation, I found that structuring the class to evoke questions was an important strategy. Here was one of the ways I tried to approach the lecture-followed-by-questions classroom pattern.

Step One: Requesting Questions

First, I introduced a fifteen- to twenty-minute lecture by saying, "I look forward to your questions at the end of this lecture. Here are the kinds of questions you might ask: questions for clarification, questions of exploration, and questions that challenge [I sometimes listed these on the chalkboard]. As you listen to the lecture, you can be noting your questions. Then when the lecture is over, I'll give you some time to formulate your questions. Hopefully, each of you will have at least one question in each of these categories." Then it was up to me to give a stimulating lecture—one that presents new material or that presents familiar material in a new way or that places information in a distinctive interpretive frame or that has a controversial edge to it or that poses a conundrum—something interesting and evocative.

Step Two: Time to Formulate Questions

Second, when the lecture was over, I would indeed give the students time to formulate the questions. I might do this by asking them to pair off and share what they were thinking about the lecture and their questions and then be prepared to report their questions. Or I might ask them to pair up and repeat to another student as much of the lecture as they could recall in order to find out if they understood it. My assumption was that if they repeated it, they would find out what they did not understand—and bingo, they had questions. I might ask the pairs to formulate their questions together in the course of reflecting on the lecture. Or I might ask students to take three minutes to reflect silently on the lecture and to formulate their questions and jot them down. This last option was especially helpful to students who needed time to process before they spoke or, conversely, to those who tended to say the first thing that came into their minds.

Step Three: Fielding Questions

Finally, when we returned to the full group discussion, I would ask for their questions. I let the questions flow. This put a value on the questions themselves apart from answers. If there was a lull in the conversation, I felt free to say to a pair or an individual, "So what questions did you two come up with?" Since they had had time to formulate their questions, I was not putting them on the spot. I might call on students to report the questions from their dyadic conversation; and they were willing to respond because the questions were formulated by both of them. In the plenary, I sometimes asked for a lot of questions to be on the table at once, without giving any responses, until many questions had been posed. I might divide these by the types of questions. "Okay. Let's hear all your questions for clarification." I might want to hear all the questions of that type first before answering any of them. I might take notes and then answer the questions all at once (briefly!) and move on to the next type of question. A few times, I had a student put questions on the board, while I sat in the back and posed questions together with the students.

Follow-Through: Questions to the Questioners

When students got comfortable asking questions, I sometimes asked a question in return, "What led you to ask that question?" or "How would you answer that question?" or "What do you think about the subject we are discussing?" In this way students could develop critical thinking around a subject. Once students got into it, often with each other, I backed off to see where the student discussion would go. Different questions led to different kinds of conversation. The responses to questions for clarification were generally straightforward. I might give an answer and the conversation went no further. On the other hand, questions for exploration and challenge required a different response, such as "Now there's a question that has no definite answer. It depends on what we think. Here's my idea . . . and I am also interested in how you all would answer it." If it went well, such responses would sometimes lead to lengthy conversations, and the reward for having asked questions would be self-evident.

Habit: Questions Become a Way of Learning

Once we do all these things in an explicit and structured way, questions just become an integral part of the class process. They become natural and no longer feel contrived. Then, the question time becomes an opportunity to deepen the conversation. It is a chance to be honest and face difficulties. It is a chance to entertain conflicting points of view. It may be a time to be vulnerable and personal. Above all, it provides the opportunity to ask the *big* questions and the *deep* questions. Study of the Bible lends itself so much to that possibility. Joseph Sittler, whom I quoted above, followed a two-part process for studying texts. The first step was to explore the text: "What is this text about?" Here the questions were straightforward attempts to understand the story or the letter. Then he would ask the big question: "Now what is it about life that this text is about?" Wow! That question opened up the conversation! Then would follow questions about the meaning of life, the human condition, possibilities for redemption, hope for the world, and much more. At this level, the questions no longer focus on the teacher. They become a shared part of the learning process.

These kinds of exercises in question asking are crucial to the learning process for a number of reasons. They enable us to see if students can understand, talk knowledgeably about what we are studying, and see the larger issues at stake. One slogan I used was: *I don't teach subjects, I teach people.* And if people are not getting it, then I am not succeeding in teaching. I could teach a subject to a wall, but obviously learning doesn't happen. *Both* teaching and active learning must take place in order for education to take place. It's a relational interaction—transformation through *dialogue*. Questions represent the collaborative aspect of the learning process. Questions also become a way to see where the students are in their learning. We could do it with tests, but that is much too impersonal for my blood. Let's find out while the lecture is still hot. If they do not get it at the time of the lecture, then why would we think they would get it later?

A QUESTION-ASKING WORKSHOP

Yet, even if students have curiosity and courage, they may also need *skills* to investigate and explore something. To address this, we could go even further to develop the skill of asking questions in structured and rigorous ways. When I first started teaching freshmen undergraduates, I became frustrated with the students' inability or unwillingness to ask probing questions; so I began my New Testament Introduction classes with a two-week Question-Asking Workshop. That was the announced subject. The whole strategy was to focus on the questions themselves. "Let's see if we can come up with interesting questions." So, the motto was: *Questions only! No answers!* Here's one model I used in my freshman New Testament classes at Carthage.

Questions About News Items

I started out sharing an opinion piece from a newspaper or a news magazine, say about the economy or abortion. Newspaper articles were not sacrosanct like Scripture. Obvious questions would abound. Then I moved to a supposedly "objective" report about something that still had an author's opinion—like a report on fashion or film. In small groups or pairs, students came up with questions about the report. I would say: "A good question is better than a pat answer. What can you come up with?" At first, they had a tendency to embed their point of view in the way they posed the questions, as if they were using questions to make statements. But after some practice, they could posit genuinely fascinating questions.

Questions About the Bible

Then I would take a brief story from the Gospel of Mark to see what questions they had. Initially, they would ask only factual-type questions about what something meant—over and over. What does the word "leper" refer to? Who were the Pharisees? What does Jesus mean when he tells people it is legal to do good on the Sabbath day? I could not seem to break them of this habit. At one point, I explained this dilemma to the chairman of the Education Department. And I got the help I needed. He suggested that I back up, develop an analogy, and ask for twenty uses of a brick. So I did. At first they would say "to make a school," "to build a house," "to erect a church," and so on. Then I would point out that these were all the same type of answers, like the similarity of questions about meaning they were asking about Mark. Could they think of anything different? Imaginative? So they came up with such uses for a brick as a door stopper, water-saving toilet device, paper weight, constructing a bookcase, breaking windows, and so on. Then I would return to the story about Mark and ask them to think of different kinds of questions. This seemed to get them unstuck.

The questions began to flow. Who translated this? What was the original language? How do we know these are words of Jesus? Are there really such things as demons? Where did this author get his information? When was this written? How long after the time of Jesus? Was the author biased? Who copied it? Were they accurate? We would list these questions on the chalk board, sometimes thirty or more. Again, no answers, only questions. A student would copy them and give me the list after class.

The next day, I would come to class with the list reorganized under the categories of methods that scholars use to study and analyze the Bible: textual criticism, source criticism, form/genre criticism, historical criticism, redaction criticism, narrative criticism, social science criticism, and so on. This way, I could show them that the critical study of the Bible came about as a way to address genuine questions people had, just like theirs. If I had taught them the methods first, it would have been academically boring. And they might have been suspicious of these "criticisms." But now they had come up with the key questions on their own; and they understood that different critical methods were not there to tear down the Bible. Rather, they were methods used to solve some really important questions about the New Testament.

Interdisciplinary Questions

I also used the following method. I would cite a biblical story, like a healing story from Luke, as the basis for an exercise. I divided the class into groups that correlated with the departments in the school, such as Literature, Physics, Biology, Geography, Psychology, History, Political Science, Cultural Anthropology, Speech and Theater, and so forth. Students volunteered for whatever group they wanted to be in. Each group was to come up with a set of questions they would ask from the point of view of that discipline. "If you graduated and became a specialist in one of these fields, what questions would you ask of this healing story?" You can imagine the great questions they raised: How can someone chemically/biologically be healed by touch or by a word? Did Jesus heal by psychology? What really happened? Why the emphasis on sickness as unclean and impure? Did they know anything about diseases in that day? What social class did this healed person come from? What political message was Jesus giving by healing? Why did the Pharisees reject him? What were doctors like then? Why is there so much word-for-word repetition in the story? Was this story told by word of mouth? Was it made up? In my classes, this approach proved to be very lively, and it gave further support for students' understanding of the methods used to study the Bible. I could point out to them that most innovations in biblical studies come from posing fresh questions to the text that had not been posed before. Often these questions come from secular disciplines and are adapted to the study of ancient biblical times—such as historical criticism or narrative criticism.

Questions About Themselves

Finally, I encouraged them to ask questions about themselves. It may be difficult getting students to realize how much their own point of view shapes how they read. I gave them a sheet that listed areas of social identification and personal experience such as race, ethnic group, class, gender, education, health, religion, and formative experiences. After they detailed these identifications about themselves, I asked them to identify which items most shaped their reading. Then they could ask: Why do I read the Bible? How does my gender or ethnic identity or social class shape how I read the Bible? What am I looking for? How am I similar to or different from the people in the story? These and other questions enabled me to talk further about such methods as liberation theology and feminist/womanist readings.

Assessment and Outcome

When the Question-Asking Workshop was complete, I would test on a passage they had not worked with before in class. In fact, I would use a passage on the baptism of Jesus from the Gospel of Peter, a writing that is not even in the New Testament! I instructed them to imagine that the translation was based on a manuscript fragment archaeologists had found in the Judean desert. Now what questions would they have about it? The entire test consisted of the questions they would ask. They were graded on the range of questions, the extent of questions, the interest of the questions, and the generative nature of the questions.

After two weeks of the Question-Asking Workshop, the students had had their introduction to method, and they were ready to study the New Testament itself. Then we moved on to the three other parts of the New Testament survey course: "How to read a story" (the Gospels), "How to read a letter" (Pauline Epistles), and "How to reconstruct history" (historical Jesus). In each section, I suggested to them a set of questions and procedures to follow for investigating narrative, rhetoric, and history. At some point in each of these sections of the class, I would model the process by thinking aloud about a passage with which I was generally unfamiliar. The whole course turned out to be an introduction to both the New Testament and the liberal arts.

WHAT'S THE PAYOFF?

The payoffs for this workshop were many. Students became awash in curiosity about the Bible. Hopefully they learned the importance of questions and the value of lingering with questions without jumping so quickly to answers. They also learned skills of question asking—how to pose questions, how to pose different questions, and how to organize them into a systematic procedure for exploring a biblical passage. In so doing, they also learned the methods that scholars use to study the Bible. Perhaps the greatest payoff was the realization that there is so much to explore in a single story. Each passage is rich with dimensions, dynamics, and layers of possibility. Once they have seen the depth and expansiveness of one passage, hopefully they will not read any other passage quite the same way again. They might not study it so thoroughly, but they will know that there is much more to it than the surface, one-look approach they might have been accustomed to before taking the course.

Yet there is also a larger potential payoff for society in general. Geared to be inquisitive, eager to learn more, having the skill to explore with questions—all these are valuable for many careers and situations in society. Pastors preparing to preach would surely benefit from posing many questions of the text, questions that are also likely to be present in the minds and hearts of the congregation. Furthermore, questions are integral to active listening, a practice in short supply. All in all, our relationships and our vocations are well served by people who by nature and by skill are given to asking questions.

7

Liberative Pedagogy

Subversive Questioning

THE CONCERN TO GENERATE a hospitality of profound respect for each other is not meant to assure that students will feel comfortable. Rather, the point is that students are safe enough to be uncomfortable, so that they can be challenged by each other and by the material we study. That is exactly what happens with liberative pedagogy.

CRITICAL PEDAGOGY: PAULO FREIRE

Early in my teaching, about the same time I was asking myself why I was doing what I was doing and when I was recognizing the political dimensions of teaching, I read Paulo Freire's *Pedagogy of the Oppressed*. This book led me to think differently about my teaching and about the world. Paulo Freire was a Brazilian educator and philosopher who became aware from personal experience how extensively poverty and hunger affected the capacity to learn. In Brazil, as in most South American countries, there is a small governing elite with wealth and power, a very limited middle class, and an overwhelming majority of people who live at subsistence level. These poor are exploited by the small ruling class for cheap labor, with little or no economic or social safety net.

Freire realized that the educational system reinforced the world of the elite oppressors, partly because the information that was taught to students was the "official story" that preserved the status quo and partly because the system of teaching and learning did not empower the poor to challenge and change things. He depicted this as a "banking model" of education. The assumption is that the teacher knows everything, and the students are like empty bank accounts into which the teacher makes regular deposits. The teacher is the authority figure, and the students are passive receptors. And the "knowledge" that is deposited reinforces the social, economic, political, and cultural status quo of oppression. Such a model—content and process—does not lead the students to question, to think for themselves, to be critical, to challenge the world around them or to be prepared to change it.

By contrast, Freire sought a liberative pedagogy that freed students from the pedagogical model that was enslaving them in poverty, marginalization, and political oppression. His approach was to empower students to think for themselves and not buy into the official line. Education would free them to challenge the assumption that what they were learning was the way the world was supposed to be and, in so doing, to *imagine a different world*. Furthermore, a liberative pedagogy was designed to enable students to discover their own power, to learn to oppose oppression, and to act in the formation of a world with justice and equality. The whole point was to change the educational system so that the socio-economic-political system could be challenged and changed. This approach was called *critical pedagogy* because it was a system of learning that gave students tools and processes to critique the world around them and to create a different world.

Freire was writing and teaching around the same time that liberation theology emerged in South America and elsewhere, represented by writers such as Gustavo Guttiérez, Leonardo Boff, and Juan Segundo. Liberation theology was oriented to free people from oppressive systems of economic impoverishment, political oppression, and cultural degradation. Liberation theology exposed and challenged the ways in which the church cooperated with oppressive regimes by teaching the poor that God wanted them to accept their suffering in this world and wait for a reward in the afterlife. By contrast, liberation theology sought to empower the poor to attain humanity, dignity, and justice *in this life*. Liberation theology was also dramatically changing the way people were reading (and experiencing) the Bible. Poor, nonliterate peasants in South and Central America and elsewhere began studying the Bible in small groups—base communities—as a means of supporting each other, as a stimulus for liberation, and as a way to discover new meanings and interpretations of the biblical materials.

Their sociopolitical situation was similar to the Mediterranean world at the time of the early church, in which there also was a small ruling elite, no middle class, and masses of impoverished and exploited peasants. The insights into the New Testament that came from the perspective of the contemporary poor were remarkable because the social location from which they were reading the Bible in the twentieth century held parallels to the predominantly peasant perspective of most early Christian communities under the Roman Empire. What the poor were saying in their conversations about the Bible in these base communities were recorded and published for others to see. Reading liberation theology and how theological and biblical studies were being radicalized by impoverished peasants interpreting the New Testament from the perspective of the poor was eye opening and convicting for many of us. They were teaching the rest of us in dominant cultures how extensively biblical interpretations in the West and North have been skewed to serve the middle and upper classes and how we have provided rationalizations that support domination and oppression.

Some years later, I would see these things first hand when I went with colleagues on a "misery tour" of Brazil. We saw the impoverished favelas where the poor lived, we talked with those who resided in huts, we spoke with social workers, and we shared meals in the makeshift tents of displaced persons. People explained to us that it was as if there were two different countries in Brazil. There was the small group of ruling elites with all the power, wealth, status, and position in the society. This group had a lifestyle like wealthy Belgium. The other country in Brazil was like impoverished Bangladesh—with dirt floors, no water or sewage systems, rags for clothes, mud for yards, and very little food. And these were people who were working!

We learned that, in the previous two decades, the government had displaced 40 percent of the people from their indigenous locations on rural lands (where they had been able to raise food to support themselves), so that the elites could produce cash crops for export and improve the GDP of the nation as a whole (for the benefit of the wealthy alone). And they drove the displaced farmers to crowded poverty conditions in cities where they provided hard labor for inhumane wages for factories in urban areas (for the benefit of the wealthy alone) and where they could not afford to buy the food they had previously raised for themselves.

LIBERATIVE PEDAGOGY IN THE US CLASSROOM

How could I learn more about this and share it with my students in a US college filled with predominantly white middle-class students who had never experienced or seen oppression and poverty like this?

Liberative Content

I took the occasion to teach an elective on the Gospel of Luke a number of times in the late seventies and early eighties. At that time, the Gospel of Luke was the Gospel drawn upon most frequently by liberation theologians and liberation biblical scholars. In that course, we looked at the ways in which the entire goal of the ministry of Jesus in Luke was "to seek and to save the lost"—to heal the sick, give sight to the blind, and announce good news to the poor. Jesus proclaimed the Jubilee Year of the Lord's Favor, an ancient Israelite tradition that challenged the oppressive structures of society, rectified inequities, and provided freedom from debt. From beginning to end, Luke's Jesus is relentless in seeking to turn upside down an unjust society by condemning the wealthy and the powerful and by lifting up the lowly so as to generate a society driven by mercy.

In the class, we read books about South American countries and about liberation theology so that students could see how Luke's perspective was fostering liberation in these oppressive circumstances. But how could we also see these dynamics closer to home? In order to connect with oppression in US life, we read an illuminating book by Michael Parenti called *Democracy for the Few*. This is a remarkably comprehensive exposé of the inequalities within the US. The book gives extensive descriptions and statistics about the huge disparities between the rich and the poor, of both income and property; the plutocracy of the rich; inequities and discrimination in housing, health care, the courts, and the prison system; the corporate control of the media; and a host of other issues.

This book was a stunner for the students. It had not occurred to them that the United States democratic political system and capitalism could be so unfair and discriminatory. Each student wrote a paper on an exploited group (such as those in the prison system or homosexuals or blacks) and reflected on what the Gospel of Luke might have to say about it and what we and our society might do in response. While I was not able to teach this class on Luke regularly, what I learned was yeast that leavened my survey classes on all four Gospels.

Liberative Process

Another issue raised by Freire focused on how our classroom ethos and procedures replicate and reinforce the hierarchical ways of imperial suppression in which the students are the objects of the teaching and not the subjects of their own learning. It was about this time that I also came across *Teaching as a Subversive Activity* by Postman and Weingartner. These authors focus on the role of the teacher in asking "subversive" questions and enjoining the students to do the same. In this book, teachers are discouraged from posing questions for which they themselves already know the answer.

Rather, Postman and Weingarten recommend asking the hard questions that can only be experienced as an invitation to dialogue, because the teacher genuinely wants to know what the students think and is genuinely seeking critical reflection from the group. The teacher may have an opinion in response to a question posed, but it is preliminary and may be shaped or changed by what students say about it. Asking the questions and pushing the questions beyond easy answers, developing ways to think critically about societal issues, honoring diverse points of view, and bringing everyone in on the conversation—this is the teacher's role. When it is modeled well, students begin to offer challenging questions of their own.

In addition to reflecting about the most constructive kinds of questions, Postman and Weingarten also suggest that students learn to spot and challenge phony arguments, self-serving propaganda, and hypocritical behavior, especially by the wealthy and powerful. A personal experience with my five-year-old daughter at that time helped to reinforce this for me as a parent. She and I and one of her friends were having supper together. My daughter Tania was awkward with utensils, so she tended to eat with her fingers. I began to tease her in front of her friend: "Tania, you are eating with your fingers. You'll probably grow up and go to dinner with your friends and eat with your fingers." I was awful. Tania knew it. She looked up at me and said, "Dad," and then paused and added rather firmly, "Bullshit!" I howled with delight—because I would much sooner have a daughter with a good "crap detector" than one who sometimes ate with her fingers. I thought of the term "crap detector," because this is the term Postman and Weingarten use for tools that expose noncritical thinking and the spin of the oppressors, obviously much more serious matters. So, that is one of my roles in teaching—to help students develop a good crap detector! I could do worse.

Subversive Learning and the Parables of Jesus

At this point, I was learning to integrate critical pedagogy with the biblical materials. In a team-taught January class with an economics professor that we titled Learning as a Subversive Activity, we read a book by John Dominic Crossan called *Dark Interval*. He argues that the worldviews and core values that we grow up with and share with the rest of our society become ossified, and we think they are Truth with a capital *t* without realizing that they are cultural constructs. Because we live inside them like fish swim in water, they seem so natural that they become idols we never question, not only social-political idols but also idols about God and the Bible. Crossan refers to this as *verbal idolatry*, idolatry on a parallel with material idols condemned in the Bible. He argues that these verbal idols, including religious beliefs, so control our world that we do not leave space for the *reality* of God to break through. We put our faith in our *beliefs* about God and about the world. It is only when our worldviews are cracked open and when seams and borders become transgressed that we open up our lives to encounter the reality of God at the edges and on the margins, which, when that happens, will change dramatically the way we think about the world, about life, about our ethical commitments, and about our relationships.

Crossan uses the parables of Jesus to make this point. The worldview in Israel was typical of most cultures, which tended to divide the world into "us and them." In the case of Israel, one of these dualistic contrasts was between Israel (us) and the Samaritans (them), hated enemies, considered apostates as Jews who refused to recognize the Jerusalem temple as the place for proper worship of God. As a first-century Galilean Jew, Jesus knew this perspective well. Nevertheless, Jesus tells the story of the "good Samaritan," an oxymoron that challenges the dualistic division and breaks open the boundaries. A venerated priest and a Levite pass by a wounded stranger on the road. The hearer would then expect an ordinary Israelite to be the third and redeeming figure to stop and attend to the man. However, a hated Samaritan comes by and shows compassion and ample generosity in helping the man, seeing to it that he will be well cared for. The story starts by setting up the cultural expectation that an Israelite will show mercy but then subverts that expectation with an enemy as the model for what it means for an Israelite to follow the Jewish law in loving the neighbor as oneself.

The story cracks apart the binary opposition for a new way of configuring the world and leaves space for a God who is inclusive, who places a premium on compassion, and who calls people to "love their enemies." God shows up in this "dark interval." It was not difficult for us as a class to apply this story to many groups that our society tends to think of in terms of "us and them"—those who are different, sinful, evil, our enemies, those of whose lifestyles we do not approve, people of "other" ethnicities or religions—both inside and outside our nation.

A parable, far from being a simplistic story that explains a difficult point, is in reality a word that breaks through conventional wisdom and leads hearers to rethink their worldview and cultural expectations. Crossan does a similar subversive analysis with Jesus's parable about the Pharisee and the tax collector who go up to the temple to pray. The twist in the story subverts the expectation that God will hear the prayers of those who are considered holy and disregard the prayers of someone like an exploitative tax collector. But God hears the prayer of the tax collector, the one who goes back to his house justified.

The class was greatly assisted in these conversations by the savvy economics professor with whom I was team teaching. And we went as a class to Loyola University in Chicago to discuss the issues with Dom Crossan in person. Crossan's insights were confirmed and expanded for students in a study by William Herzog entitled *Parables of Subversive Speech: Jesus as Pedagogue of the Oppressed.*

Learning to Change Our Mind

When we started down this path, students began to see learning not as additive but as transformative. Learning became an adventure of discovery that would change them. In that interim class, we pushed the idea that our goal was: *learning to change our mind, learning to change our world.*

With this sense of vocation, students find learning to be a deeply pursued quest of constantly questioning, abandoning, reconceiving, embracing the new—and starting the process all over again. It is what some commentators call "orientation by disorientation." Students have the world as they know it disoriented, and then they seek ways to reorient it with a new image of God, their values, and the world. And even their new reorientation cannot become an idol but is always up for challenge and reconsideration. Of course the outcome of this process sometimes affirms what one embraced before the quest began but never in quite the same way, partly because the quester takes a new sense of ownership for her or his views. It is the process itself that makes learning deeply personal, profoundly political, liberative, and transforming—for both the oppressed and the oppressors.

This approach recognizes an ethical responsibility in learning *not* to guard our current beliefs at all costs and not to refuse to change but rather to be honest and open about the ways in which the views of others may legitimately challenge us and lead us to follow that truth where it may lead. My primary role as teacher was to model this attitude, to share my own puzzlements and struggles openly, to allow conversations to shape my thinking, to share ways I have changed my mind in the past, and to be prepared to change my mind in the class. I have always taken great pleasure in saying to a student, "That's an excellent point. I never thought of it that way" or "I think you're right. I'm going to change my mind about that." Unless we ourselves share our openness and our vulnerabilities, it is unlikely that students will either.

LIBERATIVE PEDAGOGIES IN THE US: BELL HOOKS

Some years later, I became deeply influenced by the writings of bell hooks, an African American educator and author who has done as much as anyone to develop Paulo Freire's pedagogy in relation to the educational system in the United States, especially in her book *Teaching to Transgress: Education as the Practice of Freedom*. She sees education as engaged pedagogy that addresses issues of race, class, sexism, materialism, homophobia, exploitation, and imperialism. She envisions education as a practice of freedom that transgresses the repressive way things are and that resists all forms of domination. As such, education seeks to humanize students as they are liberated from forms of oppression and as they gain agency to transform society—liberation both for those of dominant cultures who (knowingly or unknowingly) participate in oppressing and for those of suppressed groups.

Early on, another book was critical to my own thinking about teaching and learning. In *The Social Construction of Reality*, sociologist Peter Berger distinguishes between primary socialization and secondary socialization. Primary socialization represents the core values, beliefs, customs, behaviors, relationships, and structures into which we are born and which we accept as our "true knowledge" of the way the world is. Secondary socialization represents the organizations we join, the jobs we take, the schools we attend, or a political party we support, which do not generally challenge the core values of our primary socialization. However, there is a third experience called *resocialization* at the primary level, brought about by experiences that challenge core assumptions of our society and lead us to rethink or change them.

In common with bell hooks's approach, this third way is what a classroom can become—a place to challenge, rethink, and resist the idolatrous "isms" that are present in our culture, perspectives that serve some and deprive/oppress others. Such a learning community goes beyond resistance to resocialization insofar as a classroom becomes a place to imagine alternative worlds of justice and peace—and even functions as an expression of them. bell hooks expresses it well when she quotes Paul in Rom 12:2: "Be not conformed to this world but be transformed by the renewal of your mind." That is the profound potential of the educational experience.

LIBERATIVE PRACTICES IN THE EARLY CHURCH

The New Testament materials lend themselves well to such a liberative pedagogy. In some sense, the New Testament writings served as a critical pedagogy for their own time in terms of the subversive nature of the writings in relation to the societies from which they emerged.

Challenging the Core Values of the Ancient World

The New Testament writings challenged many of the core values of the societies in which they arose and resocialized people into new and different communities—a world-shattering experience. These writings challenged the quest for honor and status by urging a humility among elites by calling them to be "least of all" and to "think of others as better than yourselves." They challenged the view that rich people are blessed by their wealth by calling the wealthy to sell what they have and give to the poor. They challenged the grasping for power by calling followers to be "slaves" of one another and "servants" of those below them in the social order. Almost all New Testament writings are seeking to break the self-orientation of the individual ego and of the collective in-group ego by calling people to love the enemy and seek the well-being of others. In doing these things, they seek to generate an alternative social reality.

You can go right down the line of cultural values and see how New Testament writings urge actions that are counterintuitive, communities that are countercultural, and relationships that are counter-imperial. These writings are case studies in liberative pedagogy in the first century, by presenting a vision that moves away from being self-centered to being other-centered. They are prime examples of resocialization at the primary level. Through the years, the radical nature of the New Testament writings has given me and my students the opportunity for transformation by opening us up to be "resocialized" around these issues in relation to our own contemporary society and culture.

Challenging the Bible

At the same time, as we point out in other reflections, the New Testament contains ethical admonitions and encourages relationships that compel us to critique those particular writings. There are writers who tell slaves and wives and the poor to be submission to those in authority over them. There are patriarchal assumptions that suppress or eliminate the voices and leadership of women. Same-sex relationships are condemned. There is strong anti-Judaism in some of the writings, which portray the "Jews" as foils for the goodness of the emerging Christian communities. The point is that biblical study invites us to do a critical pedagogy on the New Testament writings themselves along with the uses and abuses to which they have been put.

Challenging Scholarship on the Bible

Furthermore, the biblical classroom gives us an opportunity to critique not just the Bible but also contemporary biblical scholarship in terms of the way writings *about* the New Testament have reinforced or ignored or sought to explain away biblical points of view that are harmful, often in an effort to rescue the Bible from negative criticism. Fortunately, in the last decades of biblical scholarship, the influx of scholars and students from postcolonial contexts around the world has provided new perspectives of interpreters from many different social locations—both in supporting those seeking to be liberated from oppression and in condemning the ways in which the Bible has been used in the service of oppression. The diverse voices of people who read the Bible in order to bring liberation represent acts of resistance against repression and constitute possibilities of redemption. Because of their influence, biblical studies in many circles is becoming a practice of freedom.

In the last decades, all of these issues have become lively dimensions of the study of the New Testament both among scholars and in the classrooms. Students and teachers have an ethical responsibility to "do no harm" and to "never use the Bible to oppress people." Future pastors need to be extremely sensitive to the ways in which the Bible can be used against people. Future civic leaders need to be aware of the ways our culture engages in oppressive behavior that marginalizes and exploits. In this regard, we can urge students to use those parts of the New Testament that are incredibly liberating as means to critique and counter those parts of the New Testament that are oppressive and harmful. Several years after he graduated from seminary, a former student called to thank me for teaching him how to "preach Christ against the Scriptures"; that is, to preach our biblical understanding of the liberating Christ against the biblical texts that threaten to undo us. This advice may sound new, but it is as old as Martin Luther, who in the sixteenth century urged Christians to preach the Christ of grace *against* what he understood to be writings (such as the Letter of James) that from his point of view promoted an inadequate or a harmful picture of Christ and the Christian life.

The Bible has so many different perspectives and admonitions and visions of the Christian life that it is impossible not to be selective about what we will follow. So we can choose to lift up biblical writings and biblical perspectives that are life giving as well as interpretations that are life affirming, and we can use them as leverage to counter what is destructive.

Empire Studies of the New Testament

Critical pedagogy has been furthered by an additional development in early church studies in the last several decades with the onset of empire studies of the New Testament. This development in New Testament studies has involved a shift away from viewing early Christianity solely in relation to Judaism to studying also how early Christian communities interfaced with and stood in opposition to the Roman Empire. That shift has led many New Testament scholars to focus on the ways some early Christians critiqued the Roman Empire—often by claiming an alternative truth that trumped Roman imperial claims to truth but also by living a counter-imperial lifestyle in their communities. First-century Christians had a worldwide, indeed a cosmic vision, of the triumph of Christ as the one appointed by God to be over every principality and power. God's "servant empire" would ultimately prevail.

Because they were confident of the impending triumphant return of Christ and because of their fragile, minority status, most early Christians did not try to change or reform the Roman Empire. To be sure, in the New Testament, there are prophetic passages and writings (such as the book of Revelation) that by and large speak truth directly to the power of the empire. For the most part, however, Christians were even more radical than a prophetic stance would suggest. They were "apocalyptic" in the sense that they withdrew from the values and relationships of their world as they knew it and went about the business of creating a different world—counter-imperial communities of equality and mutual service that were contrary to the hierarchical, exploitative, and violent ways of the empire (while sometimes using images of empire to articulate it).

Empire studies have enabled us in the classroom to see how the early Christians were creating communities that shared possessions, obviated patron-client relationships, pursued mutual nonhierarchical relationships, served one another as sisters and brothers, chose humility, cared for the least, and put a premium on love, even for those who persecuted them. They saw the world upside down and inside out through the cross of Christ, which represented renunciation of wealth, status, and power. Of course, there were ways in which some early Christians writings, such as the book of Revelation, also mimicked the Roman Empire with threats of destruction and, in so doing, manifested some imperial dynamics of their own.

Imagining a Liberative World Today

The last several decades in New Testament classrooms have been exciting in this regard. It has been interesting to see students relate ancient socio-political dynamics to our contemporary situation. One way to foster contemporary reflections is to pose these questions: "If you created a parish today that was based on just this one writing in the New Testament (say, Mark or Philippians or Revelation), what would that parish look like? What would their vision of a new world order and a new creation be like? And how would they go about changing our world?" Each of the writings in the New Testament was creative in its application of the Christian message to the particular ancient community and circumstance that it addressed. I have tried to give some content to this approach in *The Challenge of Diversity: The Witness of Paul and the Gospels.*

As we seek the relevance of the New Testament for our time, we need to acknowledge that the social and cultural contexts of the first century were radically different from our own. At the same time and despite this, we can be faithful to the New Testament writers by being creative in shaping the first-century gospel perspectives in *our* contexts so as to bring the gospel message to bear on our time, as early Christians did in *their* contexts. Obviously, the Bible is limited in addressing our contemporary problems. Nevertheless, the study of the Bible invites us to see analogies, perspectives, and resources as bases on which to reflect critically on many unjust circumstances of our world today.

MY STRUGGLES IN CRITICAL PEDAGOGY

The radical nature of the New Testament and the critical dynamics of liberative pedagogy dawned upon me gradually through the years. There is no way I can say that these approaches have been front and center of my classrooms throughout the years. Different books of the Bible lend themselves to different emphases. Nevertheless, these dynamics have been present in one form or another, in small ways and large, explicit and implicit, direct and indirect, in every course—if for no other reason than that they were embedded in the material we were studying. And if I knew at first what I know now, I would have placed a greater focus on these issues, and on the process of asking tough questions that would have required us to grapple together with the issues of our time in a more intentional and open-ended way.

8

The Physical Environment of the Classroom

THERE IS A TENDENCY for us teachers to be rather oblivious to the surroundings in which we teach, in part because we are focusing on the subject matter and the students. But we would be greatly remiss if we failed to pay attention to the physical environment in which students learn. We can be severely limited in our teaching by poor or inappropriate furniture, incongruous room arrangements, drab walls, loud fans, and a singular lack of imagination in regard to décor. Unfortunately, this concern includes many things largely beyond our control. But the fact remains that teaching and learning can be remarkably facilitated by room sizes and setups, comfortable and appropriate furniture, natural and soft lighting, and interesting and relevant appointments on the walls.

"The medium is the message," said Marshall McLuhan. "And," he added, "the medium is the *massage*." The physical medium of learning gives a message, and it also has an impact. The medium in which we study will affect all that we do, making some things possible and other things difficult. We can learn something about the commitment to education on the part of an institution by looking at its classrooms. And we can also learn a lot about what kind of learning the institution expects will happen. If the classrooms are set up in lecture style with a podium in front and desks lined up in neat rows, we pretty well know what will happen there. If the rooms are set up with long tables and outlets for personal computers, we know what students will be expected to do in class. If the classrooms are small, with chairs around a table, this setup will encourage interaction. Students themselves will know the mode of learning in the course from the very first moment they walk into the classroom on the very first day—*and they will probably act accordingly*.

Classroom setups are like literary genres. They set up expectations. If we pick up a detective novel, we already know what kind of story to expect. So too with classrooms. When students see a classroom arrangement, they know what to expect, and they respond with the expected behavior. The medium is, indeed, the message and the massage. So we may need to be creative. Matching the right classroom for a given class and customizing it to the needs of that class will be well worth the effort. You may find the right room just waiting for a class to blossom.

CHOOSING THE RIGHT SPACE

I had few options at the college level. However, before the beginning of each semester at LSTC, our registrar would send out a form to teachers inviting requests for room assignments. If you have such an opportunity to choose, you might want to walk around the building to see what classrooms would work best for each particular class. The size of the classroom in relation to the size of the class is critical. So the first thing to look for is a classroom with about the same number of chairs or desks as there are students. Every year I had in mind this strange image of going past a classroom one day at Carthage College. There was the instructor standing at a lectern reading his notes to the class. There were about fifty desk chairs lined up in rows in lecture style. But there were only three students! And they were scattered throughout the room! It looked farcical, lecturing to a crowd of three, each one at least ten to twenty feet from the instructor and from each other. So I determined not ever to let that happen. In my experience, the class should look full but not crowded. Performers know that members of an audience in a theater need to sit together so that there can be group reactions to what happens as well as individual reactions. It is the same with classrooms. After all, learning is a communal as well as an individual endeavor. Students should be sitting near each other—in conversational proximity.

Arranging for a classroom of the right size is not always easy, especially if the class is about thirty to forty students and the only available classroom for this number has fifty to sixty desks. When that happened with a course, I would go to the classroom ten minutes before each class and either stack or push to the side against the wall all chairs except a few more than the number of students in the class. Then I arranged the remaining chairs appropriately. This way the class would sit together as a group. Also, the front row would not be vacant, as if proximity to the teacher was toxic! Sometimes, I also moved the teacher's desk to the side to make space for me to move around in front.

CHOOSING THE RIGHT SETUP

In a typical lecture-style classroom, the message to the students is this: "You will face and relate only to the teacher, and you are expected to listen and to take notes and perhaps ask questions of the teacher; but do not expect to talk much with other students." You can compensate for that setup with semicircles. If it is a large class of thirty to forty, you could put the desks in three rows of large semicircles with space in front. That way there is space in front of the teacher's desk to move around and interact with students on different sides of the room. It works well when no student is ever too far away from you. Also, with this arrangement, even with a large group, the students were somewhat turned toward each other for large-group discussions that could include interactions between students. And, if the desk chairs are easily moved, students can turn their chairs toward each other in pairs or groups of three or four to do some exercises together, and then turn back toward the center for plenary discussion. If the class period is treated as a workshop, you will want to be able to vary activities and therefore adjust the room arrangements throughout the class period.

When the class size is five to eighteen, you might look for a room with tables that could be placed in a circle. I prefer tables. They give the message that we mean business, that students will work together, and that all will participate. Tables also offer space for people to lay out their texts and computers and to take notes. The problem with a square or a rectangular setup of tables is that students can't see those who are lined up alongside them. In a round setup, everyone can see everyone else, and there is mutual accountability. Usually smaller tables can be placed in a hexagon or octagonal shape. The number of places at the table can approximate the number of students in the class. Again, you can go to the room before the class begins and arrange the furniture accordingly—taking down or adding tables, moving chairs, and getting the best setup for light and sound. And again, this offers great flexibility for students to work as a whole group, in pairs, and in small groups. There is no "head" to the circle (as there can be in a square or rectangle), so you can choose to sit near a chalkboard. If you want to de-center the learning process, you can sit at a different place each week.

In a Greek class one semester, I discovered that I could place individual rectangular tables at angles in the room (fan shaped in configuration so that no students sat with their back to me), four students at each table, two on each side across from each other in order to translate and do exercises together, with the tables serving as group work stations. I then also used this practice for other classes of twenty to thirty students. I would give them an exercise to do in groups of four, or I would ask them to engage in discussion in either the pairs sitting across from each other or the pairs sitting next to each other at their table. Often I asked them to move around and find other students to interact with—so they would relate with students they did not know well. Throughout a course of twenty or so, I would set up the tables and chairs one week in lecture mode (one small *u* shape formed with tables inside a large *u* shape formed with tables around the smaller *u*), and another week as work stations—depending on what we were doing for that week. Variation in the setup was helpful in retaining student focus and interest.

DOES THE SETUP FACILITATE OR CONSTRAIN LEARNING?

All of this involves a lot of planning and effort. But it made a difference for me as the teacher. And I am convinced it made a difference for the students, although they were often unaware of how much effort went into it. After I had spent ten minutes setting up a room, sometimes a few students would come late and pull chairs out of the stack on the side and sit precisely in the area I was trying to avoid.

I have a fantasy about how to enable students to be aware of the planning: Students arrive the first day of class to an empty classroom, with no furniture. Their expectations are thrown, and they have to think about it. Together we decide what we want to happen in the class, and then we determine what kind of furniture and what kind of setup we need for that to take place.

The questions are: What are we teaching? How do we want to teach it? How do we want students to learn? What different things do we want to happen? And how do the room size, the room setup, and the flexibility of the room arrangement facilitate or hinder the desired goals?

What About a Lectern?

One the one hand, standing at a lectern is an extremely helpful place to offer lectures and lead discussions, especially as a place for our notes and manuscripts. On the other hand, a lectern can represent a hierarchical symbol of authority whereby the teacher can exert power and inhibit dialogue.

A story shared with me by a female colleague at LSTC illustrates this point very well:

> In my first years of teaching, in a class where I was giving a lecture on the various forms for legitimating authority in pastoral ministry, one of the brightest students in the class expressed disappointment that my lecture was so "basic," not as exciting as the book they were reading. I remember feeling undone, a total failure. The comment confirmed every fear: I was not smart enough to be doing this work. Why had I ever thought I could teach at this level? And I was angry, too, convinced that this student (who happened to be a woman) would never have said something like that to a male teacher.
>
> My first reaction was to move back behind the lectern where I had my notes, and to try to carry on, putting more forcefulness into my voice. Then something happened—and I believe to this day it was a gift. I left the lectern, moved closer to the class, and said, "Did you notice what I did when Joanna made her comment?" A number of them responded quickly, "You moved behind the lectern!" I asked, "What kind of authority do you think I was claiming?" At that point, the conversation "caught fire." I moved over to the female student and said that I welcomed her contribution as an opportunity to learn and that I hoped she wouldn't mind if I used the opportunity to talk about what is "at play" when we take up an authoritative role. And I hoped that *she* would not feel on the hot seat, but rather that I wanted to put *myself* on the hot seat to talk about what was cooking for me.
>
> I realized that structures of inequality are not only evident in the furniture in the room but are also *inside us* as teachers, too—the images and stories we've internalized, the things we think

> make our work "count," and the experiences that evoke shame in our lives. There is such a gap between how I want to be as a teacher and what my "default settings" are. And I know those default moves I make are loaded with memories and stories of how my thinking has been shaped by my own educational formation in what were sometimes oppressive circumstances.

My colleague's story reminds us that virtually any arrangement will bear dimensions of power, often reinforcing some oppressive hierarchical structures of society that suppress voices rather than include them. We need to discern when exercising authority is appropriate to the success of the learning experience and when it can interfere with learning, when it can solidify the class, when it can inhibit the formation of a community of learners, when it reinforces some oppressive hierarchical structures of society, and when it fosters an ethos of mutuality. Also, by making students aware of these dynamics, she was teaching them to be sensitive to these dynamics when they would be in positions of authority.

OTHER FACTORS THAT HELP OR HINDER LEARNING

Other conditions in a classroom are also critically important, even though we may have little control over them. One day, for some inexplicable reason, an overhead heating fan in our classroom just stopped. We suddenly realized that we had been speaking in loud, strained tones. We lowered our voices and began to speak with each other in ways that were more intimate and personal, instead of trying to relate to each other over top of noise! It may be worth seeing if background noise can be eliminated in your classrooms. Lighting may be another issue worth considering, like overhead fluorescent lights that flicker or leave a portion of the room darkened. There is no need for these distractions and diminishments of the classroom atmosphere.

Also, a change of scenery to a different room in the middle of a three-hour class or in the middle of a semester can rejuvenate a group. Sometimes students want to go outside, although I usually found an outdoor venue to be distracting and unproductive.

CHANGING THE DÉCOR

Surely there must be an interior decorator somewhere in the world whose specialty is classroom décor. But you would hardly know it. Most college and university classrooms look bleak and institutional. How can a university, which is supposed to be a think tank, exercise such a lack of imagination? Maybe the worst examples are the portraits of past presidents or donors of the institution. Classroom décor reminds me of an essay H. L. Mencken wrote while taking a train ride across western Pennsylvania. I recall that Mencken determined the only way to account for the row after row of drab, clapboard houses that lined the railway tracks was to hypothesize a "libido of the ugly." Apart from encouraging our institutions to redecorate classrooms and hallways, how do we address these factors?

Churches are sometimes like this too. But they do not have to be. I know a congregation that was ready to build a church in Rocky Mount, North Carolina. They were a close-knit group, like a family. One of the members had a dream one night that the church they were to build would look like a large home. He shared the dream, and they did it! They built it like a large home and asked a few members to decorate the kitchen like it was their kitchen at home and another few to decorate the nursery like at home and others to do the lounge like a living room. It was amazing going into it. You felt very much at home—plants, curtains, knickknacks, vases, art, family portraits, and so on. Why not try making some classrooms look like dens or studies—with bookcases and home lighting and some photographs on display and a desk that looks like a home desk and so on?

And what about decorating the walls? The art in most classrooms is pitiful. Why not at least get reproductions of really good art in some classy frames? Why not feature art exhibits? How about stained glass? Something interesting and attractive—and educational! I always thought we should have wall decorations that served the disciplines taught in that room. Why didn't I put up a display of images of Jesus from around the world? Or aerial maps of the land of Israel? Here we could learn from elementary school teachers who know well how to make the wall décor integral to the educational process! Whatever—just so we had some imagination and some "class" in the classroom!

Lib Caldwell, who taught Christian education classes for McCormick Theological Seminary, was extremely knowledgeable about education and about teaching the faith. She also had a special appreciation for the ecology of the classroom. McCormick shared classrooms with our seminary, so I had a chance to observe her work. I never sat in on one of her classes, but I knew what it looked like. And it was fascinating. Between classes, I often passed by her classroom, where she had arrived well ahead of time in order to prepare for a class. Invariably, I was drawn to stop in and see what she was doing. Her classrooms were carefully set up for group interaction. She also had one or more tables spread with colorful cloth. On them, there might have been candles or a fresh flower arrangement. Books might be on display. Artwork relevant to the subject matter for the day might be hanging up or resting on the chalk tray. Food was often present. Every student who entered this space knew that it had been carefully prepared to provide a meaningful, enjoyable, and aesthetically pleasing educational experience. Not only that, students would leave seminary with a model for how to tend educational spaces in their parishes.

Décor to Reflect Diversity

Let's not forget the physical decor of the class as a means to foster intercultural awareness and dialogue. I am always intrigued by the pictures on the wall. I recall the Spike Lee film *Do the Right Thing*. In the film, there was an Italian pizza place. The restaurant was located in Harlem, but the management would put only pictures of Italian entertainers on the wall—no black entertainers or black cultural icons. The pictures on the wall revealed the people whom the establishment owners valued. In this case, they clearly did not value the heritage of the people they were serving in Harlem. So how could people walk into a class and know instantly that their culture will be honored? What if the classroom walls had photographs of Martin Luther King Jr., Bishop Óscar Romero, Martin Luther, Mother Teresa, the Dalai Lama, Mahatma Gandhi, Mother Teresa, Harriet Tubman, Chief Joseph, Thich Nhat Hanh, Pope Francis? Whoever walked into that room would know that there was an eagerness to reach out and embrace all races, cultures, and religions. If students enter a classroom, do they see themselves in the pictures on the wall? Or are they a stranger?

CONCLUSION

We may not all have the gift for humanizing a space like Lib does, but we can attend to these seemingly ordinary matters in ways that will provide benefits for us and for our students. In addition to enhancing aesthetic pleasure, all of these considerations can be designed to foster a good educational experience oriented toward meaningful dialogue, mutuality, and cooperative participation. One way or another, for good or for ill, the context *is* there. So why not attend to the ecology of the classroom with imagination, taste, and even a sense of adventure?

9

Overcoming Blocks to Learning

At Carthage College, I taught a course called Introduction to the New Testament. At that time, it was required of all students along with one other religion class of their choice. Every student had to take the New Testament course in order to graduate, and most students took it during their freshman year, at around age eighteen. The classes were large for our school, thirty-five to fifty, and I taught two of these classes each semester. This course turned out to be a laboratory to address every educational malady conceivable among students. It was also the crucible in which I first learned about teaching—because I had to learn how to teach in order to survive!

I wanted this New Testament course to give students a good experience. Whatever issues happened to be raised by the New Testament in its time were lively topics for discussion and potential sources of transformation. So, I wanted to challenge them to think about the poor and marginalized, about mystical experiences, about dying for what you believed in, about having integrity, about loving people unconditionally, about questioning society, about critiquing the government, and much more. However, I learned that it was not enough just to teach if people were not open to learning. Therefore, I came to realize that part of teaching involves addressing blocks to learning.

BLOCKS TO LEARNING

The experience of teaching this class convinced me that people often need "educational therapy" in order to be open to learning. I don't mean therapy for pathologies related to learning, although that was certainly occasionally the case. What I am referring to are obstacles or resistances to learning that arise from painful learning experiences from the past, from attitudes toward the subject matter, and from educational approaches that tend to frustrate learning. At first, I was discouraged and befuddled by these blocks to learning. I just wanted to get on with the business of teaching. And I wanted the students to get on with the business of learning. But I soon realized I could not do that without addressing the resistances I was encountering.

This course on New Testament Scripture had its own special challenges. In this required class, I believe I encountered obstacles to learning that might be found in most subjects in a college curriculum. Hence, although the specific blocks addressed here are particular to biblical studies in a liberal arts institution, they might be adapted to other disciplines where learning blocks are encountered.

I can fairly well quote verbatim what I heard over and over again from the students.

- I've had religion up to here (with a gesture to the neck) from parochial school; so why do I have to take another religion class?
- I have no interest in religion. Why do I have to learn this?
- I already know what the Bible says from church. So why do I have to take this class?
- I do not believe in Christianity or any religion. You are forcing religion on me, and I don't want to learn it.
- You should never question the Bible. If I take this course, I will go to hell.
- What is the point? This course will never help me get a job.
- You are just trying to convert us all to become Lutherans.
- The college is probably making us take this course in order to get money from the Lutheran denomination.

ADDRESSING THE CURSE OF REQUIRED CLASSES

I want to discuss a few of these learning blocks in greater detail, but first I need to explain how I dealt with the considerable student resentment about the bare fact that a New Testament class was required in the first place. This in itself was a major block to learning and had to be dealt with openly. So, on the first day of class, I asked each student to introduce themselves (also as a way to generate social relationships in the group), and I asked each person to give their name and then answer two questions: "Why are you taking this class?" and "What might you hope to get out of the class?" The only stated expectation I had was that they be completely honest.

When the first persons answered the first question, they invariably said that they were "taking the class because it was required"—and this was followed by considerable nervous laughter—after which I complimented them for their honesty. And almost every person in every class answered this first question by saying that they were taking the course "because it's required." In dialogue with students during these introductions, I would joke with the students about what they were saying. We had fun. At the end, I would ask the class as a whole to raise their hand if they were taking the class because it was required. There was something therapeutic about getting this block all out in the open and acknowledging it—because *every* student raised his or her hand. Then I would say, "Well, I want you to know why I am *teaching* this class (pause)—because it's required!" The students would laugh. And then I would add, "Since we are all in this boat together, we might as well have some fun doing it."

The second question I asked—"What do you hope to get out of the class?"—enabled me to flush out many of the obstacles listed above, because most students did not expect to get very much out of the course. Nevertheless, answering this second question tended to defuse the points they raised. And it enabled some students to get beyond the issue of requirement and begin to see how they could take ownership for their learning and how they might actually get something positive from the class—despite the requirement of it. And others in the class, those with predominantly oppositional attitudes, would hear and be encouraged by the positive things that some of the students were hoping to get from the class.

At the end of this exercise, I would then ask the class to brainstorm aloud together a final question: "Why do you think Carthage College requires this class?" This question tended to expose all the suspicions that students had about the nefarious reasons the college was foisting religion upon unsuspecting eighteen-year-olds. And we would joke and laugh about this also—especially when the students were honest. And it gave me a chance to explain that we were not a "Christian college" but a "liberal arts college supported by the church" (big difference!). The college did not teach subjects from a "Christian" perspective but from a secular perspective, and we were hoping students and faculty together would be seeking the truth—wherever that might lead them. And, I would add that the college considered knowing about religion to be part of a liberal arts education. I would explain that I was taking a "liberal arts" approach to the teaching of New Testament. So, already in the first class period, together we addressed most of the blocks and suggested a number of positive attitudes that might open students to learning—an effort at educational therapy! Of course, as the class went along, they would come up again.

ADDRESSING THE BLOCKS

So, more specifically, what might one come up with to address some of these blocks to a class in religion?

Too Much Religion

What about students who said they were so full of religion that they could not take in anymore? In regard to this block, I tried to address their assumptions about teaching and learning. I explained that they were imagining a container model of learning in which the teacher opens the top of a person's head and pours learning into it, an additive approach to learning. I suggested a different view of learning, namely that the new thing you learn often challenges what you might have learned before, and sometimes you even have to start over. Those who have already had a lot of religious instruction may actually be at a disadvantage, because they might have to *un*learn a lot before they could learn the new things they would encounter in this class!

This would be especially true of the students who already "knew everything" about the Bible. When they discovered how much we really do *not* know about the Bible—such as the years in which Jesus was born or died, when the Gospels were written or who wrote them or where they were written, and that some of the letters are pseudonymous—it was like I was telling them for the first time that there is no Santa Claus. At any rate, this experience of uncertainty did open students up to consider new learnings.

Dealing with Uncertainty

Nevertheless, they had to deal in some way with the idea that there are uncertainties before they were ready to move on in the course. Often students tended to attribute the problem of uncertainty to me as someone who must have an idiosyncratic view of these matters. I suggested that they check out the liberal arts approach to religion with someone they trusted, namely, that they consult with their pastor or priest, if they had one. Invariably, after they had attended their home church on a weekend, they would return with the same story: "My pastor told me that she learned these things in seminary the way you are teaching them." Why pastors do not share uncertainties about the biblical writings by the time students reach the age of confirmation classes is beyond me. The course did not focus on uncertainties. They are just there. Nor was the course designed to tear down anyone's faith. But if you already "knew everything for certain," the course did tend to pose challenges.

Some students had the opposite experience. When they started learning about the New Testament, they might not even have been sure that Jesus had existed as a historical figure. So everything they learned about the New Testament built up their picture of Jesus and in no way tore it down. And since they had started with uncertainty, uncertainty was not a problem. The reaction depends on where one starts. I would share this observation with the students.

There was also another, related issue. The main problem with those who "already knew" was complicated when they feared that if we doubt one thing about the Bible, then we cannot be certain of *anything*. The conclusion to that conundrum is: "Do not question anything."

The fear, of course, is the fear of relativism. I discovered a simple description from learning theory that depicts the stages many (but not all) students go through in dealing with uncertainty, and I would present this to them. Namely, students often start out with a dualistic viewpoint, which says that things are either right or wrong, either true or false, either correct or incorrect. When students move into the "treacherous waters" of relativism, they first encounter gray areas of uncertainty (such as the uncertainties cited above) in which, if we only knew more, we would be able to get the correct and true information. These uncertainties are hard enough.

But then there arise those other issues where we simply cannot know for certain: Did Jesus really die for our sins? Does God exist? Is it right to go to war or not? And so on. When we get to these places, we are moving into rampant relativism. If we cannot use the Bible to tell us answers in an absolute way, then any opinion seems to be as good as any other opinion. So what's the use? This is the point at which many students were ready to go back to their rooms, climb into bed, turn the electric blanket up to ten, and stay there. This is also the point at which some students emotionally returned to the safety of "true or false," closed their ears, and remained secure in their certainty. And if this was their choice, of course I honored that.

I then explained that "pure relativism" is not the only option. It is not true that any opinion is as good as any other opinion. There is evidence and there are arguments and you can weigh these and you can indeed come to firm decisions about matters of great importance. The advanced stage toward maturity is "commitment within relativism." This is a place where we stake our claim to things we believe to be true and we stay true to the values we want to embrace, based on our experiences and our considered evaluation of the evidence and of the issues. But there is no absolute certainty. Hence, we must always be open to evidence and arguments that may change our mind. But there is, nevertheless, enough "certitude" to enable us to live and die for some of these beliefs and values.

Maybe these observations did not bring all students through the crisis, but this form of educational reframing helped many to see what was at stake and enabled them to retain their sanity through (what was for them) a disturbing "loss of innocence" about certainty.

Afraid to Question the Bible

Here's another block. What about those students who were afraid to ask questions of the Bible for fear that their mortal soul was in jeopardy? In this case, I felt that it was necessary to address their view of Scripture without putting them on the spot. Many people think that there is only one way to think of the writings in the Hebrew Bible and the New Testament as Scripture, namely, that God dictated these words and every word is true and every word is to be followed. And if that is not the case, then these writings cannot be viewed as Scripture.

So I handed out a sheet showing six ways that different Christian denominations and secular people think about Scripture and the different meanings of the words they use to describe Scripture. For example, Scripture as *revelation* can mean the revelation as "words of God," but it can also mean that the human words of the Bible "reveal not God's words but God's *reality*" and it can mean that some words in Scripture are simply "revealing." Or Scripture as *the word* can refer to "the words of a book," but it can also mean that the "Word" is really not a book but the reality of Jesus (as in the "Word made flesh")—about whom the human words of Scripture bear witness. *Inspiration* can refer to "a kind of dictation by God," or it can refer to "the active presence of God" with those humans who wrote Scripture, or to the active presence of God with those of us who read Scripture, or even to the human response that the Bible can be "inspiring."

Working our way through a handout such as this on "Views of Scripture" offered options for the students. As teacher, I did not suggest what they should think or where they should end up. But the process did enable students to see how they *could* consider these writings as Scripture and *still* study them in this class (or in church) with an open liberal arts approach. They are still the Scriptures of the church, understood as foundational documents of the Christian faith whether seen as documents of absolute truth or not. And there were usually a number of students in the class for whom a liberal arts approach to Scripture was already their own approach, and the sharing of this fact made others comfortable with considering diverse options. This process enabled some students to loosen the white-knuckle grip they had on Scripture or at least acknowledge the legitimacy of other approaches. Also, the few students who were not believers or who were Jews or adherents of another religion (of which there were few at Carthage at that time) would also see some ways to be open to engaging with these writings. Of course, it was critical in the discussion not to put down any point of view but to honor all the options presented as well as the personal view of each student.

It Is a Sin to Doubt

There is another related block to learning; namely, that it is a sin to doubt. How can instructors help students open up to the liberal arts process of seeking truth by asking questions if they do not believe they should question? Again, for these students, I found it helpful to offer some cognitive reframing and redefinition. If faith equals belief in truth statements, then it is wrong to doubt the Bible or the creeds—because, in this scenario, doubt is the opposite of faith. However, if faith is trust in the reality of God, then we should be putting our trust in the *reality* of God rather than in our statements or formulations about God. In fact, in this scenario, to put our trust in some statements about God as though they were absolutes may even be considered verbal idolatry. To overcome verbal idolatry, we are invited to question our statements about God (the Bible, creeds, and so on) so that we do not end up putting our faith in our statements rather than in the living God.

In this scenario we are led to question our human, limited beliefs about God so that we might experience God in fresh ways, or so that we might come to a better understanding of God than we had before, or so that we might confirm in a new way what we believed before. In this reframing, doubt is integral and important for faith to be renewed and revived. As Tennyson wrote in "In Memoriam," "There is more faith in honest doubt / Believe me, than in half the creeds." With this explanation, students were often able to see their questions as an act of faith—the trust that in their honest exploration they might encounter God in new ways. This experience is especially important for college students, who are now having an opportunity, often for the first time, to raise questions about their childhood images of God and perhaps to embrace some more mature understandings.

What about the students who do not believe or who do not care? This approach honors such students, insofar as it affirms whatever questioning they might have done to lead them to their views. Interestingly enough, these students were often the best learners because they were not afraid to question. They were not afraid to say things that sounded sacrilegious to other students. These students did not have to unlearn a great deal before they could approach the texts with a liberal arts method. And they were not shocked to learn of the many uncertainties. In fact, it was sometimes the case that such students were relieved and intrigued that we were facing the difficulties about religion and the Bible in a straightforward way. And they often discovered that the religious views they had previously rejected or ignored were not the ones they were encountering in class.

No Religion for Me: More Reframing

All of these efforts were designed to open students up to studying the Bible through a liberal arts lens. Still, there were people who were just strongly resistant to learning *anything* about the New Testament because it was about religion. Here is an example.

Some years ago when my wife and I were going to a student conference at our grandson's high school, I recognized a teacher in the hall, and I said to her, "I believe I know you. You used to be a student at Carthage College, and you were in one of my classes. I'm Dave Rhoads."

She said, "Yes, and I'm Marna Glover. I know you. You changed my life!"

I was a bit stunned and said, "How was that?"

She said, "When I took your class I was very rigid about religion. I did not believe. I was stubborn about it, and I was determined not to learn anything. It was a course that included the letters of Paul and I could not bring myself to study and I was failing. And I had put off taking the class until my senior year. You took me aside and suggested to me, 'You have to pass this class to graduate. If you have trouble with religion, that's OK. Think of it as a history course. Learn it that way.' And so I did it that way.

"Then," she went on, "several years after college the Lord got hold of me and I had an experience like Paul did on the road to Damascus, just like I learned in the class. And when that happened, I remembered all about Paul's letters, and it all made sense."

I was delighted for her and told her how wonderful it was that she had had such a life-changing religious experience.

I did remember her and other students who held strong views against studying the Bible at all. It helped when I assured them that I was never going to ask them as a requirement for any grade to say what they believed or did not believe. I did encourage them to think of the course as a history class or a literature class or a political science class. I pointed out that in a political science course, they would learn about political philosophies that they themselves likely did not embrace. So, here they were responsible for learning about a religion in which they did not believe. Nevertheless, I explained that Christianity and the Bible have been very influential in our history and society, and here was a chance to learn about these things. I would say: "Keep your beliefs. If this is what you believe, you do not have to abandon it. But learn about the Bible and the liberal arts approach so you can understand how others believe in a different way."

The cognitive reframing enabled students to remove the mental and emotional blocks to personal participation in the class. It *was* a liberal arts class. I made no assumptions about where people began the class or where they might go from there in terms of their religious faith and beliefs—or lack thereof. However, learning is personal. Good education invites the students to engage the subject matter, to grapple with new and different ways of thinking, to imagine other worlds, to challenge and to be challenged.

In a sense, the New Testament texts have to speak for themselves and hold up against questioning and scrutiny or not, whatever the student responses may be. Our task in a liberal arts institute is to encourage engagement with the texts and with the class. But no matter what efforts I made, I would still occasionally see a student close an invisible curtain in front of them. Their eyes glazed over, and they just would not be engaged. And, of course, I honored that also, while still encouraging a positive relationship with me and an ongoing involvement in the learning process.

It Is Not Practical

Finally, maybe the toughest "nut to crack" were the students who said: "This course is irrelevant because it can't get me a job or make me money." This was an important issue and it was on everyone's mind, whatever their major. There is no answer to this that will satisfy a purely utilitarian mind. The idea of learning something for its own sake or to improve their lives or to benefit society does not seem to crack the shell here.

But we can make it clear that many companies that hire actually look for people who have a liberal arts education, companies that prefer well-educated candidates, because the company itself will train for that specific job. The skills they are learning in this liberal arts class—questioning, analyzing, interpreting, and reconstructing the past—are useful for almost any career. And students will also need to think about values and ethics, not just in their *career* vocation but also in their *human* vocation beyond securing their economic and social well-being.

BLOCKS TO LEARNING IN SEMINARY

Later, when I taught in seminary, there was no lack of motivation for the subject or concern about whether it would be useful for their future role as ministers and lay professionals. However, I confronted a different set of blocks. The main problem was that they wanted to know how they might be able to "use" what they learned when they became pastors in congregations. In so doing, they blocked the opportunity to grapple with the subject matter for their *own* lives. I would say: "If you are not changed *now* by the material you are studying, you will have no right *later* to lay it as a trip on other people in a parish!"

For the most part seminary students are better prepared to learn than undergraduates. Nevertheless, some of them were also afraid to grapple with questions but for a different reason; namely, because they had to be accepted by their church candidacy committees, and they did not want to be in the midst of a crisis of faith when they went through this process. Also, many of them were second-career students, some of whom were just eager to get through the program and get on with ministry. Others were averse to the artificial context of the classroom because they wanted to learn by practicing ministry. Occasionally, there were anti-intellectual attitudes, as if being a pastor is a soft profession and as if the professional preparation for pastors was somehow different from the demands of medical school or law school in preparing physicians and lawyers. Addressing these blocks involved different processes and strategies.

CONCLUSION

If I were to teach again, I would set aside time in the first class period to ask *the students themselves* in a straightforward way to name blocks to their learning, and I would ask how they planned to address those blocks. Whatever one may teach and whoever is doing the learning, there will likely be personal obstacles and resistances of some kind, and these blocks need in some way to be addressed in order for students and teachers alike to attain their highest potential. And we need to provide a safe space, a "window of tolerance" for students to explore freely. No doubt all teachers find ways to address the blocks. But we cannot ignore them. Otherwise, we threaten to disengage the students from personal involvement in their learning, and in so doing, we risk turning teaching and learning into a meaningless charade of detached accumulation of knowledge that robs the classroom of excitement and joy. Who wants that?

10

Performing Inside/Outside the Classroom

I GOT THE IDEA to incorporate performance into the classroom from the choir director at Carthage College. I went to the annual concert of the college choir, a wonderful Christmas event held each year in December. I was awed by the quality of the student performances. Wow! How did the director get the students to work so hard in preparation and to work together to produce such a magnificent sound?

My immediate thought was this: "What would I have to do with my students in a class to draw that level of commitment and that quality of work? Many students desire to function at a high level. So what would motivate them to do it?" At the time, I was preparing to teach a January course on Daily Life in Jesus's Time. The January term was a monthlong intensive course meeting each day of the week, a course that lent itself to innovation and experimentation. So I began to figure out what I could do that might result in such high-quality work.

MY FIRST (LIMITED) PLAN

My first idea was that the motivation of choir members came primarily from working together. After all, it was a communal project. Sopranos depended upon altos, who both depended on tenors and basses, and vice versa. I could imagine that each student knew how much the others counted on her or him to be there and to sing well in order to produce the desired sound. Only by cooperation could they together create the marvelous music that was much more than the sum of the parts.

So I devised a process for the study of daily life in Jesus's time that would replicate the interdependence I saw in the college choir. Fourteen students had signed up for the class. I determined that each student would be responsible for one area of daily life such as houses, clothes, work, synagogue, marriage and family life, geography and travel, economic life of peasants, priests, the temple in Jerusalem, festivals and pilgrimage, coins, and so on. The student responsible for a certain area would need to study so as to be an expert in those matters.

At the same time, each student would create an imaginary person out of the first century (no known figure from the Bible or elsewhere) and write an autobiographical story about that person's life—a peasant wife and mother, a farmer from Tiberias, a widow, a tax collector living in Capernaum, a priest from the Temple in Jerusalem, and so on. In order to do this, however, as each one wrote their story, they would have to depend on the other students in order to find out what his or her own character would wear and where they might live and what their labor would be like, in order to construct certain events in the life of the imaginary character they had chosen. In other words, the students would be interdependent. They would count on each other. And this would provide the motivation for quality work.

I was quite pleased with my plan for the upcoming class. So, when I saw John Windh, the choir director and professor of music, I explained to him how I had been inspired by the choir and his leadership. And I told him about my idea for the January class and what I was planning for the students to do and how it would lead them to be motivated as the choir members had been.

His immediate response was clear and direct: "It won't work!"

I was somewhat taken aback. "Why not?" I asked.

"Because," he said, "you need a performance."

Then he explained it to me, "It is primarily because the students know that they will be giving a performance before an audience that instills in them the desire to work hard and to perform well and to take such pride in their work."

Instantly, I saw the wisdom of his words.

NEXT PLAN (MUCH BETTER)

Okay. Back to the drawing board. I did not abandon my earlier idea, but now I had a new challenge. How could I incorporate a performance into the class? Well, I called several churches in the area and got an invitation to do a program for a senior citizens group on a Wednesday morning in late January. I stayed with the earlier plan for the interdependent work of the class and then added a performance into the mix. And what a difference it turned out to be!

On the first day of the class, I told the students about this plan and asked if they would like to accept this invitation to give a performance. They were enthusiastic. We decided that we would develop a program in which the students would perform scenes from first-century Jewish life. The students began choosing their areas of expertise from a list I gave them. Then they each chose an imaginary character. This freedom to choose meant that students had an investment in creating such an imaginary person. So they got to work on their research and reflections. Each day they shared what they had learned, and they conferred with each other about their projects. Then the students had the idea to approach the Theater Department and ask if we could borrow some costumes. With the help of theater students, we picked out garb that was appropriate to each of the characters. In the end, the students not only created their characters, they also *became* their characters.

Once these things were set up and the process of working interdependently took off, the rest fell into place. The students created the program entirely. The scenes were made up of interactions between the characters. A priest declaring a leper clean. A tax collector demanded tribute from a fisherman on the way to market. A Roman soldier arrested a Zealot. Three women talked at the well. And there was a wedding! There were other scenes I cannot recall now, but the whole thing was quite entertaining and informative. Someone would introduce and explain the scene, and then the students involved would act it out. The presentation took almost an hour. We arranged for the audience to pose questions to the students after all the scenes were over. The students remained in character and answered the questions as first-century persons!

The whole thing went so well that the students agreed to repeat the scenes for the Religion Department at the school—faculty members, religion majors, and any other students they wished to invite. This experience took it to another level, because now they had to be able to answer the questions posed by faculty and fellow students. As a result, the last week of the course involved more study in their areas of expertise and more refinement as they rewrote the stories of the characters they had chosen. The performance at the school went extremely well. And amazingly, the students did the performance for the Religion Department with enthusiasm at the beginning of the spring term, *after* the interim class was over!

WHY IT WORKED

John Windh was right: we needed a performance. I learned a lot from that experience. But more importantly, the students learned a lot. There is a Chinese proverb that says:

> Tell me,
> and I will forget.
> Show me,
> and I will remember.
> Involve me,
> and I will understand.

I really felt as if students got a grasp of first-century life in ways they never would have without this involvement. And as we were coming out of the church after the program, one of the students in the class who had been most skeptical said to me: "That was fun!" So I might add to the Chinese proverb:

> Make it fun,
> and I will want to do it again.

What made the difference? Why was performance so critical to the success of this class? Why were the students so engaged? Why were they motivated to do so well? There are probably a lot of good answers to these questions. But a key one is this: an activity done in a classroom just for other students can seem somewhat artificial, but a presentation for an outside audience is for real. Clearly, this is overstated, but it is accurate enough. In a classroom, we do things for the teacher or for other students. It can easily feel like it is just "practicing" or an activity done for a grade. But when there is a real audience outside the classroom, the stakes are raised and the desire to do well is intensified. It is amazing how such an event transcends any motivation a teacher may give the students as a means to bring out the best in them. In fact, as the teacher, I now became a coach or director working *with* the students to prepare for an (outside) activity, rather than as an evaluator and judge.

Also, in all of this, the initial idea to set up an arrangement in which students were dependent upon one another for their learning worked well. And the cooperative learning was enhanced by the fact that they were also working together to prepare and to put on this program. They did it *together*.

Students long to engage in learning that is meaningful, not only for themselves but for others as well. The whole experience of college and seminary often becomes a preparatory state comprised of opportunities to take in information and skills rather than an active experience of giving out in meaningful actions for others. Education often becomes a hoop to jump through, a matter of learning something that will be practiced only after the college or graduate school programs are over. The performance was a way to engage students in an activity in which they were taking in historical knowledge about first-century life, *and* they were also offering it in a way that was meaningful for others.

WRITING FOR AN AUDIENCE

Unfortunately, not many classes lent themselves to this type of performance for an outside group. There came a time when I taught Daily Life in Jesus's Time at night with a larger group, and it was just not workable to have students do scenes from daily life. I did, however, come up with another idea that worked about as well. I asked students to prepare their first-century areas of expertise in written form. These were due in the middle of the course. I quickly edited all the offerings, organized them, had them reproduced, and placed them in a spiral binder. The names of all the contributors were on the front of the book. Before the course was over, each student received a copy of *their book*! But the key was this: they knew from the start that this book they produced would be used as a textbook the next time I taught Daily Life in Jesus's Time. This process turned out to be highly motivating. Their audience was not present at the time, but the "audience" would show up in the next class and see the work and the names of the students who preceded them. And when that next class saw the book and realized that they would be revising and expanding it and that their names would be added to the front cover of the new version of a textbook for the next class, they too were motivated to do the research and to get it right! One summer school class put together a terrific book all about the Temple in Jerusalem. And, in all these cases, I got just the textbook I wanted for my next class.

I used what I learned about performance before an outside group in several other classes. I also learned from the idea of performance that we could do presentations/performances *within* the class in such a way that they too had meaning and did not seem artificial. The key was to make it clear that other students and I were counting on learning from them. In this way, everyone in the class—students and faculty—became a community of learners.

11

Learning to Fish

On Method

EVERYONE HAS A METHOD for interpreting Scripture. We may simply read and take at face value what we read without reflecting on the method we use. But that is our method! The question is: How effective is our method of reading for faithful understanding and interpretation? To answer this question, we need to become aware of our methods and be rigorous about them. This insight can be the beginning of one's education and the start of thinking independently. Certainly it is the onset of critical thinking and constructive dialogue in the classroom. And since every discipline has methods, we would do well to pay attention to them.

READING THE BIBLE IS A CROSS-CULTURAL EXPERIENCE

The process of understanding what we read is not as simple as it appears. This is why method is so crucial. Ordinarily, we have a decent chance of understanding a writing that originates from our own cultural or social location, although we know how fraught with perils even that is. However, reading the Bible is a cross-cultural experience with ancient Mediterranean societies. So, if I take the plain meaning of words, I will be taking their plain meaning from *my* culture rather than the biblical cultures. For example, if I read the word "heart," I will assume it has to do with feelings. But in the biblical world, the bowels were considered to be the locus of feelings, while the heart was the center of imagination and thinking and willing. When I hear the word "love," I think in terms of affection, whereas the biblical term most often meant fidelity and good will. If the word "guilt" occurs, I may psychologize it as "guilt feelings," whereas the ancient cultures would have been referring to the societal judgment of guilt before the public or the law (or God). The upshot is this: we need to become aware of our current method for interpreting and ask in what ways we might gain a more sophisticated method or set of methods in order to understand more faithfully when we read the Bible.

FINDING A METHOD

Too often in education we focus on *what* we think and not enough on *how* we think. We talk about the meaning of what we read without being aware of how we came to determine that meaning. The challenge of education is to make us aware of our thinking process. Michael Gelb's *How to Think Like Leonardo* is a book that identifies the creative processes that led Leonardo Da Vinci to be so inventive and innovative. Likewise, in biblical studies, the challenge of education is to make us aware of how to think like a skillful interpreter of biblical texts. So, we need to say to students: Look at what you are reading and, at the same time, *look at yourself doing the reading!* What are you doing? And how are you doing it?

In general, we teachers do not do a very good job of teaching about method. We tend to display the results of our own scholarship without revealing how we got there—without laying bare the methods we used to determine the results of our thinking. I recall many biblical lectures I have attended in which excellent scholars and teachers spoke about the interpretations they had arrived at, but they did not explain to us how they got to their conclusions. They did not reveal the steps they went through from first picking up a text to their final thoughts about it. We need a biblical crime scene investigation program that lays bare the steps from the gathering of evidence to the analyzing of evidence to the various conclusions we might (or might not) make based on the evidence.

Methods Give Independence

This is like the old saw: Give a hungry person a fish, and they will get hungry again. Teach them how to fish, and they can feed themselves for the rest of their lives. What happens when that analogy is applied to learning? Provide someone with knowledge, and they will not learn how to learn on their own. They will always have to go to an expert to learn. They will be dependent upon the teacher, dependent on secondary sources. However, if you teach students *how* to learn with a method, they will become independent learners. In this way, the teacher makes herself no longer necessary for that student. Like an effective parent or counselor or mentor, the teacher's role is to make herself or himself dispensable. There is exhilaration for the student who is capable of being creative and capable of being independent. There is a confidence that comes from knowing what methodological steps to take in order to get fresh insights that are faithful interpretations.

Early Efforts at Teaching Methods

I became acutely aware of the importance of a rigorous method in teaching years ago when my daughter Tania was in third grade. She was learning to do double- and triple-digit multiplication tables, like 254 x 87. She just could not come out with the right answers. Tania was bright enough, and the teacher was frustrated. So the teacher gave her more and more multiplication problems in the hope that Tania would finally get it. But she did not improve. There was some flaw in her method. I was puzzled also, because she knew her multiplication tables well. So what was the problem? Finally, one day I said: "Tania, I want you to work several of these problems out loud. Just speak out loud everything you are thinking while you are doing the problems, and I will just observe and listen." By the second problem, I knew exactly what was wrong. While she had her multiplication tables down cold, she did not know her addition facts. So when she came to the part of the problem at the bottom where she added, she counted on her fingers or just guessed. So immediately she went back to reviewing and practicing her addition tables. Voilà, the problem was solved.

It occurred to me that I could do the same thing with college students around a method of reading the Bible. So I invited a few students at Carthage who were interested in going beyond the basics in biblical studies to form a kind of "center for advanced learning." It was voluntary, and I engaged only a few students in the process. I had been teaching them in my classes how to do a narrative interpretation of a short biblical passage. In order to advance their learning, I set up a tutorial in which I gave them a passage; and each one interpreted it out loud step by step as I listened and watched what they did. It was amazing how clearly I could see what they had learned but also the steps they missed—where they did not stay long enough with initial questions, where they misinterpreted words, how they overlooked key details of the text, when they failed to see the thematic significance of crucial specifics, and so on. This was eye opening to me. As a result, not only was I able to teach these students concretely how to improve their method so that they would come out with more faithful interpretations, but I was also learning for myself how better to teach the method with large groups in the classroom—so that students could become more careful interpreters by avoiding numerous methodological pitfalls.

This practice of observing a student in the process of using a method put me in touch with ways I was succeeding and ways I was clearly failing in my teaching. To be honest, I was not sure I really wanted to know how I was failing. I sometimes think we teachers do not really want to know what our students have learned or failed to learn. We want to go on thinking that students not only understand but that they also actually buy into what we teach, remember it, and plan to use it! If they do not, well, then it must be their fault.

But learning is not unilateral; it is relational. We do not teach subjects; we teach people. So unless we somehow find a way to see not only *what* students have learned but also *how* they have learned it, we remain rather ignorant of the effectiveness of our teaching. After I began to make the methods of interpretation more intentional, it made all the difference. And for some assigned papers, I asked the students to turn in not only their final essay but also the notes they took and a record of the steps they made to get to the conclusions of that final paper. Eventually, students could watch *themselves* interpret. They could monitor for themselves the steps they were taking and correct the flaws in their process.

SUSTAINED EFFORTS AT TEACHING METHODS

It is not that we teachers do not introduce students to methods in New Testament courses. There are many books on the different methods that are used to interpret the New Testament. However, especially in survey courses, we tend to summarize briefly the methods and then go on, book by biblical book, to explain what the Gospels and letters mean—without connecting the methods to the results of our understanding of these biblical books. We may show students how scholars have done it, but we do not often give students opportunities to practice it. Seldom do students get a chance to learn a method well enough to employ it themselves in the process of trying to figure out what a text might possibly have meant—its range of meanings—in its original context. The result is that we leave the students either reading naïvely or needing to depend on secondary sources for the meaning of a text. How can we linger with a biblical text long enough to figure it out together from start to finish right there in class?

In the New Testament survey class at Carthage, I taught the narrative method by having students practice the same method on each of the four Gospels in turn—making use of exercises that asked them to identify plot, characters, and themes. They also applied a brief methodological process for reading letters and some steps to follow in reconstructing historical events in the life of Jesus.

When I taught at seminary, we had a required course that focused on method. The course was called New Testament Interpretation. It was a methods course (sometimes team taught) that dealt with the ways we go about constructing potential meanings of a text in its first-century context. Ironically, all of the students assumed from the title that we were going to interpret the New Testament for them by telling them what it meant. They were disappointed in the class. Also the students tended to equate "interpretation" with "appropriation"; that is, they thought that by interpreting what the New Testament meant in its original contexts, we would be determining the proper appropriation or application of the texts for today. This expectation bypasses method altogether and reads the New Testament as a document addressed directly to (all) contemporary times and situations. So we changed the name of the course to New Testament Methods of Interpretation. This worked much better in setting up the proper expectations.

More Methods Than Ever

To be honest, the task of teaching methods in biblical studies is enormous these days. When I went to seminary in the mid-sixties, there were basically four methods:

- Text criticism: To determine the original text from many copies
- Source criticism: To identify from where the Gospel writers got their information
- Form criticism: To ascertain what the oral tradition was like before the Gospel writers got hold of it
- Redaction criticism: To figure out what the Gospel writers added to the tradition and what that told us about their purposes

At that time, these methods were usually in the service of (re-)constructing either the historical Jesus or the history of the early church. Together they were referred to as the historical-critical method. The historical method drew upon literature of the period along with archaeological studies as means to construct ancient events and the meaning of ancient texts.

In the last decades, there has been an explosion of new methods. The last time I taught a methods class, the number of methods I taught was up to nineteen! In the field of New Testament, some of the more recent methods include:

- Narrative criticism: To analyze the literary dynamics of the Gospels and Acts
- Reader-response criticism: To assess the impact of a writing on an audience
- Social science criticism: To employ cultural anthropology in interpreting the New Testament
- Rhetorical analysis: To analyze the influence of classical rhetoric on the New Testament, especially the letters
- Linguistic/discourse criticism: To understand the dynamics of biblical Greek
- Performance criticism: To assess the meaning and impact of New Testament writings as oral literature

Any one of these could completely occupy a researcher or a class. These days, it is common and almost necessary not only to specialize in one writing of the New Testament but also to specialize in one method. Add to the methods listed above additional approaches such as postmodern interpretation and deconstruction theory. And these approaches need to be supplemented by liberation methods designed to grasp the ethical dimensions and power dynamics of the writings and of interpreters: feminist criticism, womanist interpretation, ideological criticism, intercultural criticism, postcolonial criticism, empire criticism, and eco-justice criticism.

Methods Are Interrelated

Another factor that complicates the teaching of method is that these methods are interrelated. That fact became apparent in the New Testament Methods of Interpretation course. In this course, I would choose one short book of the Bible from the latter part of the New Testament such as the Letter of James or First Peter as a case study for the application of methods. The methods logically followed a certain sequence. First, we had to see how scholars established a probable original text (textual criticism). Then we needed to reconstruct the context and audience (historical criticism). This led to interpretations of meaning (genre criticism, form criticism, narrative criticism, cultural anthropology, and intertextual analysis). Then we looked at the impact on first-century hearers (rhetorical criticism and performance criticism). Finally, we considered how contemporary critics from diverse social locations interpreted and evaluated the text ethically and ideologically (liberation criticism, feminist criticism, eco-justice criticism, postcolonial criticism, and so on). The students wrote several papers on the chosen text, each based on a certain method of their choice. Because the biblical writing was short and because the students went over the same text many times with different questions based on the different methods, there was a wonderful sense of discovery among them. It was a course that probed into some deep exegetical waters.

New Methods Are Comprised of New Questions

This is the delicious part about new methods. They produce new interpretations. Actually, most innovations in biblical studies come not from new discoveries out of the ancient world but from the introduction of new methods. To be sure, some developments come from new discoveries—such as the Dead Sea Scrolls, the Nag Hammadi texts, and the excavation of archaeological sites. Some innovations come from reading the New Testament writings in light of already-known ancient texts or events not previously connected to them, such as the works of the Stoics or the writings of Flavius Josephus or the events surrounding the Roman-Judean War of 66–70 CE.

However, many if not most breakthroughs in biblical studies come from adopting new methods—that is, from addressing *new questions* to the same texts. The new methods in biblical studies are usually adopted from secular disciplines in the study of secular subjects and then adapted to biblical materials—such as narratology, cultural anthropology, postcolonial analysis. The new methods do not usually produce new information. Rather, they offer new angles of vision that enable us to see features of ancient texts and past events that have not been explored before.

Take narrative criticism, for example. Until the late 1970s, we did not appreciate the narrative qualities and features of the Gospels. Then a group in the Markan Seminar of the Society of Biblical Literature began to apply methods to the Gospels drawn from secular literary methods to investigate plot, characters, settings, norms of judgment, ideal author and reader, and literary rhetoric. Before that, most scholars had been occupied with peeling away the layers of tradition and redaction to get behind the Gospels in order to reconstruct the historical Jesus, the history of the Gospel community, and the way the author put it together. Those methods taught us much, but they also fragmented the text into tradition (what the writer preserved) and redaction (what the writer added). By contrast, narrative analysis was interested in the dynamics of the final product of a Gospel as a whole. Narrative analysis looked at the entire text as it stands before us and asked about its overall impact on readers. We came to appreciate the incredibly skillful ways in which the composers of these ancient Gospels had crafted their stories to have such an impact. This had not been done before, and it opened up a new arena of interpretation.

For another example, classical rhetorical criticism was introduced to biblical studies in the 1980s. Rhetorical criticism led us to look for the first time at the ways in which the New Testament writings reflected characteristics of ancient rhetorical theory and practice. It is much more appropriately applied to letters than to the stories of the Gospels. We now analyze New Testament letters as rhetorical speeches. We discern the issue at stake, the species of rhetoric involved, the order of the arguments, the uses of ethos, pathos, and logos as means of persuasion, the tropes and figures of speech, as well as the style—all means to help us understand how a letter might have had certain impacts on ancient hearers.

As further examples, postcolonial criticism and empire studies are bringing to light the political relationship between the early Christian communities and the Roman Empire in ways never before explored. These and other methods have opened up new vistas in the dynamics and potential meanings of the biblical writings.

None of these new methods provide new sources. Rather, they make the old sources new. They have taught us how to explore the texts before us in fresh ways, how to notice what had been neglected, how to correlate and organize the material differently, and how to (re-)construct historical events/dynamics as we had not previously imagined them. All of these methods can be laid out as a set of questions to be posed and steps to be taken as a basis for teaching them to students, all as heuristic devices to investigate the text in context. Of course, methods are more intuitive and complex and artful than I am presenting here. Also, methods have their own limitations in tendencies and biases that shape interpretation. But for the purposes of launching students and introducing them to the importance and possibilities of methods, the idea of developing a methodological model to apply to the text is extremely helpful. Why give students a text without a method by which to analyze it?

Teaching a Method with a Case Study

One technique for teaching method in a course is to combine the study of a given text with the study of a certain method that works well with the type or genre of the text under consideration. This correlation of text and method works especially well in upper-level electives and doctoral seminars. Students learn a method and then apply it to the text in question as a case study, such as narrative criticism and Matthew, rhetorical criticism and Galatians, discourse analysis of Philippians, or cultural anthropology and Luke. The students are responsible for showing that they understand the method, that they know how to use it, and that it results in a cogent outcome of interpretation or historical reconstruction.

The fun part of all this is that making new discoveries from a fresh method in the classroom replicates the original development of this method among biblical scholars. Just as our scholarly use of a new method opens vistas of interpretation for scholars, so now students can awaken to ways of studying the Bible that are wholly new to them. Even more delightful is a situation where students are employing a method that has never been applied to the text they are studying! In those cases, they are on the cutting edge of biblical scholarship—not only in doctoral courses but also in college electives and seminary classes, even survey courses. I have seen innovative interpretations of texts in a ten-page paper for a class—simply because what the student was doing was something entirely fresh. What a thrill it is to share your assessment of that with the students and to encourage their further study!

THREE CAVEATS ABOUT METHOD

First, as I have said, method is much more complex and malleable than I have depicted it here. A method is not a cookie cutter. The idea is not to get a model or a set of questions that will basically determine the outcome of what one will find. Rather, the questions are designed to explore and try things out. They are meant to open up the text to new ways of seeing. They serve as a "heuristic device"—that is, as an approach that helps one tentatively and helpfully to notice things one might not otherwise have seen and to make connections one might not otherwise have made. The questions are adapted, and the method itself is adjusted and modified to adapt to the text as one goes along. In this way, the method is less like a straitjacket and more like jazz improvisation in which one uses imagination and freedom. Trial and error and intuition become as important as logic and rigor.

Second, methods are never neutral. Just as readers and interpreters are always biased and invested (in terms of what they look for, in terms of how limited they are in perspective, and in terms of how their social location and values shape their way of seeing), so also methods are not disinterested approaches to a text. Methods bear assumptions and implications, strengths and limitations, which shape what practitioners of those particular methods look for and how they "see." For example, narrative criticism looks for the unity in a text. As a result, narrative critics tend to find connections and coherences in the discourse of a narrative and in the dynamics of its narrative world. The problem is that they may find coherences that are not really there. By contrast, deconstruction criticism appreciates the fact that texts, like life, are rife with gaps and fissures, breaks and inconsistencies, contradictions and paradoxes, suppressed ideas and suppressed voices. In so doing, this method may miss coherences in the texts. Both approaches are important to complement and correct each other in the analysis of a text. And like people, methods have power dynamics. They may have an impact on life for good or for ill. They may reinforce the status quo or they may work for the liberation of the oppressed. We cannot be naïve about our methods. We must use them with full awareness of their power dynamics.

Finally, the use of methods is not designed to "master" a text. Investigation and curiosity transcend method and generate a posture of respect in relation to the subject matter. In this regard, our relationship with the text can be quite intimate. The legendary story is told about a nineteenth-century naturalist at Harvard who handed a fish on a piece of newspaper to a graduate student as a way of giving him a field exam. "Describe the fish," he said by way of direction. The student went off and made a description of the fish as it lay before him. When he returned with the fish and the description, the botanist was a bit disappointed and he handed the fish back to the student and repeated, "Describe the fish!" The student was a bit bewildered and decided that perhaps the examiner wanted the proper Latin names for what he was describing. So he did that and returned to the professor. At this point, the botanist was clearly frustrated. He again handed the fish back to the student and said emphatically, "*Look* at the fish!" The story goes that a week later with the fish now in an advanced state of decomposition, the student was beginning to *know* the fish—and in a way that transcended any initial methods he had used to describe it. There is no substitute for persistent absorption in what one is studying as a model for deep, patient, and close observation. As Yogi Berra once said, "You can observe a lot just by looking." As such, a method may turn out to be just the entry into study that transforms one's relationship to the subject matter.

MAKING THE TEACHER DISPENSABLE

In this whole process of teaching methods in the classroom, the relationship between teacher and students is distinctive. The teacher functions mostly as a mentor. The student is like an apprentice. The student is doing the work. The teacher models the method; teaches the origins, the theory, and the practices of the method; gives students an opportunity to apply the method; gives feedback to the students' efforts; has the students advance in their use of the method in the interpretation of a text; and, finally, gives more feedback. In all of this, the teacher seeks to engender curiosity and fascination with the subject matter. Through this process of modeling and giving feedback to student practice, the teacher weans the students from dependence on the instructor so that they know "how to fish." Now, on their own, they can use the same method to interpret other texts. When it works, there is a sense that the student is launched and that the formal educational part of their learning is complete. Go fish!

12

Learning to Write, Learning to Teach Writing

It is a truism to say that the way we teach is related to the way we ourselves have learned. This insight may be as true in regard to teaching the skill of writing as much as any other aspect of education. I learned how to teach writing mainly by learning how to write. This reflection recounts that struggle.

A LONG PERSONAL STRUGGLE

I thought I was a fairly good writer in high school. College, however, did not reinforce that impression of myself. In my first year at Gettysburg College, I took freshman English with Mrs. Weinhorst. She told us that she read an entire book every day no matter how late she had to stay up to complete it. She always looked tired. But I do not think it was from reading books. I think it was from grading our English papers! We must have had twenty to twenty-five students in that class, and we wrote a paper each week during that semester. It was a two- or three-page handwritten (back in ancient times!) paper on a subject we were assigned. Apparently, I did not think much about how to write the essays. I just sat down and wrote. When I got my papers back, there were red marks all over them—and I mean *all* over them. The enduring thought I had in that class was this: She obviously spent more time grading my paper than I did writing it! I was embarrassed about that. I admired her greatly. Yet, somehow, I did not succeed in learning to write any better. That was not her fault. I did not stop to figure out what I was doing wrong and then change my habits. Rather, I just kept writing, and she kept wearing down her red pencils. I envied my friends who were talented enough to write for the school paper or the literary journal. But it was obviously not my gift. I got a C for freshman English. Now *that* was a gift.

I managed to get through the many papers I wrote for college classes, as well as the seminar papers for seminary and graduate school. I did well enough, but I never got any guidelines in my head to follow for good writing. I no doubt strove to be clear, but I did not have a set of procedures to attain that. And it obviously did not come to me naturally.

Dissertation: What a Difference an Editor Makes

It was not until I got to my dissertation that I learned how to write. W. D. Davies was my dissertation advisor. He was a wonderful human being. When I went to him to set my dissertation topic, we decided on the Jewish revolutionaries of the first century. Then Dr. Davies said to me, "Come back to see me when you have something written." So I went to work. A year later I had something written. It was over a hundred pages of my own analysis of the revolutionaries based on a close study of the Jewish historian Flavius Josephus. It was time to see Dr. Davies.

How did this teach me to write well? My wife Sandy was my typist. She was an excellent writer. She had been an English major in college, and she had a master's degree in English literature from Duke. As she was typing my paper, she read it very carefully. She would get to the end of one paragraph and the beginning of another, and she would say, "Why do you say this next? What does this have to do with what you just said?" I would patiently explain the connection, and she would say, "Then why don't you write that?" So, I would go back and revise. This happened umpteen times. The revisions I made seemed numberless. Her retyping seemed endless. Finally I had these one hundred or so pages ready to give to Dr. Davies.

Now I feared that Dr. Davies would not be so pleased with my writing. I had good reason for this. One time I had gone to see him on an incidental matter, and he was reading another dissertation, making marks throughout. He looked up and said, "I should not have to be the person to edit this student's work like this." So, I was afraid of his reaction about my own work.

I dropped my paper off ahead of time. After he had read my draft, I made an appointment to go to his office and get a response from him. I waited impatiently. The first words he said were these: "I can't tell you what a pleasure it is to read something so clear." I was elated. And I knew exactly why he had had that reaction to my draft: Sandy! I went home directly from Dr. Davies's office. I went up to Sandy, and she said, "Well, how did it go?" I literally knelt down in front of her, looked up at her plaintively, and said, "Please don't ever leave me!" I went on to complete the dissertation. The only thing that Dr. Davies edited in the dissertation was an expansion of the title: "Some Jewish Revolutionaries in Palestine from 6 to 73 C.E. According to Josephus"—designed to cover my "you know what" by making sure I did not promise a whit more than I actually produced. He also added a last line to what he thought was an appropriate conclusion. I loved it.

Making Feedback a Habit

But that was not the last of my learning about writing, not by a long shot. I went to teach at Carthage College. At that time, I was revising my dissertation for publication as a book. I had a new manuscript prepared. I thought I had better get a reader. My best friend was in the English Department. Don Michie was a meticulous person and willing to help. I thought: "I bet he likes this OK. I'm a pretty good writer now, and he'll be able to do some helpful if minimal editing." After he had had a chance to work with it for a while, I was anxious to hear how it was going. So I called him on the phone and said: "How is it going?" I waited. There was a loooong silence. "Whoops," I thought. He said, "Well, I am having some problems. I am testing every line against the line that precedes it and the line that follows it. And they don't always connect." (Actually I think he said, "They don't *often* connect!") In any case, I thought, "OK. If this is the way it is, that's what I need to hear. I would sooner have the feedback *now* than *after* it was published! Besides, how many friends would read a manuscript that carefully and be honest about it?"

Ever since this experience, I have never published anything without various readers first giving feedback. Sandy continued to be an excellent reader for me. In addition to Don, another reader has been a close friend, a Markan scholar, Joanna Dewey. Years ago, Joanna and I agreed to read each other's drafts and give feedback. One of us would e-mail the article.

The other would read it, and then we would have a lengthy telephone call carefully going over the draft point by point, line by line.

In my writing, I strive mainly for clarity. I start by getting ideas down on the page. I read and reread as I reorder and refine, checking the thesis and the transitions—usually with many rewritings. A New Testament colleague, Carolyn Osiek, told me that her articles just seem to unfold before her as she writes, references and all. When she finishes, there it is, pretty much in final form. And they are beautiful articles. I wish I could do that. But I need to step back from a draft for days and weeks to read it again. And I need other eyes to tell me where it does and does not work and how I need to edit.

NOW, HOW DID I TEACH IT? SOME PRINCIPLES FOR STUDENTS

I have tried to teach others what I have learned about writing—namely, to aim for clarity. But the shift from learning it to teaching it was difficult. Any time I required an essay or a paragraph in my courses at Carthage College, I was in the business of teaching English composition. During my time at Carthage and later at LSTC, I discovered a few basic principles that students needed to know if they were to sharpen their writing. Here are five of them.

1. Your Reader Is Not a Mind Reader

The first principle is this: The reader has only the words on the page. You may think you have said something quite clearly with subject, thesis, transitions, and supporting evidence, but a lot of your essay is still in your head and not on the paper. This is what Sandy and Don taught me with their feedback to my work. I knew where I was going and what I meant, but the reader was limited in not having my mind to go along with the paper. So we must test each line to see that we have made all our ideas—assumptions and arguments, purpose and steps to get there—explicit for the reader.

2. The Teacher Is Not Your Primary Audience

The second principle is this: Do not think of your teacher as the primary audience. If you think of the teacher as the primary audience, you may tend to assume that your reader knows a lot about the subject matter and hence you do not need to explain much: "The teacher will know what I mean!" I usually suggest that students write for other students who are not taking this course, people who know generally about the subject matter but have not studied it like you have. Then it is incumbent upon you to explain to them exactly and fully what you mean. The teacher is then reading over your shoulder for the clarity, accuracy, thoroughness, and cogency with which you have written.

3. State Your Conclusion Up Front

The third principle is this: Put your conclusion at the beginning as your thesis. Many people writing essays make the mistake of thinking they will take the reader on the same process they took in researching the subject and coming to their conclusion. They state the subject, work through the evidence they found, and come at the end to the conclusion of their work. Unfortunately, this seldom works, because it leaves the reader in the dark through most of the essay. Besides, the essay ends up being a report of your research rather than an argument or an explanation. This fallacy is the most common problem with first drafts of doctoral dissertations. They take a long time to get to the point! So, if you put the conclusion at the front, make it into your thesis, and then organize the evidence into key points that support/explain the thesis, the reader will encounter a much clearer essay.

4. Make a Point and Support It

The fourth principle is this: Develop a thesis with an edge to it. Learning how to write a thesis or purpose statement is one of the most difficult processes there is. Most students think that the announcement of their subject matter is enough: "This passage in Galatians deals with the freedom of the Christian." But that is a statement of the subject, not a thesis. A thesis is a statement about what you will argue or what you will explain *about* that subject. For example, "In this passage, Paul claims that freedom is liberation from law for a life lived in response to the Spirit." If you are doing an interpretation paper on a passage of Scripture, you need to posit the overall meaning or purpose of the passage or make a point about its rhetorical impact, so as to be able to explain the whole passage in light of the thesis statement. The thesis statement cannot be awkward or too complex. Once the statement is clear, it is easier to proceed with the rest of the essay. It may take a few drafts to come up with a good thesis statement, and it may need to be revised as you write and as you edit the essay.

5. "Draw a Map" for Your Reader

The fifth principle is this: Explain where you are going, and then go there. Joanna Dewey always tells me: "I need a map. Tell me where you are going." This is the chance to foreshadow the direction of the essay and then to make the subsequent transitions so clear that the reader knows exactly what you are doing and where you are going. Here are three principles to follow.

- The essay should be *unified* around the one comprehensive statement made as the thesis. In turn, each paragraph should be unified around the one topic sentence for that paragraph. Anything that deviates or brings in extraneous points will detract from the purpose of the essay and the paragraph. Hence, to write a unified essay, you will be able to use only the research or insights that support the thesis statement of the essay and not others. It is so tempting to do otherwise.
- The essay should also be *coherent*; that is, it should be clear to the reader how the topic sentence of each paragraph relates to the overall thesis and how it relates to the previous paragraph. It should be clear how each sentence within a paragraph relates to the topic sentence of the paragraph and to the previous sentence in the paragraph.
- Finally, the essay should be *clear*. The reader should be able to follow thesis, paragraphs, and sentences, so that she or he knows at all times where you are going.

THE CHALLENGES: TEACHING FOR IMPROVEMENT

How can we teach these and other principles so that the students will actually improve in the course of the semester? Here are a few ideas.

Make It Inescapable

One problem is that many students see "writing" as a subject limited to the required course of freshman English. Almost all my advisees at Carthage College would say to me, "I want to take English in my first semester so I can get it out of the way." I would reply, "Don't you mean to say that you want to take it early on so you can use what you learn to write better papers in your subsequent courses?" Well, no, they usually didn't mean that, but it was a shot at reframing. The other problem is the idea that the students would find out what each teacher wanted and to try to do that—and as soon as the class was over, they would forget. "This is what Rhoads wants. I'll do it for this class, but I won't have a class with him again."

The best antidote to these attitudes toward freshman English was a great program at Carthage called Writing Across the Curriculum. All faculty members went to workshops to learn how to teach writing in all of our classes and to do it in a common way. Writing was inescapable, and the basic course was the *foundation* for students. Subsequently, they would get similar instructions for writing in every class! If they learned it right up front, then they would not only do better in all subsequent classes, but they would improve with repeated practice.

Engender Improvement

The idea is that the student should become a better writer between the beginning and the end of a course. The most common way to do this is to give feedback on the papers they write. In some ways, however, it is almost too late to be helpful by the time you give feedback on an essay. The students get a paper back a week or so after they turn it in, and they are mainly interested in the grade. And the teacher's comments on that essay may be long forgotten when they get to the next essay, unless you insist that they dig it out and reread it before they write the next one. I learned the hard way when subsequent essays by students in the class did not get any better than the last ones—like *my* lame efforts in freshman English.

My best efforts came when I looked at some actual essays together with the students. I would photocopy essays with common problems. I would wait several years, remove the names of the students from the papers I had saved, and project them onto a screen so that the whole class could look at them together. Then I would read aloud and comment as I read, pointing out the successes and problems with each essay—good thesis statement, no thesis statement; paragraphs making more than one point; strong or weak transitions; topic sentences or no topic sentences; and so on. Or I would put up five different examples of a thesis statement and ask students to identify what was helpful or problematic about them.

Show What a Good Paper Looks Like?

One semester, I got permission from students for everyone to read all the essays in the class *after* I had put the comments and the grades on them (I removed the names). From this exercise, I became convinced that students do not improve from one essay to the next in part because they do not know what an A or a B essay looks like. So students who make Cs or Bs will just keep trying harder rather than trying smarter and end up making the same mistakes. When they had the opportunity to read all the papers, to see the range of essays, and to understand why I gave the different grades I gave, it was a real eyepopper for some of them. They had examples before them of what to aim for. The greatest improvements came in the semesters when we did this practice.

Self-Correction

All of this became labor intensive for them and for me. So after that experience, I simply wrote out on a sheet the most common problems in writing essays along with examples, and then asked them to check their essays for these problems before they submitted them. Instead of just spell-checking, they did *essay-checking*. The goal, of course, was to wean the student from dependence on the teacher as the one to point out a lack of clarity or cogency. They could correct their own papers. Of course, this approach was adapted for adult learning from my daughter's third grade practice sheets for learning grammar. But what the heck! It worked!

Writing One Good Paragraph at a Time

By the time I began at the seminary, I had some new ideas to engender good writing and informed essays. When students were assigned an article to read for class, I asked them to submit a summary paragraph of the article beginning with the thesis or overall point of the article as the topic sentence of their paragraph and then fill the paragraph with points/details/illustrations from the article that supported and explained the thesis—sort of a mini-essay. This turned out to be an exercise that not only taught good writing but also fostered careful reading.

Another approach that worked well with students in doctoral seminars was to work step by step through the entire process of researching and writing a paper. The student would choose the subject the first day of a course and go through a series of steps week by week that included progressive drafts with feedback and suggestions from me and other students about content and style, until, by the end of the semester, they had a polished and insightful paper. Actually, with this model, some students were able to publish the papers they produced for class or present them as papers at regional conferences on the Bible. I got this idea in conversation with Amy-Jill Levine, a scholar and friend who was teaching in the doctoral program at Vanderbilt University—whose students publish an extraordinary amount of their academic work. It worked remarkably well for students who wanted to establish themselves as scholars even while still in their doctoral program.

"Free Writing" on the Subject

Another technique is the use of brainstorming as a way of developing a paper. After doing a close analysis of a biblical passage in its literary and historical context and after reading relevant secondary sources, students were encouraged to sit at the computer and just write everything they thought and had learned about the subject—sort of a stream of consciousness in which each thing you write triggers the next thought. They did not try to write a paper. Rather, they used the brainstorming exercise to help formulate and discover insights. A lot of what they wrote was unusable in their final work. At the same time, they would often be surprised at the gems that popped out in this free-thinking exercise. Then they would step back to see what focus emerged. A theme sometimes became clear first, and then a thesis presented itself from this process.

Then they saw how various points could be organized to support or explain the thesis, omitting what is extraneous and doing further research where needed. They prepared an outline. They reviewed their notes and filled in the essay with specificity. Then they edited for clarity, unity, and coherence. And voilà! An essay.

EVALUATING PAPERS FOR THREE DIFFERENT DIMENSIONS

Finally, partly as a way to emphasize the importance of good writing, I also came to develop a process of evaluating and grading papers. I used three independent but related lenses or criteria designed to give feedback on different dimensions of the students' papers: clarity, faithfulness/insight, and comprehensiveness. Here are the criteria as I would announce them to the students as part of the assignment.

- *Clarity*: Can your audience follow the purpose and train of thought easily? Do you set things up and explain things clearly for your audience? Do you have a straightforward thesis and supporting arguments? Are paragraphs unified under topic sentences? Are sentences clear?
- *Faithfulness/Insight*: Do your points represent a faithful account of the context and purposes of the passage you are interpreting? Do your points illuminate the passage in cogent ways? Does your analysis shed light on the passage? Have you been innovative and creative? Where appropriate, have you suggested an interesting contemporary application of the passage (in the opening or final paragraph)?
- *Comprehensiveness*: Do you set up your analysis with information about the historical context and the larger work in which the passage occurs? Do you cover everything in your passage that needs to be covered to make your point? Do you draw on the rest of that biblical writing in which the passage occurs (theme, ideas, other passages in the work) to develop and illuminate the analysis of your passage? Have you employed secondary sources well?

Here is why this approach may be helpful. A student may write clearly, but they may not be cogent in their interpretation of a biblical passage. Or a student may be clear in their writing and faithful in their interpretation, but they have not covered all the relevant material needed in order adequately to offer their interpretation. Or a student might have covered many points but not organized them well. And so on. How could I honor each area? How could I critique each aspect of the essay? I learned that if I gave a single grade for the whole paper, it was difficult for the student to know exactly what I was affirming and what I was critiquing in the essay. So, I gave different grades in the three different dimensions without collapsing them into one. This led me to give comments throughout the paper on these three dimensions. At the end of the paper, I also offered a brief overall explanatory evaluation of the grade I gave for each of the three areas of evaluation. The advantage was that I could value and treat writing as important in its own right while also focusing on content and comprehensiveness.

CONCLUSION: FINDING YOUR WAY

Obviously, every teacher finds distinctive ways to deal with writing—based on his or her experiences, the needs of the students, the subject matter involved, and the expectations of the program. It was a lengthy process for me to get to the point where I was comfortable with teaching the skill of writing, and it was well worth the effort for the students—and for me! But this is a new age with the ubiquity of the internet and artificial intelligence aiding research and writing. So, creative efforts will be needed.

13

Silence

It may seem strange to consider silence as an integral part of learning and teaching, but I am convinced it is essential to good education. I am *not* talking here about the silence that the students are exercising while listening attentively to the teacher and to each other. Or the silence involved in reading in preparation for class. Or the anxious silence after a teacher's question that is meant for the student to guess an answer the teacher already has in mind. Or, most emphatically, the *silencing* of students through rules, shaming, and intimidation, often experienced by students in any number of classes in their educational experience as a means to suppress and control their participation and their opinions.

CREATIVE SILENCE IN THE CLASSROOM

No, I am talking about silent silence, purposeful silence, creative silence. Such silence belongs to the mystery of learning, indeed to the mystery of transformation. But this seems odd in a classroom, doesn't it? After all, when we talk about education, are we not talking about verbal teaching by the teacher and verbal responses by the students? Or students talking among themselves? Aren't talking and speaking what teaching and learning are all about? I have sometimes lurked briefly in the hallway outside classrooms just to overhear what goes on inside. If you listen to the conversation inside a classroom, you will no doubt hear speaking of some kind going on virtually 100 percent of the time (unless the students are taking an exam). And most of that time, it will be the teacher speaking. It would be unusual to "hear" much silence.

Being Comfortable with Silence

Nevertheless, one of the primary qualifications of an effective teacher is the capacity to be comfortable with silence. Typically, when teachers ask a question worth pondering, they may need to wait a long time for students to formulate answers or gather the courage to speak. If teachers are not comfortable with silence, then they may quickly fill any void themselves. If a teacher asks a question and there is no forthcoming response in fairly short order, the teacher may think the students have nothing to say or do not know or will not answer, and so they become impatient. The result is that teachers fill the silence by answering their own questions. Furthermore, in so doing, they will be giving to the students the message that if they just keep quiet long enough they will not have to speak at all—because the teacher will always rescue them! If it is true that people often learn best by speaking their thoughts and ideas out loud, then we need to be patient in silence while students prepare their hearts and minds to speak.

Being silent does not come naturally to most of us. So, the practice may involve a transformation of us as teachers up front so that we are at peace with our silence and not anxious about filling the void. Only then might the silence happen organically without manipulation.

The Practice of Silence

I developed a practice in which I tried to address this problem. When I posed a genuinely reflective question inviting student views on something (not a fact-finding question), I sometimes encountered a long, awkward silence. The first time it occurred, I would say, "I want you to know that I'm very comfortable with silence, and I'm in no hurry. So speak when you're ready to speak, because I really want to know what you think about this question." Then I returned to silence, and waited. I had to be prepared for silence after the first and second and third speaker, and so on. Otherwise, I found myself picking up the beat again after one or two students spoke, and the value of the initial silence was obviated. Sometimes I would say between speakers, "Others?" And then lapse into silence again. I tried to be careful not to correct or add to answers as they came up. Sometimes, praise God, students would even begin speaking to each other!

Silence is crucial to learner-centered education and a sign that the teacher takes student views very seriously. It is captured with precision by the title of a recent book, *Teaching with Your Mouth Shut*, by Donald Finkel. I was privileged several times to team teach with Don Michie, an English professor whose comfort level with silence was legendary. In a course on business English, he began the first class with the words, "Well, what do you think?" And those were the last words he spoke the entire first fifty-minute period! And the students spoke the whole time. What a message those students got about what would be expected of them through the class! It was crystal clear that they were going to be taking responsibility for their learning.

I had another team-teaching experience with Don that was quite formative for me. At Carthage, there was an honors program among freshmen students that was almost entirely learner-centered. In one given year, there were three of us team instructors who decided to try an experiment. We would give an initial assignment to read, say, something from Plato or Virgil. When the students arrived for class the next day, they all sat in a circle and were invited to discuss what they had read. After they had discussed it for a while, one of us teachers would say, "You don't get it" (a statement, incidentally, that was true). When the students would ask what they did not get, the faculty would revert to silence. So the students would return to discussion. Again a faculty person would say, "You don't understand." And then revert to silence. After several class periods of this, the students were completely baffled and frustrated—accusing us teachers of not doing our jobs. So one student finally said, "Okay, if you're not going to teach, we'll just go to the library and figure it out for ourselves!" Bingo! They got it! And when they returned for the next session, they took over the class. And the silence, the refusal to fill the void, the refusal to give "answers," the refusal even to engage in leading conversation—all led to the desired outcome. Without the silence, I doubt this would have happened. We could not guarantee it would engender the desired result, but when the process worked, it served to foster independent, self-motivated, and creative learners.

I have not repeated this exercise. Frankly speaking, in general it frustrates students unnecessarily. Most students really do need *some* direction or process or framework to proceed. Nevertheless, I learned from that dramatic experience how the power of silence can shift the responsibility for learning from teacher to students.

SILENCE AS A SIGN OF INTIMACY

Ultimately, however, the meaning of silence does not lie in its usefulness as a pedagogical technique. Rather, silence is an end in itself. It is the act of being present in the present. In this regard, silence is a sign of intimacy. To be comfortable with silence is to be comfortable with people. I know that I have reached a level of friendship with someone when we can just sit together in a car ride or over a meal and simply enjoy the silence together while we think. Then when someone is ready, they will speak.

I learned this in conversation with a friend and fellow scholar who is somewhat reserved. We had a tradition of meeting for dinner each year at our national conference of biblical scholars, the Society of Biblical Literature. In conversation over our meal, I would speak, but then it would seem to me that it was a long time before my friend would speak. At first I filled the void. But then it became a discipline for me just to wait. I love my friend, and it was always worth waiting for him to share, because he had such insightful things to say. I learned to relish these slow-moving conversations. I discovered that just as people have a zone of *personal space* in which they are comfortable (how physically close they feel comfortable being next to another person), so also people have a comfort zone of *personal time* in conversation. And what I would have missed if I had filled the time!

Silence can even be a chance to be intimate with oneself. Our space is so filled up with games on the phone and social media and news feeds. We seldom stop to be with ourselves, just to think, just to experience solitude as a precious gift to be nurtured. I once assigned students to meditate for twenty minutes on one of the symbols for Christ in the Gospel of John. The students had the hardest time with this assignment because they were not doing something. So, practicing solitude in the classroom as part of the learning process just might contribute to our personal well-being, even to our deeper sense of humanity.

A Quaker Pedagogy?

Consider the meetings of the Society of Friends. If you are not comfortable with silence, do not become a traditional Quaker. Some Quakers meetings are done almost completely in silence. They do not fill their time with structured liturgies of hymns and litanies and sermons and prayers. Rather, they wait for the Spirit to lead them. So they may sit for a long time in silence until the Spirit leads someone to speak. And what is spoken is usually thoughtful and inspired, worth pondering with even more silence. What about honoring silence in a classroom periodically just to think? We have to make space so that the Spirit can get a word in edgewise!

How about a Quaker pedagogy? What if we gave an assignment for people to ponder and reflect about ahead of time, and then had "Quaker" meetings. What would the conversation be like in class if we invited people to wait and listen for reflective guidance before the next person should speak? Of course, the subject matter would have to be conducive to such a process. You would not want to do it every class period. But when you did it in one class period, it might change the dynamics of every succeeding class period because the whole group would be more comfortable with silence and probably more thoughtful about what they said. They would be trained to think a while and to think more deeply before they spoke.

A Word from God Maybe?

I imagine the void that preceded creation in the story in Genesis was characterized by a profound silence that lasted billions of eons. Then God spoke. And what a word! "Let there be light," and there was light! What if we considered that many ordinary acts of creation might well share this dynamic: first silence, then a word, and possibly then a creative transformation of some kind. Silence is the matrix out of which thoughts, ideas, feelings, and actions are born/created in a person or in a group. Consider the purpose of some meditation programs, namely, to think of nothing. What eventually comes forth is indeed "creation out of nothing." Sandy tells the story of the high school teacher who asked the principal if she could begin each class with meditation. The principal okayed the request as long as the teacher called it relaxation and focusing. The result was significant in the learning that followed. Occasionally, I would begin a class with a brief silent meditation, and it generally served to make the class discussion more focused and thoughtful.

I recall Tommy Tyson, a Methodist pastor/evangelist, telling this story. He went to lead a revival, an evangelistic retreat, for several nights at a church in an inner city. Next door worked a prostitute who walked prominently around the neighborhood and in front of the church in the evenings. As Tommy and the leaders prepared in prayer for the revival, the elders began to say terrible things about this woman and to ask God to judge her and keep her away from their meetings. Tommy stopped them and said, "If we offer these thoughts as prayers to God for this woman, the thoughts might tear her to shreds. These might be our human thoughts, but do you think God has a thought about this woman?" Then they returned to prayer. There was a long, long silence. Here was the seedbed out of which something new might emerge. And finally one of the elders spoke the word: "Let the one who is without sin cast the first stone!" As a result of this experience, the entire atmosphere of the group and of the revival changed. And in the end, according to Tommy's account, the woman came to the revival. And she even came forward to be saved! Maybe silence in our classrooms might evoke an authentic human word or even a word that comes from God.

SILENCE AND FEELINGS

But there is more. There are often so many words in a teaching/learning experience that we do not take the time to attend to our *feelings*. Perhaps we do feel, but we do not take the time to be aware of what we are feeling. Feeling is essential to learning and transformation. Just as we have rational intelligence, we also have emotional intelligence. And the integration of the two may be essential for outstanding learning. Emotions are indeed connected with how people learn, from whom they learn, what they remember, and how it affects them. The ancient rhetoricians knew this well. They pursued the art of persuasion by engaging the emotions as well as the mind, feelings as well as logic. I am not talking about an appeal to emotion that is manipulative. I am talking about the natural inclusion of emotions in the learning process.

So, what if we took silence as an opportunity to enable students to get in touch not only with what they are thinking but also with what they are feeling? There are dimensions to the biblical texts that can evoke powerful emotive responses. How can future pastors tell about the healing of a blind man or preach about the blessing to the poor or teach about a conflict between Jesus and the authorities over some vital issue without expressing emotion or without the hearers experiencing emotion? I often did an exercise immediately after I did an initial performance of a biblical passage we were studying in which I asked each person to sit in silence and get in touch with what they were feeling as they were seeing/hearing me perform the story. Then they shared their feelings, and they identified what it was about the passage that led them to feel that way. Very insightful conversations invariably ensued about the meaning and rhetorical impacts of the passage.

THE CHALLENGE TO BE SILENT

Personally, as a very outgoing person, I have struggled all my life with the challenge to be silent. On the Myers-Briggs personality test, I am far to the right on the extrovert versus the introvert side of the scale. The overall role assigned to me by my profile in the Myers-Briggs test is that of a field marshal! Frankly, that's embarrassing. I began my adult years acting as if I should say aloud everything I was thinking internally. I not only said what *I* was thinking; I also used to finish *other people's* sentences—including my wife's. But early on, due mostly, thank God, to the women's liberation movement and to therapy, I was able to change (somewhat!). As a result of those experiences, I learned to hear myself speaking, and I did not like it. So I sought to become more of an active listener than an active speaker.

Even God got to me. In the early seventies, I participated in the Christian charismatic movement. Along with others, I was praying for the gift of speaking in tongues. God said (you know how God speaks to us in our minds), "You? The gift of tongues? No way! You already talk too much in English. Why would I add tongues? No, I am giving *you* the gift of silence. Then maybe *other* people will have a chance to speak!" That was pretty clear. Soon it became obvious to me that *not* talking was indeed a gift of the Spirit and should be practiced as a spiritual discipline. On the same excursion, this message was reinforced. When it was my turn to preach, the group leaders encouraged me to open the Bible and preach on the passage that appeared before me. So I prayed and opened the Bible. I may be the only person doing this exercise who opened to the two blank pages between the Testaments! Oh well. I got the message. No need ever to do that exercise again.

THE CHALLENGE TO SPEAK

However, for others, for introverts, the problem is the opposite. They have the challenge to speak up, especially in a group the size of most classes. Many such students have told me that they set as a goal for themselves to speak up at least once in each of their class periods. That was a very courageous goal. Their silence did not mean that they were not engaged. Nevertheless, they realized how important it was for their learning and involvement that they express themselves verbally in class. And for the usually silent students to speak up in class invariably affected the whole group in very positive ways.

Sometimes, after a discussion was underway for a while, I would say, "Now I want only those who have not yet spoken to share their thoughts." Sometimes there was considerable silence before they began to speak up. However, it was then that we all learned the true wisdom of the group as a whole. Some of the most profound insights came when I was patient and when I insisted (but without manipulation), even after much silence, that everyone be given an opportunity to speak.

SILENCE AND FLOW

In the end, there are no methods or strategies or techniques for incorporating silence into the learning process. We cannot repeat an exercise of silence and expect the same results from the same group or from a different group. We need to be prepared to improvise on the spot when it seems judicious to give students the chance to reflect and become aware of feelings in quiet meditation. How to work silence into the classroom may not always be plan-able, but, clearly, silence can be an important dimension of the educational experience.

14

Oral Communication

It has always puzzled me why we teachers put such a premium on student writing and not on student speaking. We privilege writing in a way that absolutizes it and at the same time often serves to denigrate the value of oral communication. Apart from oral communication classes in college and preaching courses in seminary, we tend for the most part to assign students a paper to write but not a speech to give. We will give a significant portion of the course grade to a paper, but we will give token credit for class discussion. Usually we evaluate writing by a series of criteria we have developed. However, we evaluate class discussion either in terms of mere presence/absence of the student in the class or in terms of active participation rather than the quality of the contributions. Seldom do we give students criteria for an effective speech. Almost never do we give guidelines for constructive class discussions.

WRITING AND SPEAKING AS PROCESS

Part of the problem is that we tend to see writing as an end product of thought, whereas we think of oral communication only as a step in the process of thinking. This is a false dichotomy. Actually, writing can be experienced as a step in the process of thinking. As Norman Mailer once said, "I can't wait until I get to the typewriter—to find out what I think!"

The point is that when it comes to communication, not just writing but also speaking can serve *both* as the process *and* as an end product of our thinking. For oral communication, we can assign students a variety of opportunities to give different kinds of speeches. In a few of my classes, students would be given a topic, then process their thinking on the subject in conversation with a partner, get feedback and suggestions, take some time to formulate their thinking, and give a brief speech of persuasion or explanation.

This oral exercise is social, both as process and as end product. By contrast, writing usually is a solitary process. The student writes in private, and the teacher evaluates in private. This means that a person is evaluated more on what they learn by themselves rather than on what they learn together in conversation with others. It will help to find ways to provide guidelines and protocols for oral communication in order to balance the equation.

GIVING GREATER WEIGHT TO ORAL COMMUNICATION

The emphasis on writing to the diminution of oral communication is all the more puzzling in a seminary where people are being trained more for speaking and for group conversation than for writing. What about a commitment to teach oral communication across the curriculum: biblical studies, Christian education, theology, history, and so on? If, in addition to giving assignments for writing, we gave students opportunities to solve problems in conversation, to lecture, debate, perform, engage in constructive dialogue, and give an interview, then we would be preparing them for a full range of pastoral and civic activities. Some students have taken speech and debate classes in college; but even these students may need to hone their oral presentation skills.

Furthermore, with regard to seminary, we have traditionally taught students to *write* their sermons first and then preach what they have written. This process leaves the sermon in a writing mode rather than in an oral mode. To deliver orally one needs to learn how to *compose* orally, to compose in mind and memory—to compose as though one were in conversation with another or as if one were speaking to a group. The importance of composing orally lies in the fact that preparation for delivery involves tone, pace, intensity, volume, pitch, and inflection, along with body language such as facial expressions, posture, gestures, and movement. These need to be part of the preparation of a presentation. They are not just add-ons. They are a natural and an integral part of the meaning of what is being said and a constitutive part of its impact.

In addition, in order to be most effective, there are distinct features to oral communication that might not appear when composing in writing. For example, oral communication is often punctuated with proverbs, pithy sayings, parallelism and contrast, alliteration, stories, catchy sayings, repeated motifs—all of which can be memorable and persuasive. Anyone who studies oral cultures and the contrast between predominantly oral and written cultures (for example, Walter Ong's *Orality and Literacy*) knows that these elements of style are typical features of oral expression.

The best way for all those elements to be included is by composing orally. Consider the stand-up comedian as a model. Most stand-up comedians do not write down their material. The humor comes as part of the oral flow of composition. Comedians who do lengthy monologues create them mentally and then practice their material at nightclubs and in front of small audiences in order to get the wording and the timing—and many other aspects of performance—just right. Then they are ready to present their polished material. So, can we not experiment with giving students assignments that will encourage them to compose in mind and memory and present orally? And can we not take this work seriously enough to give feedback and grades?

One reservation. Requiring and evaluating oral communication may inhibit students. In fact, some students say that, constitutionally, they just cannot speak publicly before a group, including a class. We might appropriately treat this as a learning challenge and seek to find alternative learning modes. We need to find ways to address such situations creatively and compassionately, but we should not give up our commitment to teach orality. What if someone said that about writing? What if a student said, "I just cannot stand to put my thoughts out on paper." Initially, we would probably say that they would not be able to pass a class without writing a paper or taking an exam. We might wonder how a student with such a limitation got this far in the educational process. I have in fact had two students at the seminary level over the years with a learning challenge with regard to writing. In each case, I substituted oral assignments for the written ones. However, our common responses, our default choices, usually reveal our preferences in favor of writing. So why do we not expect people to learn to speak effectively?

THE EXAMPLE OF ORAL CULTURES

In antiquity, the Greco-Roman educational enterprise was only for a small percentage of elites, and it was overwhelmingly based not on writing but on oral rhetoric—delivering speeches of famous orators of the past, learning to create speeches, and practicing oratory for participation in the public arena. The ancient cultures of the West were predominantly oral, with as few as 2 to 15 percent of the people able to do any kind of writing or reading. The vast majority of the people, mostly peasants working the land and the urban poor, experienced the compositions that have been preserved (in writing) in the New Testament as oral performances. The New Testament writings are examples of *performance literature*, like music and drama—meant to be performed before gathered communities. When I explained this in class, students were able to see examples of oral language and memory techniques embedded in the very subject matter they were studying.

Oral cultures experience the spoken word as an expression of power. Words are often treated as actions, because words have the capacity to impact and change situations. In the biblical world, words share something of the creativity of God's words at creation. Words go out, and do not return empty. Words are expected to *do* something. They create, heal, forgive, evoke the spirit, reconcile, bless, curse, judge, accept, among so many other things. Studies of the functions of language show that, at some level, all words/sentences *perform* something in the act of communication. They are speech-acts. The works of the philosopher J. L. Austin and the linguist M. A. K. Halliday on the functions of language have been extremely helpful in explicating for students the nature of oral communication.

Once students understand the power of words, their grasp of the rhetorical dynamics of the biblical writings expands considerably. The Gospels and the letters were meant to generate new communities, transform worldviews, trigger actions, inspire for mission, and enculturate into alternative ways of living. In the Reformation, preaching was talked about as an event, a happening that led to change and transformation. The study of oral cultures re-enlivens the view that speech has tremendous impact.

ASSIGNING ORAL PRESENTATIONS IN THE CLASSROOM

How can we incorporate speeches in the classroom? I tried a few different approaches. Sometimes, I asked students to read a book and then in class make a five-minute presentation on it without writing it out and without notes. They picked a theme or idea from the book they read, stated it clearly and faithfully, and then either elaborated on it or challenged it and explained why. Or two students would elaborate several key themes from an assigned book and then pose questions so as to generate discussion among the whole class. In other situations, I have asked people to summarize orally an article clearly and cogently in three minutes so we can get input about many articles from a number of students in a short period of time.

Sometimes, I assigned a theme in a Gospel in which several different interpretive hypotheses could be supported by the text. Then students prepared by taking a point of view and gathering evidence to debate the issue. In class, several people presented their thesis and the support for it as an oral debate, while others participated in the discussion that followed. Here are two brief examples of such assignments.

The Gospel of Luke

One of the major themes of the Gospel of Luke is the dynamic of wealth and poverty. After reading and taking notes on Luke, consider the following: In the Gospel of Luke,

1. In order to be saved, people with wealth are to sell all they have and give to the poor.
2. Wealthy people can give to the poor, keep much of their wealth, and still be saved.
3. Wealthy people can keep their wealth and will be saved as long as they believe in God and follow Jesus.
4. Other

Choose one of these options and prepare a brief speech, making your choice of the options above into your thesis statement, and then, based on evidence from the Gospel, explain your support for that point of view. Be prepared to debate your position in class.

The Gospel of John

One of the major themes of the Gospel of John is the experience of eternal life. After reading and taking notes on John, consider the following: In the Gospel of John,

1. Eternal life is life with God that will be experienced only after one dies.
2. Eternal life is tasted in this life, but the full experience of eternal life will be experienced only after death.
3. Eternal life is a reality that can be experienced fully in the present and will continue beyond death.
4. Other

Choose one of these options and prepare a brief speech, making your choice of the options above into your thesis statement, and then, based on evidence from the Gospel, explain your support for that point of view. Be prepared to debate your position in class.

In these and other ways, the preparation of speeches not only trained students in public speaking, the speeches also served as a generative way to evoke meaningful class discussion. The key for the effectiveness of their brief speeches was to give students guidelines (just as we have criteria for written essays). The class as a whole learned also by experiencing many styles of speaking. They saw what worked and what didn't work.

CRITERIA FOR PUBLIC SPEAKING

What kind of criteria might we use to evaluate oral speeches? Some criteria overlap with criteria for written essays, but they are also different in some sense just by virtue of the practice of oral composition. Other criteria take account of the distinctly oral nature of speeches. For example:

- *Clarity*: Is the speech clear in language and structure? Can listeners follow the train of thought?
- *Content*: Is there a significant point to be made, and does the speech adequately support that point with explanations, evidence, and

arguments? Does the speech counter opposing opinions by clearly outlining the contrast?

- *Presence*: Did the presenter communicate in a personal way with eye contact and make a connection with all parts of the audience? How much were the presenters able to work from memory, and how much did they depend on notes or a manuscript?
- *Style*: Did the style include features of oral communications such as stories, memorable sayings, repetition, questions, and imaginary dialogues with interlocutors? Was there a beginning to the presentation that engaged people?
- *Manner*: Did the presenters express themselves in ways natural to them, using gestures, pace, volume, inflection, movement, and facial expressions that enhanced the persuasiveness of the points being made?
- Was there an overall focus that made a striking impact on the audience? What did the speech want the audience to think or to do or to become?

The criteria were given ahead of time to those preparing speeches and to those giving evaluations.

The most dramatic improvement in public speaking I have ever witnessed came in a course I co-taught in a doctor of ministry program in preaching. The program set out the following steps for the process. After a weeklong summer class, the participating pastors had two assignments to be completed one after the other. After several months, each pastor prepared a sermon to preach at their church, which they videotaped and made available to the teacher and to a group of ten parishioners. I watched the video and submitted an audiotape of comments and reactions, using the criteria for oral speeches outlined above. Then the group of ten parishioners would watch the video of the sermon and also listen to the audiotape of my evaluation, *together with the pastor who had done the preaching*. The ten would then give their own feedback and recommendations to the pastor. After the pastor had had a few months to process the feedback, the same process was repeated. The difference was like night and day.

How to account for the growth? Maybe it was because of the public accountability with ten parishioners, or perhaps it was the opportunity for the pastors to see themselves preaching on the video. In any case, it was an extremely effective process. Some regular preaching classes for seminarians do indeed incorporate video feedback into the standard semester timeline. Clearly, this exercise could be adapted for other classes as well.

WHAT ABOUT CLASS DISCUSSION?

In class discussion, there is often a great disparity in student involvement. Some students are not inhibited and seem to say aloud whatever they are thinking. It is salutary to find ways to encourage such students to be circumspect, to see themselves as one contributor in a class conversation, and to learn how to draw out others. Other students will be reluctant to share ideas in nascent form. These students may process ideas and information more slowly than others, and this phenomenon disadvantages those (often introverts) who prefer to think through their ideas before speaking. Sometimes, such students will explain that "by the time I got my thoughts together, the conversation moved on and my point was no longer relevant." Writing gives them a chance to be much more in control of their verbal expression. Even so, if we privilege writing in an exclusive way, then we disadvantage those who do well in thinking out loud with others about a subject and who excel at presenting their ideas orally. And by privileging writing, we fail to give reluctant speakers the practice of making presentations and speaking out in class discussion.

Perhaps we can level the playing field by giving students quiet time for reflection and for processing in the middle of a discussion. Also, we can lighten the pressure by inviting students simply to say "I pass" if they are called upon but not yet not ready to speak. We can ease some anxiety by encouraging individual students to request the school for permission to take the class pass/fail rather than for a grade, if this is an option. Also, it is important to be aware that sometimes there are cultural reasons that some students (for example, some Asian students and Native Americans) might not speak unless they are invited to do so. The works of Eric Law have been very helpful to me in demonstrating how these cultural differences can be acknowledged and addressed with sensitivity.

Guidelines and Practice

How do we foster effective class discussion? Just as we give students criteria for writing well, so also we can give students criteria for constructive conversations. How do we engage in a group process that involves expressing our own point of view, listening care-fully, understanding others, being open to changing one's mind, developing ideas together, and coming to a decision *as a cooperative, communal effort*? Such skills involve being able to engage in a conversation while *also* being aware of the dynamics of that conversation. Most of the time when we listen, our minds are too busy formulating our response! If students can contribute their ideas and *also* be active listeners who follow the train of thought and who help to guide the common discussion in productive ways, we will have trained students to be able to learn well together.

Because my approach to teaching involved so much dialogue, I found it important to learn how to teach a class so as to have more constructive dialogue both with the class as a whole and in small groups. The focus of the following guidelines is not on students scoring points or knowing the most. The emphasis is on the idea that the whole group knows more than an individual. So it is important to get all ideas expressed. The guidelines were also designed to keep the group on track and to guide the discussion toward a conclusion, which may result in a consensus or in the clarification of differing points of view. Furthermore, the guidelines helped individuals to express, explain, and support their views and at the same time to be open to changing their point of view. I tried to employ these guidelines in ways that rewarded people for listening carefully and changing their minds. Here are the guidelines.

GUIDELINES FOR CLASS DISCUSSION

Principle: Every statement should further the discussion constructively toward the group goal.

1. Assume responsibility for the whole discussion.

a. Help formulate the purpose of the discussion.

- "Let's clarify the purpose and goal of this discussion."
- "Let's discuss how the protagonist changes/develops in this story."

- "Let's see if we can agree on the dominant theme."

b. Suggest a procedure for carrying the discussion forward.

- "Let's each state what we think is the dominant theme and then lay out the evidence together to see if we can move toward a consensus."
- "Let's brainstorm all the ideas and then narrow them down."
- "Could we talk first in pairs or small groups and then put our ideas together?"
- "Let me state a thesis and see if we can agree or not."

c. Summarize the discussion to clarify what has been resolved and what is yet open for conversation.

- "We have agreed on the main theme but we have not shown how the other themes relate to it."
- "Where are we? What have we done and where are we going?"

d. Keep the discussion on track.

- "Let's get back to the main purpose of the discussion."
- "Could you show how that pertains to the main point?"

e. Observe yourselves in the process of discussion.

- "I wonder how our social location is determining our views here."
- "What are the personal issues that are blocking this discussion?"

f. Bring the discussion to a close.

- "Are we agreed then that . . . ?"
- "Then we have two opinions. Can we resolve this, or should we leave it open?"

2. Provide comments about the subject matter or the material under discussion, comments that carry the discussion forward.

a. Raise a question for discussion.

- "Here's my big question about this passage . . ."

- "I'd like to know why the author includes this theme. What do you all think?"

b. Give evidence for or against certain views in the discussion.

- "Here's a passage that also supports your notion."
- "But other facts do not support that idea. How would you explain . . . ?"

3. Listen well. Let the views of others be fully expressed and weighed.

a. Avoid dominating. Listen and get others involved.

- "Sally, what do you think this passage is about?"
- "George, with whom do you agree in this discussion?"

b. Draw out the views of another.

- "Why do you say that?"
- "What evidence leads you to say that?"
- "How do you relate that to the story as a whole?"

c. Challenge the view of another, not for conflict but for exploration.

- "Show us where you get that from the text."
- "But how do you fit your views with the passage that says . . ."
- "Are you sure you have the right meaning of that term?"

d. Clarify your understanding of someone's views by summarizing them in your own words.

- "Let me feed that back to you to see if I have it right."
- "Do you mean that . . . ?"

4. Try out your own ideas and get reactions.

a. Test a hypothesis.

- "Here's what I think the theme is . . . How do you react to that?"
- "I argue that . . . Tell me if you think I am on the right track."

b. Debate your views.

- "I don't agree with that, and here are my reasons."

- "I think the evidence leads to a different conclusion. Here's what I am thinking."

c. Change your mind.

- "You have a point there. I'll have to adjust my views."
- "Okay. You may be right. Here's what convinced me . . ."

5. Plan for the next discussion.

a. Suggest the best use of the next class.

- "Next time, let's discuss the characters and how they display the theme."
- "Let's try to figure out what 'freedom' means in this story."

b. Suggest appropriate assignments.

- "Why don't we each study a different aspect of this story and then put it together next week?"
- "Let's each study that theme and come up with a brief statement of our views."
- "We should study the whole story and be ready to discuss these questions . . ."

When I introduced these guidelines and asked students to try them out, I would back off and let the conversation go in order to see how the group as a whole did with them. Or I stated an issue for discussion and then said, "I am going to give you twenty minutes to decide this issue together." Then I was silent the rest of the time. Afterward, I invited the students to look at the guidelines again and assess how they did. What went well? What was most helpful? What might have been done differently? Also, I offered my own evaluation of the conversation. Then they went at it again in the next focused conversation. At first, the use of the guidelines was stilted. But after a group got used to them, participants became more comfortable.

An Oral Communication Course

At Carthage, I taught a course on the Old Testament with a completely oral approach. The class was a survey of the Old Testament with about ten students. It was an intensive summer course in which the class met three hours every weekday for a month. I gave the guidelines and illustrated them by my own participation in discussions early in the course. I would point out when students followed the guidelines.

After about a week of modeling the process, I would give the students as a group a purpose or goal for a discussion each day. Then I would turn it over to them and be silent for about a half hour. At that point, I would give feedback on their discussion—how they had succeeded in their goal, what seemed to block the group process, what contributions served to carry the discussion forward, what they might have done differently.

Their final examination was a targeted conversation about the book of Jonah. I gave them a hypothesis about the purpose of Jonah and asked them to explain from Jonah how this thesis could be true or not. Then I observed for an hour while the group struggled with this assignment and came out with their conclusions. It was quite exciting, and I was pleased with the outcome. I then verbally evaluated each person for their positive contributions to the discussion. My evaluation addressed not only insights that individual students contributed but also an assessment of the process as a process. The group was also given a grade as a group, and the grade depended in part on how much *everyone* contributed in a variety of effective ways to the discussion.

None of the guidelines seemed to put students in a straitjacket. Quite the contrary, the guidelines seemed to expand the ways in which individual students contributed to discussion. At the same time, they brought order and focus to the group and led to meaningful conversations. When students followed these guidelines, they learned to recognize when something significant was being said; and when that happened, we all just listened and gave that person time to share. We reflected on ways to bring more people into the conversation. We talked about not posturing or dominating or withdrawing or making points or playing games with the discussion. We encouraged people to be honest and to speak from the heart, to use evidence from the text to support their points, and not to try to impress others. We talked about listening well, without thinking about what *we* might say next.

The classroom payoffs for training students in constructive oral conversations were many. And the training was preparing them for future staff meetings, board meetings, citizen forums, church council meetings, teaching opportunities, and pastors' study groups. Being able to participate in a discussion and also to give constructive direction to the group conversation was a skill well worth developing.

CONCLUSION: PROCEED WITH CAUTION

Having said all this, I am nevertheless conscious of the many legitimate reasons we teachers do not assign more structured oral communication in the classroom—the elusive nature of grading it, the intimidation of students by the prospect of being graded on it, the time-intensive work needed to hear many speeches, and the fact that it is so new for many students. Nevertheless, the students themselves would be well served if we incorporated more instruction and practice in oral communication. And the course might also turn out to be more fun and engaging.

15

Generating Dialogue

There is often quite a difference in point of view among faculty about the inherent value of discussion groups. The concern is not so much about plenary discussions, those where the discussing is between the teacher and the whole class. In that situation, the teacher is actively involved and can assure that the conversation is constructive, that the discussion stays on track, that the class as a whole stays engaged, and that the students are learning what the teacher considers to be important for them to learn. Rather, the concern is whether anything of value can take place in small group discussions when students are on their own and the conversation can meander ineffectively or get completely lost.

WHAT'S IN A NAME?

Maybe the problem is in the language. Perhaps the name we give to discussion groups would make a difference in how people participate in them. We could call them "discussion groups," but perhaps that is all we would get. Calling them "conversation groups" would not prove to be much better. We used to call them "buzz groups," which are merely discussion groups with pizzazz. Perhaps calling them "focus groups" would at least make it clear that the group discussion has a clear task that will lead to a definite outcome. Maybe "working groups" would do the trick. If we call small group discussions "dialogue groups," we also might be moving in the right direction. There is something intentional about dialogue that is not present in discussion. Dialogues are more formal interchanges in which people representing two or more points of view are explaining and exploring their beliefs and values, perhaps even engaged in negotiations.

To explain the potential for the concept of "dialogue," it may be helpful to reflect on developments in interreligious dialogue. It used to be that dialogue between religious groups meant: "We will demonstrate that our beliefs and values are superior to others, and in so doing we may be able to convert them to our way of thinking." Now interfaith dialogue has come to mean: "We will explain our beliefs and values, and we will listen carefully to what we can *learn* from our dialogue partners, with the possibility that both may be changed by the dialogue or that something new may emerge." Such dialogue may include the conviction that the beliefs and values of others ought to survive and thrive in the world, even while we may disagree with them. Given this last definition, there is the possibility that dialogue groups can lead to transformation.

Perhaps the solution is to give the small groups a variety of names, depending on what we want the small groups to do or to accomplish. Of course, we would need to explain the rationale for the suggested makeup and purpose for each type of group. In a way, such attention to group dynamics would give a seriousness and importance to them that they might not otherwise have. It might also greatly clarify for students what we hope will happen in small groups: discussion groups, focus groups, reflection groups, feedback groups, debate groups, dialogue groups, working groups, or even proposal groups.

A descriptive name may also help to distinguish your expectations as the teacher from the expectations students bring with them from other classes. Perhaps this would also clarify in the minds of us teachers exactly what we ourselves want to happen in small groups. We might also clarify that these are a critical part of the learning process and even explain what we do *not* want to happen in the groups. If we are unclear, this is not helpful. If we are clear but do not communicate it, this is also not helpful. As my own teaching progressed, I found myself being quite prescriptive in my directions about what small groups were meant to do in each case and what they were not to do. Along with clear directions, the teacher needs to provide the groups with what they need to carry out the instructions—and, also, where appropriate, to provide some means of accountability.

THE VALUE OF DIALOGUE GROUPS

But what is the value of dialogue groups in the first place? If we have a focus-on-information approach to education, discussion can certainly be of value. It can serve to give students an opportunity to make sure they have understood what they have read in the assignment or heard in the class lecture, using the time to prepare comments and questions. This process sets up a meaningful plenary discussion in which students are prepared to ask the teacher questions to make sure they understood the material. If needed, the teacher can call on one or more of the participants to explain their understanding as a means of confirming the teacher's communication of the material. Or ask students just to turn to the person next to them to talk about the material. Clearly, an important part of education is to make sure the students understand certain information and ideas clearly.

But of course the experience of learning is more complex than learning information. In fact, the pedagogical fact is that the more actively students are involved in their learning, the more they will remember and understand and think for themselves. We do the students a disservice when we make them so dependent upon us for their learning that we do not give time for independent thinking and dialogue. We do not have to be in charge of all the learning that goes on in a classroom, nor do we have to be the "idea police" correcting every questionable comment made by students. In addition, by organizing dialogue groups, we ourselves might often learn from the students. In my experience, there have been students in virtually all my courses whose native intelligence and gifts are greater than mine, even if I have had more experience with the subject matter. And all students come with personal history and angles of vision from their social locations that are different from mine, which gives us reason to expect that they will have insights to contribute.

Furthermore, extensive group work in class gives us a chance to flip the usual expectation that students get information from class and then do the work of study and learning on their own. In this reverse scenario, students get their information by reading and listening to lectures online *outside* the classroom and then make use of the time *inside* the classroom for working together to evaluate the material and reflect on it together under the teacher's guidance. This conceptual switch was critical for me to use as a basis for organizing the classroom as a "workshop."

Some principles from learning theory confirmed for me the importance of dialogue groups:

- In contrast to a plenary discussion, small groups assure that everyone is actively engaged in speaking and listening.
- Explaining one's point of view to others helps a student to formulate and clarify it, especially if others ask questions. This may strengthen, deepen, or adjust one's points of view.
- Hearing diverse points of view in a thoughtful dialogue may also relativize one's position and lead that person to be open to hear, understand, and respect the points of view of others even if not persuaded by them.
- Diverse points of view help lead students to a better understanding of the subject under discussion.
- In respectful dialogue, students learn how to be passionate and persuasive without imposing their views on others.
- Dialogue groups allow for more creativity, independence, and responsibility on the part of students.

HOW DO I GET A GOOD DIALOGUE GOING IN MY CLASSES?

Good plenary discussions of the class as a whole in conversation with the teacher are not always easy to generate. Time and again, I have heard faculty express their frustration at not being able to generate class discussion, especially after pouring themselves out in a lecture. I recently heard a teacher say: "I gave this lecture and then asked for questions and reactions. There was nothing. It was very discouraging."

I recall my own frustration at the beginning of my teaching. I expected students to read and understand the assignments and then come to class ready to discuss them. Didn't happen. In fact, I recall one incident in which I became so exasperated at not getting responses for a discussion in a class of about forty students that about halfway through the class I said, "Let's try again tomorrow," and I walked out. That was a shipwreck. I was not angry at the students. I was upset at the situation. That was my breaking point when I decided that I had to figure out some way to pretty much guarantee there would always be meaningful class discussion in a positive and constructive way.

So how can we get students motivated to participate actively and enthusiastically in class discussion? How do we get students engaged so as to take responsibility for the success of class discussion? How can we get dialogue groups to function effectively?

A Fantasy

Some of it has to do with student self-motivation and interest in the subject matter. Here is a fantasy about how I wish it would work: instead of a course being published in the catalogue and students signing up to take it, what if we had a group of students come to us and say, "We would like to learn about the parables of Jesus. Would you be willing to assist us in selecting books and consulting? We will do our work and then gather for class to talk about it and to stimulate each other's learning. Would you be willing to be present at some or all of these classes to give us some guidance and evaluate what we do?" In this scenario, the dialogue in the class would be: "Let's teach each other what we are learning. Let's talk about it to see what we think about it, where we agree and disagree. Let's come together to try out our ideas and get feedback on them." In this case, the learning would be fully student centered, and everyone would be teaching and learning in conversation. The role of the instructor would be to recommend resources, suggest procedures for the classes, help the students avoid dead ends, give occasional input, and offer some informed feedback about their progress. Now that would be a community of learners!

Actually, I did have a scenario similar to this in several semesters at Carthage. We had an arrangement called a "directed study." This was different from an independent study in that it was done with a small group of students rather than an individual. When several students approached me about learning some subject, we met and arranged a syllabus, a course of study, and set up dates through the semester when I would meet with them to go over what they were learning and a means of evaluation. When we met in the course of the semester, the conversations led by the students were quite lively. This extra instruction was not officially a part of my teaching load, but the students got credit, and it was a pleasure to teach students learning on their own like this.

A Step-by-Step Example

The following example was one solution I hit upon to address my frustration at not being able to engender meaningful class discussion that engaged everyone. It involves thinking about the role of dialogue groups as one part of a *sequential process*. It was a sequential process I used for most of my classes over the years: I would make an assignment designed to prepare students outside of class for small group work, which was followed by the work in small groups in class, which in turn prepared them for a plenary class discussion to follow. This strategy is sometimes called a "ladder" exercise in which each step builds on the last and "ups" the level of the engagement.

Step One: Individual Assignment for Class Preparation

I would give the students an assignment to do in preparation for the class period (say, for example, a character analysis of the disciples in the Gospel of Mark). As they read, they were to gather details (for example, on worksheets under categories of "What the Disciples Say," "What They Do," and "What Others Say About Them"). In addition, they were to bring three questions that emerged from their study.

I collected these worksheets at the end of each class, reviewed them briefly, recorded them as the "completion" of an assignment, and returned them the next class, perhaps with one comment but without a grade. Making these written exercises a regular part of the requirements of the course ensures that the work was done before each class; and I could then count on the fact that the students would indeed all be prepared for the small group dialogues. If the students had not been prepared, the small groups would not have worked.

Step Two: Dialogue Groups

When the students got to class, I asked them to form small groups (usually comprised of two or three, maybe four participants) but *not* in order to repeat what they had already done. That would be busy work and needless repetition. Rather, I asked them in small groups to do something more with the information they had collected. That is, I gave them a worksheet with a set of open-ended interpretive questions. For example, in the study of the disciples in Mark I would ask: "Why did the disciples follow Jesus? Why are the disciples afraid? Why do they not understand? Would they be faithful in the end?" These questions involved differences of opinion and a closer reading of the evidence in the text. Students were to add into the mix the three questions they prepared. The mantra for this exercise was: *Show in the text the basis for your point of view.*

Step Three: Plenary Discussion

Then I followed with a plenary dialogue of the whole class. Again, I did not ask them to repeat or report what they had said in the small groups. That would also be repetitious and time consuming. Rather, I asked them broader questions that made use of what they did in small groups but went beyond it. For example, I asked: "With his portrayal of the disciples, does Mark accurately reflect the human condition?" or "In what ways is Mark's depiction of the disciples true also of you and the people you know?" or "What traits of the disciples reflect groups in our society?" or "How is the situation of the disciples under persecution different from the situation today?" Such open-ended questions about contemporary society made the discussion especially relevant for students. In turn, they also served to illuminate the Gospel of Mark in its original context.

This whole process would bring the conversation to a more informed and meaningful dialogue. I seriously doubt if it would have been successful or constructive without the first two steps. The questions went from gathering information to interpreting that information to asking open questions (to which the teacher does not know *the* answer and/or there is no one right answer). Because students had time to chew on the issues in the dialogue groups, I could ask individual students what they thought as a means to make sure everyone was involved in the plenary discussion. Because the students came to expect this process in most if not all of the class periods, they did the assignments faithfully so that they would be prepared for the dialogue.

Giving Mutual Feedback in Small Groups

When students were doing individual projects that did not replicate what everyone else was doing, small groups offered an ideal way for students to give each other feedback, often in triads. For example, if students were writing papers, they would give a draft of their paper ahead of time to the other two members of their triad. Then, when they met in class, they were prepared to give each other detailed and extensive responses to the papers. Each student got responses from the other two peer evaluators based on criteria of assessment that I provided ahead of time. I then set a time limit for the discussion of each paper, and when that time was up, the group would move on to the next paper. In this exercise, the focus of the small groups was clear, and the conversations that occurred were constructive.

Other Uses of Dialogue Groups

Additional uses might include: giving students time to practice a skill or method with other students (for example, reading Greek or doing a narrative analysis together in pairs); providing a forum to solve a problem posed by the teacher or students; and offering an opportunity to role-play, with each member of a small group taking a different role and having a conversation with each other in their respective roles around a relevant issue.

Larry Hamilton, who taught psychology at Carthage College, had his own distinct way of provoking meaningful dialogue. He wanted every student to deal in a personal way with the dynamics of human life and behavior. He himself was a voracious reader, and he would collect the most provocative quotations he could find. When he came to class, he brought photocopies of a handful of quotations dealing with critical matters such as facing death, wearing social masks, having the courage to live, and being authentic. He would then read one of the quotations in a lively manner several times and comment on its significance. Next he told the students to pair up and say what they thought this quotation meant for them and for society. When he returned the group to plenary, he walked around and challenged individual students to explain what the quote meant to them, all the while making his own comments and posing probing questions of the students as he proceeded.

It was actually a rather enthralling experience. The students knew that Larry wanted them to be authentic about their engagement with the ideas he was presenting. As a result, there were remarkable interactions between Larry and the students. And neither the small groups nor the plenary discussions were ever dull. Not all of us have the personality to engage students as Larry did, and some students may be intimidated. But it worked. And, for the most part, the students who engaged in these dialogues of transformation found what they learned to be life changing and unforgettable.

BENEFITS OF DIALOGUE GROUPS

The idea is to make the small groups as meaningful and as productive as possible within the larger learning process. When we see the groups working constructively, we realize how they can serve many purposes. In addition to engaging all students and clarifying student learning, small groups can serve to strengthen the bonds between class members in forming a community of learners. They also allow students to try out an idea or give feedback to each other that they may find difficult to say in front of the whole class. In addition, they give space for students to share intimately in a way that would not happen in the whole class; for example, sharing personal experiences of awe or curiosity or fear.

GUIDELINES

While we want the dialogue among students to be transformative, we cannot guarantee that will happen. Yet we can do a lot to set up the conditions for it to happen; that is, we can set an atmosphere of expectation and we can model it ourselves.

Facilitating Dialogue Groups

Here are some guidelines that served me well in facilitating dialogue:

- Be aware of the size of the groups, and consider what kinds of purposes will work best with what size groups: pairs, triads, groups of four to seven, eight to fourteen, and fifteen or more. Each size will facilitate or hinder a task or a dialogue, depending on what you want the groups to do.
- As we have indicated in an earlier reflection, consider the flexibility of the classroom. What diverse arrangements are possible given the space, the furniture, and the arrangement of the room? The shift from plenary to small groups and back to plenary should be easy to

accomplish. If the groups are eight or more, consider arranging for them to go as breakout groups to different classrooms.

- Clarify about how much time you expect them to work in small groups. Timing is tricky. They must be given enough time to do the task in a satisfying way but not so much that they finish before the time is up. I used to walk around among the groups—trying not to be intrusive—to get a sense of how they were coming along and to answer questions. If all the groups were actively engaged, I would extend the time. When a few groups came to completion, I was prepared to give those groups an additional question to discuss. I usually returned the class to plenary dialogue before all the groups had finished the task.
- The groups are an important means to form learning partners. If it was a large class and the students did not know each other, I made sure they introduced themselves and learned names.
- The makeup of the groups can be important. In smaller classes, you might choose ahead of time the particular people who would be in each small groups. Or, depending on the task, the small groups could include males and females and reflect ethnic and age diversity.
- Have students change dialogue partners so that they are in small groups with different people. If they sit in the same place and with friends, they may already know what the others think or they may begin talking about extraneous matters. Often, I would ask everyone in a large class to stand up, walk around, and partner with people they did not know well.
- It sometimes helps to ask the groups to give each participant a turn to talk. In the midst of their dialogue, you might remind them to give everyone a chance to speak. Give them instructions for constructive oral communication.
- At the outset of the course, remind people to practice hospitality in the small groups. Share guidelines for respectful dialogue.

Facilitating the Plenary Dialogue

It is important that the whole class be engaged in the plenary discussion that follows small group work. Here are some ideas I used:

- Ask the groups to report briefly. If each small group is doing a different task, the reports of the groups contribute different things to the plenary discussion. This emphasizes the value of their work for the rest of the class. However, this can also be time consuming and does not necessarily result in dialogue among the class members.
- In the plenary dialogue, carry it on in a way that allows the dialogue to focus on student interaction. Room setup will be important if students are to address each other.
- If desirable, seek to detach yourself from the center of the discussion. This is often difficult. Students may tend to address every comment to you as instructor. Request that students address each other, not just you. Move around. Sit down in a student chair, or stand on the periphery.
- Keep the conversation moving among students. Ask one student to respond to what another has said. Or push the conversation deeper by posing a question in response to a student comment. Or be comfortable with silence as you wait for other students to speak.
- Avoid intruding unnecessarily to direct the conversation. Let the dialogue go for a while, even where you might not want it to go. It is often more important that the students own the dialogue than that they get everything right.
- Avoid correcting what students say in the course of the discussion or adding something you think is important. There will be time at the end of the discussion or even during the next class period for you to say what is important to you.
- Don't answer questions, but acknowledge them and offer them back to the students for discussion. Or answer the question briefly and redirect the conversation back to them.
- Model what you want students to do, learning from the conversation by listening carefully, maybe asking questions, and taking notes for yourself from what you are learning.
- If the conversation gets stuck, ask someone what came out of their small group discussion.
- If you want to achieve a goal with the plenary conversation, push for that.

- It may be helpful for you to summarize in the midst of a discussion what you have heard so far in order to clarify the issues and move the conversation toward a goal. Or at the end, you might name the state of the conversation, identifying issues that seem to have consensus and those issues that were left open and unresolved.
- End the conversation before the energy runs out and before everything is resolved.

CONCLUSION

The key to constructive dialogue in small groups and in the class as a whole starts long before the conversation begins—with a particular assignment, a thought-provoking question, or a process to engage everyone. There are lots of ways to do it, but it usually takes forethought and planning. Often, it also involves improvising in the moment as a way to generate or enliven a dialogue. No strategies or mechanics, however, can guarantee a good dialogue. When the planning does not work, it can be quite frustrating and boring. But when it does work, it can be energizing, engaging, and potentially transformative.

16

Social Location and Biblical Interpretation

THERE HAS BEEN AN important movement in biblical interpretation that leads interpreters to lift up their social location. "Social location" refers to a person's country and culture and to the place one has within that particular social order. It is no longer enough to ask about the *personal* biases and beliefs and values of the individual interpreter as the means to discern perspectives that shape interpretation. Though these are important, we must also look at the *social* factors that shape interpretation; that is, the ways in which individual scholars are shaped by their nation, society, culture(s), communities, groups, particular eras in which they live, and particular geographical/ecological locations. Grappling with this movement over the years has had a significant impact on the scholarly and teaching community.

One of the difficulties in grappling with the concept of social location is that people from the Global North tend not to realize how much they speak out of their social location. For example, students from the dominant Global North tend to experience the world through the lens of individualism, through which people are defined primarily by their personal traits. They do not always grasp how much people who live in collectivist cultures get their identity primarily in terms of the social groups of which they are a part: nation, ethnic group, race, tribe, family, village, class, gender, and so on.

DYNAMICS OF SOCIAL LOCATION

We are aware that it makes a difference whether biblical interpreters are male or female and whether interpreters are part of different racial and ethnic groups. But we may be less aware of other factors, such as socio-economic group, city or rural roots, health or disability, and age. What about gender identity and sexual orientation? What do these social locations mean in different countries and cultures? People come to the biblical text with certain assumptions and experiences that are to a great extent rooted in the groups with which they identify and into which they have been enculturated. We share certain presuppositions—ways of thinking, ways of relating, values, beliefs, and customs—that are determined (or at least greatly shaped) both by the overall culture and by the subgroups in which we find ourselves within that culture. Hence, when students read the biblical text, they come not only with personal predilections but also with important influences out of their social location.

Complexity

These social dynamics are often very complex. At its simplest, people come from a rather homogeneous social location. However, many folks are mixed in their racial and ethnic background. Such hybrid identities caution us against stereotyping social location of any kind. Furthermore, it is a mistake to lump together all Hispanic Americans or all Native Americans or all Asian Americans, as people in the dominant culture tend to do. People originate from many different countries or cultures or indigenous nations within these ethnic groups. And those who are European-Caucasian Americans often forget that *we* have diverse geographical and cultural roots as well, about which we, as a historically dominant group, are often unaware.

Unfortunately, there is a tendency to think that all those who belong even to a particular narrowly defined social group are pretty much alike and stay the same. Indeed, people with the same social location may have some prevailing traits, values, worldviews, and patterns of behavior. However, the identity of a person cannot be exhausted by recourse to her or his social location. Some people resist the dominant values of their group and seek to counter them or to overcome them. There is no "essential" makeup of an individual or of a group. Groups contain diversity, and they change over time. As teachers, we have much to learn about these dynamics, because they represent potential pitfalls and stumbling blocks both to teaching and to learning. At the same time, they also represent enormous opportunities for dialogue and transformation.

Power Dynamics

Social locations are fraught with power dynamics between different social groups to the extent that they are polarized in a society in such categories as dominant culture/suppressed minority culture, male/female, wealthy/poor, educated/uneducated, healthy/sick, young/elderly, and positions of authority/subordination. These power dynamics enable certain groups to take things for granted, while others cannot.

Most often, people from dominant cultures—for example, being white and male in the United States—do not reflect often on the social dynamics that characterize what it means to be white or male. Historically, they have the power that has made their identity and patterns of behavior "normative" in the society groups. There is a tendency for them to think that their way of relating is just the way things are and the way things ought to be. In so doing, they dominate and marginalize others, often without being conscious of it, just by what they take for granted. On the other hand, people in subordinate groups and cultures are often well aware of how different they are from the dominant culture because they think and relate in ways that are not predominant and may not be acceptable to those in the dominant cultures. In addition, people in subordinate positions usually know not only their own patterns of thinking and behavior but *also* those of the dominant culture—because they need to understand the mentality and patterns of behavior of the dominant culture in order to survive and thrive.

The power dynamics of social location are often extremely complex. Some groups experience multiple forms of discrimination. Womanist thinkers point out that women of color, by virtue of their social location, generally experience three levels of oppression: economic exploitation, racial discrimination, and gender domination. And their gender oppression differs from the gender oppression that white woman may suffer. For example, black women may experience gender oppression from black males, but they are in solidarity with black males in their common experience of being subjected to racial and economic oppression by whites.

Also, someone may be in a dominant position as part of one group, but they may be in a subordinate or marginalized position as part of another group. One African American student at our seminary had a personal crisis over this dynamic. She had experienced various forms of oppression and discrimination throughout her life in the United States as a black female. However, when she took her seminary internship in India, the people there were indifferent to what color or race she was. But she was American, and, in that role, many people saw her as one of the oppressors. After struggling throughout her life to overcome oppression, she found it difficult to experience herself in a dominant social location as an oppressor. Conversely, in the 1980s, as women rose in number as students and teachers at the seminary, there were some male students used to being in a dominant role who found it very difficult when they experienced being in subordinate positions to women.

SOCIAL LOCATION AND BIBLICAL INTERPRETATION

One of the results of this awareness of social identity has been that some biblical scholars started to name their social location in their publications so as to acknowledge the influences and perspectives from which they interpreted. Traditionally, writers would suppress their social location under the misapprehension that they could be objective. This has changed significantly.

In this regard, I found the *Global Bible Commentary*, edited by Daniel Patte et al., to be very helpful in the classroom. Each contributor identifies and describes the contemporary social context from which they write. He or she then interprets the biblical book they are analyzing in light of that context. I asked students to report on each article they read from this volume—such as the commentary on Galatians by Nestor Miguez (Argentina), the commentary on First Thessalonians by K. K. Yeo (China), the one on Philemon by Jean Kim (South Korea), and the one on Philippians by Demetrius Williams (African American)—identifying first the social location of the author and then explaining how that social location informed their interpretation. Other commentaries and books have now become available from feminist and same-gender/queer orientation perspectives. Identifying one's social location clarifies so much about the approach one takes; and the practice of doing it encourages others to do the same.

What these commentators from different social locations bring to the biblical text is highly illuminating. Identifying their social location makes it clear and explicit that they are interpreting with a purpose—looking for insights in the text that address their situation, that provide avenues to overcome their oppression, or that offer direction for personal renewal and social transformation. Of course, approaching the text from a suppressed social location means interpreters also discern oppressive dynamics in the biblical text itself, dynamics that they expose and resist. One of the great benefits of these diverse resources is that when students encounter their own social locations in such commentaries as the *Global Bible Commentary*, they are emboldened to find their own voice in the classroom.

Naming Dominant Culture Social Location

European Americans from the dominant culture frequently cannot see how their social location informs their interpretation of the Bible. Perhaps they can in terms of religious denomination or gender and race but not in regard to many other factors. In the classroom, it is especially problematic when the student group is comprised overwhelmingly of people from the dominant culture. At Carthage College, where the student body was quite homogeneous, I would do an exercise of asking students to identify *my* social biases simply by looking at me visually before them in the classroom. Almost invariably they would name only those things that made me different from them. I was a male; I was older than they were; I had a beard; I was a teacher; and I wore a sport coat. They looked and looked for other things, but they could not see the things about me that were like them and that made us different from other groups in society. I needed to point out that I was white; I was European American; I spoke American English; I was well fed; I was without disabilities; I had a watch (Western view of time); and so on. Then I would begin to elaborate on some of these biases, explaining how they might influence "my" and "our" biblical interpretations in distinction from people of other social locations.

Self-Examination

Unless we who are in dominant positions examine ourselves and think about our differences in relation to others, we will not see our privileges or discern what we as a dominant culture or group can take for granted. A personal example. I grew up in a small town in Pennsylvania. There was only one black family in town. Later, in the sixties, I was living in North Carolina, where I came into more frequent contact with African Americans. I knew little about the hardships, suffering, and discrimination blacks were enduring, and I wanted to "help." I went to a church anti-racism encounter experience between blacks and whites. My intent was to learn more about what it was like to be black, so I could give support to African Americans. I was taken aback when I was told that this was not what was needed. They could take care of themselves. Instead, they thought it was a good idea for me to find out what it meant for me to be white! And as I was finding that out, I could work with my white brothers and sisters to change the things we did that contribute to conditions of discrimination and oppression.

That early shock and reorientation have been with me throughout my life as I have sought to understand all that I take for granted as a result of *my* social location—all the privileges I enjoy, all the cultural patterns I can take for granted, all the actions I take that are marginalizing of others, all the de facto segregation that takes place simply because of the groups of which I am a part, all the things I say that are thoughtless and hurtful, all the things I do—consciously or unconsciously—that serve to exert power over others. And it is not up to people of other ethnic groups to show me what I do as a white male. That has clearly helped; nevertheless, I have to examine these things for myself, to take my own responsibility for my harmful actions and attitudes.

For me, awareness of social location has required of me honest social- and self-reflection to ferret out and admit my biases and cultural perspectives, somewhat as those in Alcoholics Anonymous take a "fearless moral inventory" of themselves and their actions. And the process of self-reflection and social examination does not end. This was one of the lessons I learned from the women's movement. In the sixties, I thought I would develop an awareness of the dynamics of sexism in my life and then become some pristine self that was without sexist bias. Not a chance. It is layer upon layer of sexism all the way down, just as it is layer upon layer of racism. As such, it is a process to be engaged proactively for a lifetime.

IMPLICATIONS FOR THE CLASSROOM

The classroom can model healthy interactions reflecting justice between different groups. The classroom may initiate the process of reflection on social location for some students, and it may advance the process already in motion for others. Many students may be ahead in the process and able to help the rest of us. But what the classroom experience must *not* do is to hinder or reverse that process—or be ignorant of it. That principle applied to my students *and* to me.

So what specific implications does this have for learning in the classroom? Actually, it has implications for how we imagine the entire learning enterprise. Justo González proposed an image of the classroom as an ethnic roundtable with people from many different cultures gathering at a "round table," an arrangement in which *no one is privileged* and *no one is marginalized.* We can extend the image to the study of the Bible, in which the text is in the middle and there is a dialogue that is mutual with one another and with the biblical text. Because certain voices have traditionally been suppressed in our culture, the group needs to assure that these voices are indeed expressed and that they will be heard.

Implications for a Teacher

Of course, as noted earlier, in order for this to be effective, we have to create a classroom atmosphere of mutual regard in which everyone can contribute and challenge each other in a common quest for understanding. Three specific implications come to mind.

Be Self-Aware

The first implication is that we have a responsibility to express an awareness of our own social location. If I am not aware of my social location and how it informs my interpretation of Scripture or in terms of how I relate to people from other social locations or in terms of the power dynamics involved in my position, then I will not be able to empower others to speak from their social locations. I needed to name explicitly the factors of my own social location: model it, state my desire to resist anything negative, and express my commitment to empower others to speak.

Part of my personal difficulties as a teacher in a position of authority was that, in terms of social location, I am the quintessential oppressor in my particular culture—white, Anglo-Saxon, Protestant (WASP), male, heterosexual, middle-class, educated, older, American—and the teacher! I had to acknowledge the power dynamics that resulted from my presence and role, dynamics that were negative for many students. It was a burden and a liability to some students that I bore actually and symbolically the blindnesses and limitations and history of much oppression. In this reflection, I may appear confident as I talk about issues of social location, but inside I shudder. In spite of that, if I was to be effective as a teacher, I had to do my best to deal with these dynamics.

Model Liberative Practices

The second implication of social location for the teacher is to model liberative practices. In this regard, our role as teachers is to limit our power in some ways and to use our power in other ways so as to assure that students have a safe place to claim their voice and express it. The poet Wendell Berry once said that people in my circumstance should stop thinking they will contribute to the salvation of the world and just spend a century or two "cleaning up after ourselves"—which, in this situation, I take to mean that we make sure not to perpetuate the problem and that we seek to reverse it.

It is important to acknowledge that teachers from groups that have traditionally been suppressed have a different power dynamic to deal with. On the one hand, their very presence gives encouragement to others who have been suppressed. And their position empowers others without voice to speak. What a difference it made to women in the church and the seminary when finally they had female pastors and seminary teachers! I have seen the same empowerment take place with students whose leaders in authority were Native American, Asian, Hispanic, and African American women and men.

At the same time, at LSTC, a few female faculty members had some students in the doctoral program who, because of their social location, had difficulty acknowledging the authority of a female instructor in their courses. This placed the teacher in an awkward position and undermined the goals and effectiveness of the instruction. Fortunately, conversations were able to alleviate the situation so that the teacher and the students could move forward.

Know the Students

The third implication is that the time is now over when it is enough for a teacher to know only his or her subject matter. Now we also need to know our students. And this is fortuitous, because the best people to teach us about the students are the students themselves. This approach places the teacher in the position of the learner, the inquirer. I was able to model what I wanted students to do with the subject matter by having an appetite for learning about the students—their social location, their point of view, and how this was informing their interpretation of Scripture. In the classroom mix, without denying my position as a teacher or my social location, I struggled to generate a classroom of interpreters, all of whom at different times could be teachers and learners.

Implications for Students

Here are three implications of social location for students.

Be Aware of Social Location

First of all, if students are to engage in the act of reading and interpretation, they need to know the factors in their own makeup that affect how they read and interpret: what they are interested in, what they look for, how they understand it, how they frame it, what assumptions about life they bring to the task, what they ignore or simply do not see, why their perspective differs from that of others, and so on.

Perhaps the most important thing for students to learn is that social locations bring both assets and liabilities to the task of interpretation. Factors of our social location have the potential to hinder our understanding of the text because we may be imposing a framework from our time and culture onto the text. At the same time, our social location can never be a reason to dismiss an interpretation. Quite the contrary, the social location can help us understand the text in fresh ways, because diverse interpreters are looking for things that others have not heretofore discerned in the texts and their contexts. Our role as teachers is to assist the students to embrace this awareness of strengths and limitations from their social location and the social locations of others. That is to say, it is no longer enough for students to look just at the text. They must "look at themselves looking at the text." In terms of social location, *students must interpret themselves and each other interpreting the text*.

How can we give some time and tools for students to do this? One way is simply to ask what it is that students are looking for when they read the Bible. Are they looking for spiritual guidance and insight? Are they looking for inspiration to work for justice and liberation? Do they want to know how they can minister in a church? Are they looking for affirmation? Are they seeking the Gospel message of salvation for preaching or witness? Often it is possible for them to correlate their quest in reading the Bible with some dimension of their social location—their gender or ethnic identity, their family background or the church group to which they belong, or their vocational choices. A simple exercise can help students see more clearly how these factors contribute to interpretation. At the same time, such questions can broaden their perspective when they interpret with others who have differing social locations and different goals for reading.

In this regard, the main strategy I employed was to provide students with a "Social Location Profile." The handout lists the following categories on one side of a page with space between each item for students to put notes:

Country of origin

Language(s)

Race/ethnic group(s)

Gender identification/sexual orientation

Economic system and personal level

Occupation

Education level

Religious affiliation

Political party

Geographical origin

Health

Legal status

Other

I made it clear that these categories were not meant to label or to stereotype anyone but only to give some suggestions about social factors that may shape one's interpretation of texts—and that the students could revise the form itself accordingly. I also added two other categories of an individual nature, because they helped to qualify and sometimes even to counter a social profile.

Personal experiences

Personal commitments

I then asked students to make brief notes on these factors (not to be turned in)—identifying how they related to each category. Then I invited them to share in pairs or triads (only as much as they felt comfortable sharing) the factors on the profile that *they* thought were important as lenses through which they interpret the Bible.

On the back of that sheet of paper, I then gave another list of factors that would have shaped ways in which people from the first-century biblical world might have seen their lives:

Jew/gentile

Gender identity

Family position/position in family

Work status

Village location

Urban location

National/imperial context

Position of social honor or shame

Scale of purity or defilement

Economic position

Elite/peasant/expendable (no "middle class")

Other

Making use of this profile, I asked students to identify the social location of the biblical writer under study, say the author of Gospel of Mark or the apostle Paul. Not only did the students realize how much their own social location impacted their way of seeing the text in contrast and comparison to other students; they also realized how different the social location of the biblical writer was from their own, and how the social location of the biblical writings differed from each other. Overall, they learned that their interpretations of the text and their appropriations of it for contemporary situations needed to take account of all these dynamics.

Be Aware of Multiple Perspectives in Dialogue with the Class and the Bible

There was a second implication of social location for students. The students became much more dialogical when they were aware of their own distinct perspective, the perspectives of others, and the multiple perspectives of the biblical texts. They saw how inappropriate is our tendency to understand what we read in the Bible in the framework of our contemporary social location rather than the social location of the biblical text under consideration. This insight reinforced the cross-cultural nature of a biblical text and the importance of reading a text in its original context. Words, concepts, examples, stories, and relationships all take on new meaning when seen in the context of an ancient social location.

At the same time, students learned to read and interpret with self-conscious awareness of their own social location, namely, that they had something distinctive to see and to say as they made connections in comparison and contrast with biblical social locations. What do you see when you read from the position of the dominant culture? What do you see when you read as a female? And what do you see when you read with an illness or disability? What do you see when you come from a collectivist culture? Obviously, such factors in no way exhausted the grounds of their reading. Nevertheless, the goal was that each student find her or his own voice and begin to speak out of it in relation to the biblical text and in relation to other students. When this happened, students came to value the diverse perspectives in the class and to depend on this diversity as a means to see dimensions and meanings of the text that they would not otherwise have noticed. They could more clearly see the interpretations they had chosen and the ways they could challenge each other. They were eager to hear what insights each person had and why/how that person had them.

Be Aware of Power Dynamics in the Classroom

A third implication for students is that the concept of social location affects students (and, of course, teachers) in terms of power dynamics. The students become attuned to the power dynamics in the biblical text in new ways; and they also become more open about the power dynamics in the classroom. Why not talk about the fact that there are men and women, people of different ethnic groups and races, people with disabilities, people who have wealth, and others who come from backgrounds of poverty? One seminary student who previously had had a Wall Street career was committed to demonstrating how the biblical materials made it clear that wealth was not the source of happiness and well-being. Another student was reading the biblical materials from his social location as one with the fatal condition of cystic fibrosis. It was important in the classroom not to privilege or to marginalize but to honor equally the very diverse social locations from which students interpreted the Bible.

Transformation through dialogue will not happen if we do not challenge each other or if we talk only with those who agree with us. The goal is not to avoid conflict but to overcome interactions that suppress or exploit or marginalize and to practice dialogue that is liberating and empowering. To deal with this, the teacher needs to be comfortable with conflict and have a sense of when to remain silent and when to intervene to make sure the classroom is a safe place to have conflict. On a few occasions, there were some heated exchanges between black and white students in several of my classes. I trusted the students to play it out. In each case, they stuck with it, explained their views, listened carefully, acknowledged each other, and even changed somewhat—to the point where these incidents turned out to be positive examples of how to relate through differences.

Equality with Difference

The basic concept that underlies justice among diverse social locations in a classroom is equality with difference, mutuality amid diversity. Maintaining this dynamic without either losing the equality or collapsing the differences into sameness is not easy to accomplish. Individuals have to affirm their own distinctive voice; and the group members need to appreciate each other. On the one hand, the process involves not letting others define you; and on the other hand, it involves not being presumptuous about your point of view. I used two slogans to convey this phenomenon. Both apply to every interpreter.

- The one adage was this: *Don't let others interpret for you.* That is to say, find your own distinctive approach and interpretation. This may apply more frequently to people from subordinate places whose voices have been traditionally suppressed.
- The other adage was this: *Don't trust yourself to interpret alone.* In other words, our perspective is limited, and we need to see more clearly the biases, limitations, blind spots, and distortions of our own interpretations by being in dialogue with others from differing social locations. This advice may apply more frequently to those in traditionally dominant positions.

Implications for the Institution

Institutions of higher learning may imagine that once the makeup of the faculty, staff, and students hits a critical mass of diversity, then the job is complete and diversity will take care of itself. It does not seem to work that way. It is precisely when diversity has been achieved that the hard work may really begin. Even more will the institution need to be intentional about the conflicts and stresses that inevitably occur between people of very different backgrounds, understandings of power and decision-making, and visions for the educational process. We live in a world of incredible diversity. That diversity is also present in the classroom. As such, the classroom is a laboratory. If we can learn to appreciate the rich diversity of social locations and the related power dynamics in the microcosm of the classroom, we can go a long way toward generating the macrocosm of a just society in which we live together, work with our differences, and work out our differences.

17

Experiments in Intercultural Dialogue

It is one thing to have a classroom makeup that is multicultural. It is another thing to have intercultural conversations and study. Unless we draw upon the dynamics of diversity, the class can end up being not much different from classes we might teach with a monocultural makeup. On the other hand, when we have interactions between cultures, we greatly enhance the educational experience.

My classes ranged from courses with predominantly European Americans, often with some African American and Hispanic American representation, to courses in which there was extensive international representation. Each of these courses offered different challenges for introducing social location, expanding student experiences of diverse points of view, and fostering intercultural dialogue. Here are some things I experimented with as means to do that.

PLANNING A COURSE FOR INTERCULTURAL DIALOGUE

Being open to a multicultural class is only the very first step in the process. It is important to have a thoroughgoing approach to planning a class from the ground up, so as to attract a multicultural group of students and to foster intercultural dialogue in the class dynamics. What follows is a checklist of factors I used for planning, promoting, and carrying out courses that embraced multicultural diversity.

Course Title and Description. Prepare a course title and/or description (for example, Reading the Bible from Many Cultures) that indicates people will be reading from different social locations.

Syllabus. Make clear on the syllabus the commitment to honor diverse voices as an integral part of the effectiveness of the class. State an inclusive language-sensitive policy. Include guidelines for respectful conversation.

Subject Matter. Highlight themes, events, situations, and case studies in the course that give an opportunity to deal with issues related to diversity. Choose primary sources that address and reflect diversity.

Readings. Assign secondary sources—books, articles, and other media (such as films)—that originate from and reflect different social locations, cultures, and subcultures. The required (and not just the recommended) books should reflect this diversity.

Teacher. Make explicit your own social location and explain the power dynamics of a classroom.

Colleagues. Consider team teaching the course with someone from a different social location. Include guest speakers who reflect diverse social locations.

Room Setup. Does the arrangement of the room give the message that there will be conversation with each other? Do the pictures and artwork on the walls reflect a multicultural atmosphere?

Composition of the Class. Through the use of an exercise to identify student social locations, make explicit the different perspectives of students in the class. Make the most of the differences in social location, even where the makeup is largely monocultural. Compare and contrast these with the social locations of the authors and implied audiences of the primary and secondary works under study.

Subject Matter. Highlight the diverse cultural locations of the biblical writings under consideration in the class. Imagine the biblical writings in dialogue with each other.

Class Discussions. Give voice to all members of the class as means to identify and foster dialogue from various social locations. Arrange small groups to maximize opportunities for students to meet both with others from their own culture and with people from diverse cultures for intercultural dialogue.

Assignments. Give assignments that engage students in intercultural reflection, action, and conversation. Give group projects.

Evaluation. Make sure the evaluation forms employed in the middle and at the end of the class ask: Have students encountered resources and voices from diverse social locations?

CLASSES WITH SIGNIFICANT DIVERSITY

I have been extremely fortunate on occasion to have a genuinely multicultural makeup in a few of my classes. In an elective on Justification in Romans and Galatians, students included a Korean Presbyterian, a Mandarin Chinese Methodist, a Korean Baptist, two German Lutherans, a Norwegian Lutheran, an American Roman Catholic, and three American Lutherans. A doctoral class on Luke was comprised of students from Korea, Lithuania, Hungary, Cameroon, Guyana, Tanzania, and the United States. I learned a great deal from the challenges and opportunities these classes presented.

My main fear was that if someone were to make a transcript of the class, would an independent reader be able to discern a significant difference in this class from one in which students were all from the US culture? Would my teaching open things up so that diverse perspectives were integral to the entire course? Some examples of my efforts included these: When we dealt with a passage from Paul, everyone worked out of his or her own-language Bible. They contributed cultural insights in conversation, through a sermon, and in a paper. I performed biblical passages in English, and each student reflected on the experience from their cultural context. Students gave presentations out of their cultural perspective and their social location. These two classes were highly stimulating and generative for the students—and for me.

IMPROVISING IN A CLASS WITH LIMITED DIVERSITY

Part of the difficulty is that no matter how hard we recruit, the makeup of the class may still be largely monocultural. When that is the case, intercultural dialogue can still be introduced as part of the subject matter under study. The following exercise proved to be very helpful. I prepared a list of articles (more than the number of students in the class) that offered interpretations of the Bible from diverse cultural perspectives. Here are some examples from more than thirty articles that I used:

- "The Danger of Ignoring One's Own Cultural Bias in Interpreting the Text," by Randall Bailey
- "The Bible from the Perspective of the Racially and Economically Oppressed," by Katie Cannon
- "Toward a Post-Colonial Feminist Interpretation of the Bible," by Musa Dube
- "Borderless Women and Borderless Texts: A Cultural Reading of Matthew 15:21–28," by Letitia Guardiola-Saenz
- "A Korean Feminist Perspective of John 4:1–41," by Jean Kim
- "Discovering the Bible in the Non-Biblical World," by Kwok Pui-Lon
- "A Nice Jewish Girl Reads the Gospel of John," by Adele Reinhartz
- "Biblical Studies after the Empire: From a Colonial to a Postcolonial Mode of Interpretation," by R. S. Sugirtharajah
- "Reading for Liberation," by Mary Ann Tolbert
- "From I-Hermeneutics to We-Hermeneutics: Native Americans and the Post-Colonial," by Jace Weaver

I took a hard copy of each article to class as well as a printed list of them to give to each student. Each student picked a different article from the list, took the article, read it, wrote a half-page paragraph, and came to the next class prepared to read that paragraph and answer questions about their article. In their paragraphs, they were to identify the author's cultural and social location and then explain how that social location had shaped the interpretation put forth in the article. For this exercise, I arranged for us all to sit in a circle, regardless of the size of the class. We had five students read their paragraphs in a row, after which we would stop for questions and reactions, then five more.

In a single class period, therefore, students were introduced to many new insights about the Bible coming from a plethora of social locations. It opened up a wider world—a new world of interpreters and a new world of interpretations. The experience led them to see the relative nature of their own perspective. Experiencing this diversity also gave voice to students from suppressed groups, empowering them to speak out of their heritage and cultural tradition.

AN IMMERSION EXPERIENCE

As part of a course on First Peter, I organized a daylong workshop for students from the community of seminaries in the area. The goal was to take participants through a process whereby they would become aware of the particularity of their own responses to First Peter and the reasons for it, to appreciate the interpretations of people from other cultures and the reasons for their interpretations, and to engage in intercultural conversations. In addition to the fifteen members of the class, about fifty other people participated, representative of many cultures around the world.

When we gathered, each person filled out a worksheet identifying key features of their sociocultural location and personal convictions. Then I performed First Peter orally for the whole group to experience together. Although this was performed from memory, it could be also powerful as a dynamic reading. Immediately after this, they wrote down their own reactions to hearing First Peter and how they would correlate these reactions to their social location/personal conviction indicators. Then they met in small groups to share these reflections with others from different cultural locations.

After a brief break, several faculty from nearby seminaries gave talks that reflected their cultural reactions to and their own interpretations of First Peter, including their appreciation for and their resistances to dynamics in First Peter. The speakers included an African American womanist from the Adventist tradition who taught at Chicago Theological Seminary and an Asian American male from Chicago Theological Seminary, along with a European American female and an African male, both Roman Catholics who taught at the Catholic Theological Union. At the end of the morning session, all participants were asked to identify on their worksheets what they had learned from the speakers and in what ways their own views had been confirmed and challenged. In the afternoon, a number of participants in the workshop who were from diverse cultures were invited briefly to offer their interpretations in plenary session, followed again by small group conversations. In concluding, participants were to write down what their interpretations/evaluations of First Peter were at the end of the workshop in comparison with the beginning of the day, and to identify what they had learned from the process.

There was an overwhelmingly positive response to the event. Many issues arose around the interpretation and evaluation of First Peter: the author's view of women/men and marriage; the treatment of slaves; the attitude toward the state; whether there was accommodation to the larger culture or not; the idea of "submission" and what that entailed; the apparent glorification of suffering; among other things. These issues proved to be of critical importance to people from diverse cultures and social locations.

Afterward, people kept saying that they had not before this event imagined that there would be such different and surprising reactions to this biblical writing. In the process, they became clearer about their own views. And they came to respect other views. They could see how other views were legitimate; and they could even understand why others held those views, even when they themselves did not and would not hold those points of view. Many also learned, for the first time, how to distinguish their own views from those of the Bible, especially when they disagreed with the view presented in the Bible and when the Bible itself had been a source of harm to so many.

Here are some verbatim comments made in participant evaluations from that workshop (I have noted how they each identified themselves on their worksheet).

- *Male from Iraq*. "Hearing people from different cultural backgrounds express their views helped me realize the richness of this text in terms of how many aspects of life it addresses and how these aspects are suppressed by reading or hearing the text from one point of view or from a single cultural background."
- *Female from China*. "I love the honest statements of the presenters and what sounded offensive to them. To me this kind of openness was comforting. I believe that if we take this text as a whole in a group it can yield insights for us."
- *Male from Poland*. "Listening to others talk about their perspectives on 1 Peter leads me to consider that no one has a complete understanding of any part of the letter. I need to be humble in the way I appropriate 1 Peter, knowing that others also have a valid perspective from their vantage point. I need to challenge my limited horizon and my social location and have the humility to enter into a dialogue with others, especially someone of the opposite social location."
- *Male from Kenya*. "One sees how dangerous it is for women to be told to submit to husbands, yet in my country before Christianity

it was customary for men to beat their wives. But when Christians came they were told to stop beating their wives and help the children, and they quoted 1 Peter. Now which Bible did they read? How could the same Bible oppress women in one situation and liberate women in another?"

- *Same speaker.* "In my interaction with other readers I have learned that we all respond and are impacted differently by a text. Many would agree that in its original context, 1 Peter was not meant to oppress or give license to oppression. Even those who feel resistant to 1 Peter agree to this. It is a good beginning point. So what do we do with a text when it becomes abusive and marginalizing?"
- *North American female.* "It was affirming to know that other people of diverse contexts struggled with portions of the text, and it was essential to hear from people who heard many positive things that my own experience tended to block out. I do not feel particularly changed in my own view, but empowered to own it."
- *Same speaker.* "One way at least is by adopting the humility that the text suggests, which enables me to be in solidarity with many different folks, never feeling better or superior to anyone."
- *Male from South Korea.* "We should be open to all kinds of voices. But it is difficult to endure dominating voices and the power that controls different voices. So reading the Bible out of our social location is not only interpreting the text but also interpreting our context, because interpreting and engaging is related with power."
- *White North American lesbian.* "I know the systems of domination. I know the cost of silence. I do not know the cost of raising one's voice in the context of persecution where the threat of death is real. From people who come from cultural experiences that include persecution for faith and identity factors, I have learned to soften my opposition to the text and listen more attentively to the places in which the text can be liberating."
- *Male from Ireland.* "I want to use 1 Peter in a positive way, but I also want people to know the possibility of misuse of it by the powerful."
- *White North American male.* "I realize that 1 Peter is not the entire Bible. So what do John, Paul, and Mark have to say?"

- *Same speaker.* "I realize that the concept of being 'chosen' must encourage insiders, but that being chosen cannot be used with outsiders to express superiority."
- *White North American Roman Catholic sister.* "Hearing this as a woman is entirely different from a man's perspective."
- *Male from Burma.* "My own social location is the same as that of 1 Peter's condition. As Christians suffered under the Roman government as Peter says of Babylon, we are suffering. My military government is like the Romans. By the grace of God, 1 Peter affirms my suffering for people in terms of faith in God."
- *Mexican American male.* "I heard the text from the stance of being marginalized, not accepted in either culture, Mexican or American—not Mexican national and not considered American, but hyphenated Mexican-American, criticized by both cultures, being told what I have to do to appropriate a rootedness in one or the other. I have my feet, my identity in both. This challenges me to do what my society does not permit. I was brought up to assimilate, but I need to honor my social location, values, my person, my experience, and culture. Those resident aliens in 1 Peter were just like that."
- *North American white female.* "The closing small groups affirmed the great variety in the levels of authority we grant the Bible in general."
- *White North American male.* "This text is oppressive to those who are part of a social location where the text has been historically used to oppress. Others who are part of a culture where Christianity is oppressed by the dominant culture are comforted by the encouragement it seems to offer. We have to distinguish between what the text meant in its original context and how it is being used to oppress or to liberate since then."

ANOTHER IMMERSION EXPERIMENT

This immersion in intercultural dialogue was repeated on other occasions. For example, the Chicago World Mission Institute took a similar approach by sponsoring a three-day conference organized under the title: "The Bible in Many Cultures: Reading the Book of Revelation from Your

Place." The program followed a similar pattern to the earlier immersion. On the first evening, I offered a dramatic performance of Revelation, which gave the group of more than a hundred people a shared experience of the Apocalypse. On the next days, plenary lectures were presented by a Chilean scholar working in Costa Rica and an African American womanist scholar. Different workshops were led by professors on reading Revelation from a Chinese perspective, a postcolonial Brazilian perspective, an African perspective, and an ecological perspective. In order to make this experience more widely available, we added some additional voices, and I edited the essays as *From Every People and Nation: Reading the Book of Revelation in Intercultural Perspective*.

CONCLUSION: DIVERSITY IS THE LIFEBLOOD OF SUSTAINABILITY

Diversity—biological, cultural, social, religious—is integral to God's creation and critical for our human survival on planet Earth. It is an ecological fact about our world. The diversity of wheat strains is crucial for the continuation of wheat on our planet. If we had only one or two strains, then soil conditions, plant diseases, and insect infestations would wipe them out. Unless we have many strains that can adapt to changing conditions, the few strains of wheat would be lost.

Likewise, we need many cultural formations and diverse social structures and economic systems and religious communities to enable us to adapt to changing circumstances on Earth or we will not survive or thrive. One culture or one economic system does not fit all times and situations and peoples. And we also need great diversity of religious beliefs and expressions to meet the needs and visions of different communities in different situations. For adaptation to occur, for renewal to happen, for justice to be enacted, we need to hear the clear voices of many people. It is in our best interest for diversity to survive and thrive. This is what we should cultivate in the classroom.

18

Performing Scripture

Unfortunately, most adults have memories of some horrible moment in their childhood when they were expected to recite something by memory in class or in church—and they froze. The mind goes blank, the muscles tighten, and the eyes dilate. We do not want to recall such moments, and we do not ever want to be in that position again in our life. Memories of such experiences of teachers and students alike have tended to eclipse the development of a "pedagogy of performance."

It is tragic in a way, because people are kept from opportunities that could change their lives. What an opportunity it is when students of any age are challenged to learn and perform the "I Have a Dream" speech of Martin Luther King or Lincoln's "Gettysburg Address" or President Kennedy's inaugural address or a speech by Harriet Tubman or a sonnet by Shakespeare or traditional Native American stories. Oral performance in the classroom has become a lost art.

NOT SO HARD TO DO

The shame is that it is not that hard to do. Consider the number of songs or hymns most people can sing all the way through practically in their sleep. My teenage granddaughter could follow along by heart with the words to almost any rap or R & B song that came on the car radio. How many children know the multiplication tables by heart? How many people have a repertoire of jokes? How about the people who learn pages of lines for a play? I am sometimes stunned by youth who know by heart the full dialogues of a movie they have seen umpteen times. To do some memorizing and the performing of poems and speeches and passages of Scripture is not far removed from this. And the natural ingredients needed to do it are not far away: interest, incentive, some determination, a model of how to do it, a process for doing it, a safe place to practice, a place to present it, and the assurance that forgetting and recovering (always with a script nearby!) can be as natural as falling and getting up when learning to skate.

Learning something so that it becomes part of you is a unique experience. Learning something by listening to it is one thing. Learning by putting yourself in the place of the writer/narrator is an entirely different thing. These are things you may never forget. Even if, later in life, you do not recall any passages verbatim, there will be lines and emotions and angles of vision that will stick with you like burs for a lifetime.

PERFORMING THE GOSPEL OF MARK AND OTHER WRITINGS

I did a lot of memorizing as a child—poems, Bible verses, and speeches. But I had pretty much forgotten about memorizing until I read in *TIME* magazine a story about a British actor, Alec McCowen, who was performing the King James Version of Mark on stage to audiences in the major theaters in England and in cities across the United States. From the rave reviews, it was clear that the audiences were captivated and delighted by it. The reports expressed surprise that a biblical narrative would lend itself so well to theater and be so engaging and entertaining. Some even suspected that McCowen must have made up some of the stories!

In response to reports about McCowen's performance, I thought, "I could do that!" I had already done my own translation from Greek for a book I was working on, *Mark as Story*. That same year I severely wrenched my back, and I was in bed for a month. It was then that I set myself to memorizing Mark. It takes over two hours to recite/perform Mark. I learned it and practiced it one line at a time, over and over and over. It took the whole month of doing little else to get it initially in mind. Then it seemed like only a week would go by and much of it would be gone! At first, I would work fifteen to twenty hours before each performance just to do the memory work. As I gained control of the material, I began to ask for guidance on how to tell the stories so as to bring out the dynamics of the narrative and to have a greater impact on an audience.

I chose to memorize and perform because I thought it would help my students to experience Mark in a fresh way, as hearers or "theatergoers" rather than as readers. And it worked. Students heard things they had never noticed when reading. They said that it brought emotion back into the Bible and a sense of humanity they could relate to. They said it felt like they were encountering the Gospel of Mark for the first time. I was very encouraged by the results and decided to offer it to other groups. Before I retired from performing, I was privileged to perform Mark several hundred times, for classes and in churches and in auditoriums around the country. Over time, I learned and performed other books and sections of the New Testament for the same purposes, such as the Sermon on the Mount, Galatians, Philemon, James, First Peter, Revelation, and selections from Luke and John.

These immersion experiences with Scripture changed my life. In fact, translating, memorizing, and performing became a primary research tool for my scholarship. If I wanted to study a particular book, I tried to become the voice of the text, live inside the worldview of that story, learn every detail, bring it to life in performance, and seek to convey the impact of the work for the engagement and transformation of an audience. For me, there is no better way than performance to understand a biblical writing—its potential meanings and the dynamics of its rhetorical impacts. As I have shared these experiences with students, the process and practices have proven to be effective pedagogical tools—for students not only to *hear* but also to *perform* biblical passages. The shared experiences have significantly transformed the dynamics and relationships of my classes. In the framework of transformation, the voice of Scripture became a significant part of the dialogue.

THE NEW TESTAMENT WRITINGS AS "PERFORMANCE LITERATURE" LIKE DRAMA AND MUSIC

The New Testament writings were not originally experienced in writing except to a very few. The writings were oral in inception—told by early Christian storytellers and heard by audiences hungry to experience the stories and letters being told. The writings that are now in the New Testament were not originally written or received as Scripture. They were stories, letters, and apocalypses. Some of them were created in mind and memory or composed orally in performance and then transcribed into writing. Others were composed in dictation to a scribe with the goal that they would be performed orally.

In the oral/scribal cultures of the first centuries, probably 2 to 5 percent of the people could read or write (often up to 15 percent in urban areas), and then only with varying degrees of skill, some able only to assist with letters or documents. Everyone was steeped in the orality of the culture, even those who could read and write. The writings we now have in the New Testament were originally handwritten on scrolls between 50 and 100 CE. During that time, there were few scrolls available to early Christian communities. With no punctuation or spaces between words, just one uppercase letter after another from beginning to end, handwritten scrolls were not designed to be read with facility before a group. Even when one was reading a scroll publicly, one needed to know the composition practically by heart in order to read with ease. Vastly different from modern books, these handwritten scrolls functioned as aids to memory retrieval for a performer preparing for a performance.

These New Testament writings have all the marks of orality. We can see that they were composed "by ear" to please the hearing and to assist in remembering—with alliteration, chiastic patterns, chain linkages, antithetical and synonymous parallelism, contrasts, proverbs, maxims, parables, type scenes, and other mnemonic devices. And just as we have people with photographic recall in contemporary print cultures, so in predominantly oral cultures people come to the fore who have audio-phonic recall—the capacity to hear and reproduce something with astounding faithfulness (as some musicians do today). Indeed, to some extent, in such a predominantly oral culture, everyone was accustomed to hearing and remembering, because that was the way people learned and retained their traditions. The experiences of performance generated in my New Testament classes were meant to recover some small taste of the original ethos of the early Christians—experiences of oral performance that have been fundamentally eclipsed for nearly two thousand years.

As such, the New Testament writings are examples of "performance literature," every bit as much as music or drama. They were meant to be performed by memory or by reading aloud. The New Testament writings that have been preserved in writing are like the fossil remains of what were once flesh-and-blood performances. Imagine a musicologist studying scores of music without ever hearing a performance. Imagine a

Shakespearean scholar studying the plays without ever experiencing an enactment of them. Imagine that we biblical scholars have studied the texts of the New Testament for centuries without ever hearing them in their entirety! When was the last time in the history of the church that people heard the wisdom of the Letter of James or the Epistle of First Peter, for example, being performed by memory or being read in their entirety for a communal gathering, as they were in the first century?

For us, the task, based on clues from the text itself, is to put flesh and blood back onto the fossils and make them into live performances. This is not simply a matter of giving sound to the text, as if performing literature was a matter of creating a talking head or listening to a recording. A performance involves the performer, the audience, and the context. A performance is embodied. It includes inflection, pauses, pace, volume, pitch, gestures, posture, facial expressions, and movement. And the text provides clues, like stage directions, to what a performance might have been like when it tells the performer that someone "screamed" or "pleaded" or "laid on hands" or "flogged someone."

Although we can learn a lot about ancient performances from rhetorical handbooks and descriptions of storytellers, we clearly cannot reproduce a performance the way it was done in the first century. So, in our class we did not seek to replicate the dynamics or the mechanics of performances from the first century. Nevertheless, the experience of performing in a modern context shifts the *medium* of the New Testament from print back to oral performance. As such, our goal is to find contemporary techniques of telling stories and of giving speeches that make sense to a modern performer and audience. Just as we add punctuation, provide spaces between words, and mark paragraphs to bring out the meaning of the text for reading, so we invest voice, movement, and body language to bring out the potential meaning and impact of the text for listening. And just as we translate the Greek text into a modern language as a means to understand it better, so we "translate" the printed text into contemporary methods of oral storytelling. In this way, the performance itself is an *interpretation* of a text, every bit as much as a commentary or an essay on the passage.

ENGAGING STUDENTS IN PERFORMANCE

When I first began performing for students in this enterprise, I was taken aback by the level of student engagement in experiencing these performances. One evening I started performing Galatians late in the class. At exactly 9:30, I stopped about two-thirds of the way through Galatians and said, "The class time is up. I will have to pick this up next time." The response was immediate and overwhelming: "No way! You're not going to stop in the middle and leave us hanging. You have to finish this!" And of course I did.

After doing my own performances for students, I began inviting each student in my class on the Gospels to learn and present one story to the rest of the class, such as the parable of the unjust steward or the healing of blind Bartimaeus or a conflict over the Sabbath laws. It was amazing what happened. Each student presented one story, and all students heard twenty or twenty-five stories by different people from different social locations with different styles and approaches. The encouragement for the student performers was considerable. It was one thing to hear the teacher perform; after all, they might have expected it from me. But to hear their peers tell the stories was jaw dropping for them. And each student came away knowing that *they could do it*! I incorporated this unit of memorization and performance into many different classes at the college, seminary, and graduate levels.

Then I took it a step further by having several students together in tandem perform an entire letter. For my last years of teaching at the seminary, I regularly taught a course on the shorter letters of Paul, covering Philemon, Galatians, First Thessalonians, and Philippians, in that order. In the first half of the course, I performed Philemon and Galatians. Both performances helped us immensely to dig into the meaning and rhetoric of each of these letters. The familiarity with the letters created for them by a performance was significant. And the communal nature of the experience enhanced our conversations about letter structure, narrative analysis, discourse analysis, social science analysis, theological themes, and rhetoric, as well as efforts to imagine ancient scenarios of performance as a basis for further interpretation.

Then, for the second half of the course, I asked students to volunteer to learn and perform one of the chapters from First Thessalonians or Philippians. So, five or more students chose the chapters and presented the whole of First Thessalonians in preparation for studying that letter.

For the study of our final letter, four or more students presented the four chapters of Philippians. I never failed to have enough volunteers to cover both letters. Sometimes, two students would do the same chapter; and the class got to hear it twice by different students with different approaches.

I also encouraged students to perform in their native language or in a second language of their choice. Over the course of several years, there were performances in Korean, Japanese, Chinese, Arabic, Spanish, German, Thai, Swedish, and Swahili, among others. Several performed it in the original Greek. What a thrill it was to have these different voices of men and women, old and young, black and white and Latino and Asian American and Native American, people from diverse countries and languages and social backgrounds, giving their rendition of a chapter from one of Paul's letters—and then sharing what they learned from the experience.

For students who have read the Bible over and over in print to now hear it and tell it fosters a fresh encounter with the Bible. And it becomes clear to everyone that *reading aloud* the text for an audience does not have the same impact as a memorized performance. With reading, there is less immediacy, less liveliness, and less interactive relationship with the audience. Reading aloud tends simply to replicate in public the act of reading in private. There is not a substantial shift in medium. But with performance from memory, everything becomes oral and aural in a new way. It has an immediacy and an emotive effect with gestures and eye contact and facial expressions. The performer makes a personal connection with the audience, and the audience experiences an impact. This process has deepened and reshaped the learning of the students in significant ways.

Going from written text to oral performance is a fundamental paradigm shift for scholarship as well. To study the Bible with the assumptions of print culture, with a single author writing at a desk, a fixed text, and a reader reading alone and privately, is very different from interpreting with assumptions from oral cultures, with an oral composer, a fluid oral composition in performance, and an active, communal audience.

IMPLICATIONS FOR INTERPRETATION

There are four important implications for interpretation that characterize this shift from print to orality, all focusing around interpretation.

The Audience Has a Sensual and Communal Experience

The first implication for interpretation is the experience of the class members as an audience for the performance of the text. The sound itself affects the experience of the text in a fresh way. Sound envelops a person and is a vehicle not only for meaning but also for emotions. And the experience is temporal. When we read, we can stop and go back and forth spatially looking at the pages of text. But a performance does not stop. It just keeps going, and the audience has to keep up. Furthermore, a performance involves seeing as well as hearing. The presenter is acting out the story and thereby generating visual images. It is a holistic experience for an audience to be drawn into the imaginative world of a story or a letter.

In addition, the experience of a performance is communal. And in the classroom or in a worship setting, the audience is not just a gathering of people who do not know each other, but an audience that is already a community of people who know each other and who share various allegiances. The communal audience responds to the performance as it goes along—the changes of mood, the tension of suspense, the humor, the rapt silence, and sometimes the tears. The responses of the audience in turn affect the performer. It becomes clear that performer and audience *together* generate the experience and therefore also the meaning and impact of the composition. And the quality of the conversation after the performance, including the sharing of diverse interpretations by members of the class/audience, reinforces the communal nature of the experience.

The Performer Experiences the Point of View of the Speaker

The second implication for interpretation is this: when a student performs a passage from the Gospels, she or he assumes the role of the narrator—the voice of the text—and of the many different voices within the world of the text. When performing a letter, the performer takes the role of the sender, much as an ancient performer did, by standing in, for example, *as Paul* speaking to the community being addressed. If *hearing* a performance as an audience changes the relationship with the text, the shift to being the performer of the text goes much further. The experience of performing can actually change the performer's opinion of the narrator of a Gospel or the sender of a letter. One student reported: "I must admit I am forced to change my image of Paul from an angry person who rails at people to one who loves those to whom he is writing." Another said, "I got in touch with the Paul who is concerned about the people he is addressing."

Performance Illuminates the Writing: What the Text Means

The third implication for interpretation is this: students find that the experience of performance provides fresh access into the meaning of the text. You cannot screen out details that you do not understand or disagree with or find objectionable. You have to make sense of them. Seeing the texts from the inside gives these stories and letters new meaning and life. And the performer comes to realize that the text can mean different things, depending on how it is performed. Performing makes you aware of the fullness of the text, including the cues to performing it—when to move, how to speak, what gestures to make, what tone the narrator or a character is taking, what emotions to express, and much more. Most students end up writing their interpretation paper on the passage they have performed, and it always improves their grasp of that text. In relation to their performance and their paper, students would say, "I never knew this passage was in Paul's letters, and it changes everything" or "I have read these lines all my life, and, for the first time, I think I know what they mean."

The Performer Creates a Rhetorical Impact: What the Text Does

The fourth implication for interpretation is that students get in touch with the rhetorical impact of the text. This may be the most important pedagogical payoff of all. The performer becomes acutely aware of the text as an act of communication. More than simply communication, performance is an act of persuasion and of transformation. When we read the text as print, we put our focus on what the text *means*. But when we perform it, we also put our focus on what the text *does* to and for those who hear it. Does the text lead the audience to share possessions, overcome fear, experience the power of love, be brothers and sisters to each other, resolve a conflict, follow Jesus in facing persecution, or welcome an outsider?

The potential impact of a New Testament writing is not just on individual behavior; rather, the performance fosters a certain kind of community, characterized by freedom or acceptance or holiness or wisdom or mutual relationships. The performance can be seeking to change the way people think about the world—affirming or challenging their most fundamental assumptions. The performance offers a world and draws the audience into it—so that they will be different for having experienced it. This potential rhetorical impact is a dimension of the text often neglected by interpreters operating with a print mentality. But when communicated orally, the performer must ask: What is the possible impact that this text was meant to have? How does the story or letter work so as to generate that impact? And how can I perform it so as to be faithful to that impulse of the text?

Talk about the potential of "transformation through dialogue." Recovering biblical speech as a performance event brings dialogue and transformation to a new level.

THINKING THEOLOGICALLY ABOUT PERFORMANCE OF SCRIPTURE

The theological implications of this paradigm shift in the medium are significant. One implication is the *incarnation* of the word that takes place within the performer. An oral Bible is in the hearts and minds and bodies of those who know these stories. As a class doing performances, *we were the Bible*. Together with others, the Bible *becomes* the community of those who bear the memory and tell the stories.

Another theological implication is that the biblical word *becomes an event*. It is off the page and into the world. The oral dynamics of the word can, for some people, dislodge an approach to Scripture based on the fixed text of a print mentality. One can see in the performance how different each presentation can be even when the words are exactly the same, how some things are emphasized more than others, how much the audience participates in creating meaning, how powerful the word can be in speech, and how much the spoken word challenges the audience to change. This experience of words as *event* can change the way students understand the Bible as Scripture, how they relate to the church, how they go about their ministry of worship and education, and the possibilities they see for transformation of the world.

CONCLUSION: A TESTIMONY

I became so convinced of the pedagogical efficacy of this approach to interpretation that I began regularly teaching a class wholly devoted to learning and performing biblical selections, called Scripture by Heart. For a detailed description of this course, see Appendix 1. For a guide to learning biblical stories and performing them, see Appendix 2.

One consequence of all these experiences in the classroom is that there are now pastors who present the Gospel text by heart at worship. They learn the story in about half an hour at the beginning of the week, repeat it often during the week as they drive or go to sleep; and by Sunday they know it well enough to tell it in worship. Many of them say that the experience of living with the text in mind and in memory all week enables them to connect their daily experiences to the story and suggests associations with memories and other stories—and the sermon just seems to unfold out of their experience of having this Scripture passage on their minds and in their hearts all week.

As a conclusion to this essay, I share an e-mail from a student who had the experience of performing in two of the classes described above. She was a second-career student who had spent many years teaching high school English literature before studying for the ministry. She describes an event that occurred in her first call process as an ordination candidate.

> *Hi David:*
>
> *Just thought that you might enjoy hearing how our time together in "The Shorter Letters of Paul" and "Scripture by Heart" continue to impact ministry. Today I interviewed for a call at a redevelopment church in the town where the church is located. The people are aware of the need to change, but they are hesitant about sharing their feelings about this. The congregation asked me to preach during my interview, but the Synod did not want me to do this. The committee asked me if there might be something else that I could do.*
>
> *I started toying with the idea of performing Paul's letter to Philemon. My synod contact person thought it was a good idea because it would demonstrate my "preaching" (quotation marks are the contact's and not mine) and my capacity to lead worship. The more I prayed and thought about it, the more I could see a correlation between Philemon and the situation the congregation faces. Philemon faced change, too. What would happen if he did not do what had always been done regarding Onesimus' misconduct?*

One of the people on the call committee was not a member of the church although he assists the church a great deal. He said that he wished that church was more interactive. It was the perfect time to perform Philemon. I assigned each member of the committee a role as listener in relation to the people referred to in the original letter and asked them also to listen for how the letter might connect to the current situation experienced by the congregation.

When I finished they were in tears. The Holy Spirit had touched their hearts through the Word, and I got to watch it unfold as they made connections. They saw themselves as leaders on the spot as was Philemon, saw themselves as other slaves who would ask why Onesimus should receive special treatment and how they might respond that way when today's youth did not do things as they had. Most significantly, they asked if Paul "could have commanded Philemon like that ('though I am bold enough in Christ to command you to do your duty . . .)." This led to an interesting discussion about the changes that Paul had experienced himself, how as a follower of Christ he had to learn a new way of relating to others; that they might need to learn new ways of relating to others in order to grow. I couldn't have planned it better if I tried. Isn't God amazing?

If I am called to this congregation, I could imagine performing Paul's letter to Philemon for the entire congregation as an introduction to our visioning and mission statement work.

Thanks so much for learning experiences that lend themselves to such ministry.

Peace and Joy

19

Teaching as Research, Research as Teaching

LIKE MANY SCHOLARS, I have always had more ideas for research projects than I could ever have published. And I have begun more projects than I could ever complete. When I retired a number of years ago, I had a "retirement coach" who showed me how to make a healthy and meaningful transition to a different lifestyle. I shared with her that I had lots of research and writing projects that I wanted either to complete or delete. She asked me to make a list of them so she could help me prioritize them. I came up with six books and ten articles, all of which were in various stages of research and writing. At that point, I think my retirement coach was considering retirement. As for me, I would need to retire from retirement!

IT'S A CHALLENGE

One of the main challenges faculty members have is this: How do I devote myself to good teaching, to thoughtful advising, to conscientious administrative work for the school, and *still* find time to work on research and writing projects? Some professors have jobs at universities in which their primary work is to do research. Other faculty members are so prolific in writing that they are able to produce a prodigious amount of scholarship in the limited time they can set aside for writing. However, many of our projects involve immersion in the subject matter for a concentrated period of time; so just catching a few hours or a day here and there during the semester won't do it. Most of us are gasping for air during the semester and planning for every holiday break, summer months, and the occasional sabbatical as the time to get to the research and writing we love to do. Add to this the fact that many faculty members are under the gun to produce a certain amount of published scholarship in a short period of time in order to get tenure or to qualify for promotion.

In the midst of this is our genuine love of research and writing as well as our sense of responsibility to stay on the cutting edge of a broad swath of scholarship for the benefit of our students. Furthermore, we also have a desire to make some contribution to the academy and/or to our religious community and/or to society at large. This is often the reason we go into academic work. We hope that our scholarship as well as our teaching will have some socially redeeming value. In any case, the weight of so many responsibilities on faculty can squelch the muse and make it difficult to do any scholarship at all. Sometimes, too many good things can ruin everything. How do we cope?

FINDING TIME FOR RESEARCH

There are no magical answers to that question, and there is no advice that can solve it. One promising piece of advice often given to new (and seasoned) faculty is to coordinate the classes we teach with the research fields in which we are working. That way we can double up; we can bring our research into the classroom and in turn use the subject matter of the class to further our research. Easier said than done! Many faculty members have a certain number of courses they are obliged to teach for the curriculum, often with few opportunities to offer elective courses. At Carthage College, I taught two sections of the required New Testament survey course with about forty students in each class every semester, with limited opportunities for seminars. Even when we are able to teach electives, we are eager to teach subjects that students need for their program or courses that interest them. These may or may not cohere with our scholarly interests. Of course, many of us have specialized research projects that wouldn't translate into viable courses anyway.

CROSS-FERTILIZATION

However, when research and teaching do overlap, the situation is greatly improved. This has been my good fortune through many of the years of my teaching. And I would like to give some examples of those opportunities in this reflection as a way to encourage others to think about the possibilities.

Basic courses, electives, monthlong January courses, seminars for majors, doctoral seminars, and dissertation subjects are ripe for various forms of cross-fertilization between the classroom and the study. I was extremely fortunate, on the one hand, to have research that lent itself to course content and, on the other hand, to have courses that provided fertile ground for research endeavors. These courses gave me an opportunity to try out my research, to learn together with students, and to learn from the students. Many of these courses were team taught with someone who enhanced my learning in the field. Even when I did not have time to write during a semester, the courses nevertheless enabled me to be immersed in the subject matter during the teaching semester.

FROM RESEARCH TO CLASSROOM

In some cases, the direction went from my scholarship to the classroom. Here, I shared my scholarship with students in the course of teaching. They benefitted from my enthusiasm about material that was on the cutting edge of scholarship, and I expanded my knowledge of the subject by interaction with the students. Here are a few examples.

Teaching My Dissertation Subject

In my first year at Carthage College, I came upon just such an opportunity. I needed to revise my dissertation in the hope of publishing it, having submitted it to Fortress Press. So I offered a January course on the subject of my dissertation: *Israel in Revolution 6-74 CE: A Political History Based on the Writings of Josephus*. After all, January terms are for odd subjects and experimental teaching. So why not? Astoundingly, ten students signed up. Among other things, I had students read Josephus and view the miniseries *Masada* about the Roman mopping-up conquest of a mountain fortress near Jerusalem just after the Roman-Jewish War of 66 to 70 CE.

As part of the course, I asked the students to read my dissertation and give feedback for revisions. I kept track of their suggestions and then, on a lark, sent a list of them to the publishing house, asking the editors to get back to me on what they thought I should revise, should they decide to publish it. One of the suggestions that students made was that I should add more about the Jewish sects of Pharisees, Sadducees, and Essenes. The letter came back from Fortress: "We will publish your book if you expand the work on Jewish sects and explain them to the reader. We have a book on Jewish sects that is currently going out of print, and this will fill that void." In other words, thanks to my astute undergraduate students, my dissertation was accepted for publication. In the process, students learned not only about the Roman-Jewish War but also about writing lengthy papers, critical thinking, and how to critique and edit a manuscript. In addition, they had the satisfaction of being part of a publishing project.

First-Century Israel

Another early example of cross-fertilization from research to teaching came in the subsequent process of revising my dissertation.

Part of my research for revising the dissertation involved a trip to Israel. While my main goal for this trip was the revision of my dissertation, I was astounded by the ways a visit to modern Israel, with such a plethora of archaeological sites and artifacts, could enlighten one about the realities of antiquity. The ways we imagine places and events are transformed by firsthand experience of the geography and the historical remains. I brought back from the trip (and another later trip) a fascination with details about everyday life in ancient Israel: topography, climate, houses, clothes, farming, trades, travel, festivals, temple, and much more. These details informed my research. And they also enabled me to share what I was learning with students in class. And I began teaching a course on Daily Life in Jesus's Time, which once again melded together research and teaching.

Cultural Anthropology

Just before I moved from teaching at Carthage to seminary teaching at LSTC, I immersed myself in the study of models from cultural anthropology as a means to interpret the New Testament writings. The field was new for me as well as for other scholars. I began teaching a course on Cultural Anthropology and the New Testament as a way to share with students what I was learning and also as a way to expand my knowledge by teaching it. Reading books with students, preparing lectures, discussing passages, and (on two occasions) team teaching the course with Carolyn Osiek, a colleague from the Catholic Theological Union who had written a basic text on the subject—all these enhanced the student experience of this new field. Of course, the subject was new for the students, too, which meant that they were applying the method to texts that had not been explored this way before. This engagement with a cutting-edge method led students to do outstanding work. Papers written by the students were often innovative and illuminating, and I learned a lot from them. Later, I also supervised dissertations of students using this same methodological approach. Again, the interaction between teaching and learning paid rich dividends.

FROM CLASSROOM TO RESEARCH (AND BACK)

In other cases, the benefits came from the other direction. In these cases, my research projects emerged from the classroom, from pedagogical efforts to make the classroom a better learning experience.

Narrative Interpretation of Scripture

For example, research into narrative criticism grew out of my classroom teaching. This occurred in my survey course in New Testament at Carthage. I had become friends with an English professor, Don Michie, who had recently completed his dissertation on Shakespeare. As we talked about our classes and my interest in the Gospel of Mark, Don jokingly suggested that I should teach it like a short story. So I posed this challenge: "Come to my class and show us how to do that." And he took on the challenge. And when he came in and spoke, we were all blown away. He talked about Jesus as a very human character who was limited in his efforts to achieve his goals, frustrated by the obstacles presented by the crowds, crotchety with his disciples, determined in his purpose, and contingent upon a variety of circumstances that led to his death. He was talking about Jesus in a fresh way, as a character in a story rather than as a "Christological figure." There was much more, but to say the least I was deeply intrigued. How did he as a teacher of literature look at this story? What did he *see*? And *how* did he see it? More than this, I was taken by the fact that Don himself, unexpectedly for him, was utterly surprised and delighted by the artistry of Mark's story, calling it "the most tightly written narrative I have ever read."

The narrative method led me to change my pedagogical approach to teaching the Gospels. I jettisoned the traditionally indispensable textbook, a comparison of the Gospels that focused on differences between one Gospel and another and broken up into short episodes. Instead, I began having the students read each of the Gospels over and over as a whole narrative—comparing character analyses, contrasting the plotlines, and identifying distinguishing themes. I was delighted by how much more engaged the students were with this approach and how much I was learning from this process.

The upshot of all this is that Don and I decided to write a book together about Mark taking this approach, an approach that only a few people in the academy had taken at that time. After a lot of research on my part into literary criticism on a sabbatical leave, the result was *Mark as Story: An Introduction to the Narrative of a Gospel*, which helped to bring narrative criticism into the mainstream of biblical studies.

I came through this experience with the realization that *when it is to the benefit of the students*, one can do research and develop innovative scholarly work for and in collaboration with them. In fact, I have found that the primary way I seem to be able to understand a research area well for myself is by grasping it so clearly that I can explain it to students who come to it with little understanding of the subject matter. The need to explain it to them is what enables *me* to "get it" at a level that is required to be worthy of a wider scholarly audience.

Performance Criticism

The opportunity to perform biblical texts gave me a unique pathway to develop what has come to be called biblical performance criticism, which is built on the insight that the writings now in the New Testament were originally composed to be presented by memory or by reading aloud to a populace that was overwhelmingly nonliterate. I began performing for the students: the Gospel of Mark, Galatians, Philemon, and others. Then I moved to having students perform. Eventually, the process of translating, memorizing, and giving dramatic performances became one of my basic approaches to doing research. Gradually, through research and classroom experiences, the discipline unfolded before me: the oral culture, the functions of scribes, the role of memory, the dynamics of performance, and the integration of these elements into many disciplines of the field of biblical studies such as historical criticism, rhetorical criticism, narrative criticism, as well as the activation of disciplines new to New Testament studies such as speech act theory, ancient theater studies, and modern performance theory. These came together for me in a two-part article entitled "Performance Criticism: An Emerging Methodology in Second Testament Studies." Other articles followed. I am confident that these insights would not have come forth without the interaction with students in the classroom. Along with the contributions of others, this work helped to establish performance criticism as an important disciple in biblical studies. For more on this process, see chapter 18 on "Performing Scripture."

OTHER EXAMPLES

There are other examples of interaction between scholarship and classroom that involved cross-fertilization. Studying intercultural criticism with students from many different national and cultural backgrounds led to a different kind of learning, an awareness of our own social locations and how it affected our interactions in the classroom. Also, reading the biblical materials with students through the lens of the modern ecological crises led to some scholarly work on eco-justice criticism of the New Testament. In another situation, I taught a doctoral seminar on rhetorical criticism to learn what I needed to know in order to supervise a dissertation on that subject.

RESEARCH IS COLLABORATIVE

Scholarship and learning are always communal, with a wide variety of colleagues in many groups and relationships. I have been fortunate that students were an integral part of communal relationships that led to my growth as a scholar. Teaching and research were leaven for each other. Yes, we do a lot in solitude. But even then, the communities are in our minds as collaborators, as audiences of our publications, as colleagues looking over our shoulders, as students engaging with our work.

20

Bits and Pieces

THERE ARE A FEW dynamics of pedagogy that were important to my teaching but that do not merit a separate reflection: role-playing with case studies; teaching by slogan; evaluation, grading, and assessment; and having fun.

ROLE-PLAYING CASE STUDIES

Case studies address actual events or fictional stories that give students an opportunity to deal with principles, values, and beliefs in real-life or in lifelike situations. Role-playing with case studies is a very effective way to decenter a classroom, enable everyone to participate, and learn a great deal in the process.

Case Studies in Environmental Ethics

In a course called Greening Your Congregation, I was positing the idea that congregations can function as a safe place for their community to have ethical conversations around controversial ecological issues. We used a text by James Martin-Schramm and Robert Shrivers called *Christian Environmental Ethics: A Case Method Approach*. The book is a series of well-elaborated case studies that identify the context, lay out the issues, and unfold lifelike situations in narrative form with imaginary people who had a stake in the issue and who expressed their points of view in dialogue. No resolutions are given, so that readers are left to come to their own conclusions.

Our process was this: I would summarize briefly the case study for the next class period, name the various stakeholders depicted in the case study, and invite class members to choose which character in the case study they would like to represent in the debate to take place in class. For example, in a case study on "Sustaining Dover," the question was whether or not to accept a proposal to bring a Walmart supercenter into this small town. The issues were habitat loss, water pollution, economic sustainability, and the distinctive ethos of the town. The stakeholders were a local businessman and city council member, the chair of the local River Alliance, a Walmart representative, the director of Citizens for Sustainable Development, and a professor at a nearby university consulting on economic impact, among others. Students would then study the case and be prepared to articulate and defend their position for the following class. Other examples of case studies in this book include such situations as "Saving Snake River Salmon" (dealing with habitat restoration), "Chlorine Sunset" (on toxic waste), "Market Mountain Takeover" (about protecting old growth forests), and "Taking on Water" (species conservation).

The most interesting part of the process was that, in addition to the human characters, we gave voice to the creatures and features of the natural world that were being affected by the choices made by humans. Hence, a person in the class would speak for a threatened wetland, another for the animals in the wetland, another for a forest of trees about to be stripped for logging, for salmon prevented by a human project from reaching upstream to spawn, and so on. We had no illusions that we could adequately speak for entities of nature. Nevertheless, it was illuminating to hear the point of view of the natural world given voices, indeed quite passionate and persuasive voices, in the debate—something that rarely happens in conversations and decisions involving human actions that have a significant impact on the environment.

After the debate was over, students playing the roles would reflect together from their personal point of view. The exercise served to enlarge, deepen, and sometimes change the perspective of the students. The open-endedness of these conversations, which often became quite lively, led to many ongoing conversations beyond the classroom.

Role-Playing Philemon as a Case Study

The Bible is filled with material for case studies. Think of the stories about Jesus, the parables he tells, the interactions Jesus has with individuals in John's Gospel, and the letters of Paul addressing situations in his churches.

One letter that works well as a case study is Paul's brief, personal Letter to Philemon, a rhetorical tour de force. Paul is writing from prison to Philemon on behalf of Onesimus, Philemon's runaway slave. I am personally convinced that Paul wanted Philemon to exonerate and free Onesimus, welcome him as a Christian brother, and send him back to Paul as his (Philemon's) representative. However, the situation was tricky due to a very complex matrix of relationships between Paul, Philemon, Onesimus, the members of Philemon's household, and the brothers in prison with Paul, as well as the members of the house church who met regularly in Philemon's home and who would have been present for the reading/performance of the Letter to Philemon.

As a class, we would study the letter and then I would perform it, taking the role of the one who performed the letter on behalf of Paul. In this exercise, students took various roles. The performance was addressed to a student taking the role of Philemon (sitting directly in front of me), while newly arrived Onesimus sat nearby. The rest of the class assumed the roles of people in the house church gathered to (over)hear the letter—Apphia, Archippus, Philemon's household (other slaves of Philemon?), members of the house church (men and women), possibly including other Christian masters (slave owners who would probably have expected Philemon to punish Onesimus). After the performance, everyone shared their insights in experiencing the letter from their imagined roles and their ancient social locations, explaining what they experienced and what they thought Philemon ought to do in response to the letter. In this role-play, students brought to life suppressed voices in the text.

Then we would have an imaginary reunion after Paul was released from prison months later. In our scenario, Paul and Onesimus returned to visit Philemon. In groups of three, each of the three students chose one of the roles to play, and the triads discussed their new, imagined relationships. Finally, we went through the letter line by line, interpreting it in light of our conversations. The "experience" of the letter made clear the profound issues involved in the letter. For example, the event was a homecoming for Onesimus (like the prodigal son), and the letter deepened a commitment to God as *true* Father (patron) and Christ as *true* Lord (Master). We also saw how Paul used the situation as a *teachable moment* to move Philemon and the entire community away from all human hierarchical relationships to mutual relationships of sibling love.

Everyone was fully engaged in the case study. For example, one student who participated wrote this in her evaluation: "Designating specific people as Philemon and Onesimus brings the letter closer to home. As Onesimus, I was watching Paul and Philemon, trying to gauge how it was going, what Philemon was thinking. The letter came to life in a way that made sense. And I no longer think of Paul as being manipulative in the letter, but pastoral and caring. He even gave Philemon a way to save face in the honor/shame culture he was in."

TEACHING WITH SLOGANS

Slogans are an important form of rhetorical expression. They are used to convey common wisdom and sell products. They are usually brief, rhythmic, and quite memorable. They can be proverbs, mottos, or even bumper stickers. Social media have generated many phrases that stick to us like burs. Repeated again and again, they become mantras that can change a person's life. For example, "One day at a time" and "Let go and let God" are two of many slogans for Alcoholics Anonymous, sayings that have sustained the sober lives of many alcoholics and their family members.

We should not underestimate the power of such slogans in the educational process—even when we think it is not making an impact. Decades ago when I first began raising teenage grandchildren, I read a helpful book by Anthony Wolf appropriately titled *Get Out of My Life, but First Will You Drive Me and Cheryl to the Mall.* The key wisdom I got from the book is this: Teenagers may show every sign that they are not listening to a word you are saying, but if you just keep calmly repeating your best guidance, it will stick to them through a lifetime. That may also be true of some of our educational wisdom with students. For example, last summer I had a former student call from a parish in Texas asking me to do a program at his congregation. During the conversation, he said to me: "I will never forget when you said, 'Reading Paul's letters is like reading someone else's mail.' I think about that every time I preach on one of Paul's Epistles." The slogan he recounted was a line by Krister Stendahl, the wonderful New Testament scholar and dean at Harvard

Divinity School, explaining how we misread a letter if we think it is addressed directly to us.

Throughout teaching, I often identified the most important things I wanted to teach in one class or another and conveyed it repeatedly with a memorable line:

- Show me in the text.
- Don't pretty up the text. Let it say what it says.
- Learning to change our minds, learning to change our world.
- A good question is better than a simple answer.
- The text should be the source of the sermon and not simply the occasion for it.
- Don't let anyone else interpret for you, but don't trust yourself to interpret alone.
- Never use the Bible to oppress people.
- When the Bible is harmful, preach Christ against the Scripture.
- You are justified by grace, not by grades.
- Interpret yourself while you are interpreting Scripture.

Such sayings were sometimes guiding lights to students in what they learned, how they learned it, and to what use they put it. Slogans are certainly worth formulating, promoting, and repeating as words of wisdom for lifelong learners.

EVALUATION, GRADING, AND ASSESSMENT

Evaluations of teachers, students, and the classroom process are critical dynamics of teaching and learning. Evaluation and assessment can obviously be done in a great variety of ways.

Evaluations of Me and the Class by Students

At the end of every semester the students would evaluate me and the course they had taken. Of course, the goal was to improve teaching and the classroom experience. For the twenty-two years of teaching at LSTC, I used the end-of-semester forms provided by the seminary. I left the room during the evaluation, and a student delivered the completed forms in an envelope to the dean's office. Students chose whether to identify themselves or to remain anonymous. Most of these evaluations through the years were based on a set of statements about which the student circles a numerical rating on a scale of one to ten: "The teacher respected the students" or "This course exposed students to a diversity of gender, racial, and ethnic points of view" or "I would recommend this class to others." And so on.

After each semester was over and my grades had been submitted, I would review the evaluations in the dean's office as part of my assessment of the course and as part of my preparations for the next classes. The statements and numbers were an appropriate format. However, the problem was that while the numbers might "alert" me to a problem, they did not specify what that problem was or how I could correct it. Sometimes I could infer the problem, especially if there was a pattern to the responses. Often, however, I had to search my memory for what I might have said or done that led a student or students to give a negative evaluation on some item or another. Some time ago, the dean revised the forms to provide a space below each question for the student to explain their rating. Big help.

In addition, I also used my own form. It was fairly simple, with three questions about the effectiveness of the learning experience: "What worked well? What did not work well? What suggestions do you have for the next time I teach this class?" Students also did this same evaluation shortly before the *middle* of the semester. At that point, the last question was posed this way: "What do you think needs to be changed for the remainder of the semester?" When I had read carefully and taken notes on these midterm evaluations (also anonymous by choice), I would report back to the class the very next class period, summarizing what seemed to be going well for them, the issues they raised, the number of people who might have raised them, and how I planned either to keep things the same (with explanation) or make changes that would help them learn better. I then asked them to discuss in small groups both their evaluations of the class and my responses. I asked them to share with the whole class suggestions for further revisions. I usually had some further adjustments to make that assisted the learning experience.

On the basis of these evaluations through the first several years at the seminary, I made one major decision. I stopped giving exams. I was usually expecting too much in my exams. There was too much student anxiety and uncertainty around exams. And I just do not think human beings by a certain age (mid-thirties was the average age of our seminary students) should be subjected to exams. Of course, this was not true for the field exams of the doctoral students. But it certainly helped the spirit and the learning in my seminary classes.

A few final questions about this process were not an evaluation of the course as such but a way to see some of the results: "What are the most important things you have learned in this class? In what ways have you changed as a result of this course?"

Evaluation and Grading of Students

Then there was my evaluation of the students, usually in the form of grading, an unfortunate and ill-advised description because it focuses on comparison. Many schools have all pass-fail classes. As a faculty person, I was occasionally able to offer a whole class on a pass-fail basis. Also a student could individually request to take a certain number of classes in a pass-fail mode. This information was not shared with the teacher lest it influence his or her time and effort in relation to that student. In any case, generally speaking, I am in favor of grades. You can give all the feedback in the world, and students may still be unsure at just what level they have performed unless there is a grade or grades attached to the work. On the other hand, if a student gets a grade but receives no clear, extensive, and specific feedback on their work, they have no meaningful way to know why and no helpful way to know how to improve the quality of their work.

I wanted to establish solidarity and partnership with students in the learning process. I wanted my authority to reside intrinsically in my knowledge and expertise in the field and my skill and capacity to offer effective and humane leadership in the educational process. Nevertheless, the task of evaluating and grading students on behalf of the institution was what ultimately distinguished me as a teacher from the students and clearly identified me as the authority figure. I did not want to do anything to blur that distinction between me and the students. I became friends with students but never in a way that would diminish my authority or influence their grade. I encouraged students to call me Dave, but I never suggested by this invitation that I wanted to be pals with them. I wanted to give academic support to students but not in a way that compromised the standards. In some sense, the standards are separate and independent both from me and from the students. And we are to honor the standards together so that we all seek to maintain them. Therefore, I had a set of principles about grading and some procedures to carry them out.

Some Principles of Evaluation and Grading

In retrospect, I wish I had stated these principles for grading explicitly earlier in my career. They were in my mind, and I often shared one or the other in scattershot manner, but it would have helped me and the students to make them transparent. What follows is a summary of the main principles that guided me, with some explanations.

- There should be high academic standards at a seminary. Sometimes people who want to become pastors imagine that it really takes only a commitment to the faith and kindness toward others to be an effective pastor. Indeed, these traits are critical. In fact, however, effective parish ministry also requires a depth of knowledge and insight and a wide range of skills. One can readily see what is at stake in medical school or law school as students prepare for these professions. Who would want to go to a doctor who did not treat them with the best knowledge, skill, and wisdom available in the profession? The same is true for pastors. The lives and well-being of people and communities are at stake, and we teachers have a responsibility to see that students prepare to live up to them.
- Make the standards as explicit and as transparent as possible by providing a full set of expectations. Avoid pedagogical games that cause needless anxiety and fruitless work. There is inevitably a problem of consistency in standards across an institution. It is a problem that different faculty members inevitably did their grading according to different standards. At minimum, faculty should engage in conversations with each other about these matters. Team teaching, which involves team grading, is an important way to maintain consistent standards across the curriculum. As for grade inflation, I did not worry about giving too many A's or too many C's in a class. We had excellent students at LSTC, and if, in my view, most students in a class deserved an A, then that is what I gave them.

- My authority as a teacher is that of a servant. There is tension and paradox in that role, but so be it. The point is that we use our authority/power to benefit students. Hence, truth in evaluation is critical. At the same time, I often measured my care as a teacher by maintaining relationships with students who did poorly or who failed the class, while also maintaining the standards. I followed these principles: empower students in achieving the standards without enabling them and without compromising the standards, give clear directions about how they can improve, and provide tutors for extra help. These approaches represent an ethical commitment to the most vulnerable in the class. I never wanted to lose a connection with students who were not doing well or who were failing. Quite the opposite, I empathized with them and consulted with them about how they might respond both academically and personally to failure.
- Invite students to identify any learning disabilities they may have, so you can work together to address them.
- Address the needs of students who work at an advanced level. If students are not challenged by the assignments, encourage them to speak with you about doing alternative work. I encouraged outstanding seminary students to sign up for one of the doctoral seminars as an advanced course.
- Announce the school's honor code. Make it clear that students are not to plagiarize from other students or other materials. They are to give attribution for all the quotations and ideas they get from print or online sources, according to the guidelines set out. I imagine there are now guidelines for using AI to write papers.
- Set firm deadlines, but be flexible in regard to personal situations. When students seek "grace," such a request translates into academic support or some flexibility regarding a deadline. It does not mean compromising the standards.
- Do interventions by alerting students to a possible poor grade ahead of time. Taking the student aside, explain your concern about his or her work and ask how they are doing. Or e-mail or phone your concern. Avoid addressing their situation in front of others.
- Do not use shame or guilt as a motivation, such as "You can do better." We are not responsible for a student's success; and they do not

owe it to us to succeed. Students are where they are. Our frustration that they are not where we think they should be is immaterial. Do not take their work, good or bad, personally.

- At the same time, we need to own up to our part. If our failure to communicate or our negligence is the cause of grading problems for students, we need to acknowledge that and seek to make it right.
- Take students' work seriously and evaluate it with care. Give extensive and concrete feedback, positive as well as critical. Do your best to give timely feedback. It is often hard for students to move on to the next unit of learning until they know how they have done on previous work.
- Work hard to be fair about grading. Although I never arranged for papers to be submitted blind with a student number but no name attached, I think that is a good idea. My problem in grading was a matter of getting confused about my standards when I read an A paper, then a C paper, then a B paper, and so forth. I would lose track of my expectations for each grade. To offset that concern, I would read once through all the papers and put them in piles tentatively representing different grades based on my first read through. Then I would read all the provisional A papers together in a careful way, making many comments and assigning a grade or grades (all in pencil). By reading all the likely A papers together, I could more easily tell if a paper did indeed merit an A or if it clearly belonged further down the scale because it did not match the best papers. Conversely, when I read all the papers provisionally in a C category, it was easier to see that one or another paper should be bumped up to a B or an A. Finally, I went back through the papers for a final check, adjusting some grades before I finalized them for return to the students.
- Invite students to talk about their grade. The grade on a paper does not need to be the final word.
- Give opportunities for students to improve. This works when there is a midterm paper upon which a student can improve for their final paper. In addition to comments on individual papers, it may help to share with the whole class some generic feedback on their midterm exams or papers, summarize the main strengths of the exams or

papers, and identify key ways they can improve when they write their final paper.

I told students (in seminary) that they are justified by grace, not by grades, be they good grades or poor grades; that is, we do not grade students, we grade their work. Such a distinction is helpful in clarifying our relationship with students and at the same time maintaining the standards expected in their work.

Assessment

In addition to grading, I wish I had done what might be called "assessment" or an exit interview with (at least some of) the students in each class. I would have sought to find a way, after grades were submitted, to meet with students and ask them how they evaluated themselves in relation to the standards that I and the seminary expected from the biblical class they had just completed. Meeting with them in small groups, I would like to ask them: "What were the most important things you learned in this class? Do you have an adequate grasp of the subject matter from the class? Do you know better how to use methods to study the Bible? How were you changed personally by your study of this material? How well are you prepared to carry out the various functions of ministry related to this course?" By pursuing these questions in a personal conversation after grades were submitted, I think I would have gotten a better picture of what the students had learned, how they were changed or transformed by the class, and how successful I and the school were in preparing them for their future vocation.

MAKING IT FUN

Learning works better if it is fun, if there is humor involved, and if laughter is common. Humor engages students, makes the time go more quickly, and enhances learning and recall.

I am not talking here about entertainment for its own sake, although I have considered the idea that stand-up comedy might be an effective way to lecture on some important subjects. Rather, I am speaking of humor that is appropriate to the classroom and integral to the subject matter—never at the expense of a person or subject, whether inside the classroom or not. There is a proverb that says: "A wise teacher makes learning a joy." I figure that this kind of joy includes spontaneous humor and plain enjoyment. I hoped that this approach would also make it enjoyable not just for me but for the students as well.

I have also sought to teach classes by making a game of them. I mentioned in another reflection that we played the popular game Trivial Pursuit with our homemade cards to learn facts about daily life in Jesus's time. In a Quest for the Historical Jesus class, we set up a debate and a question and answer time with the audience in conversation with students standing in for modern Jesus scholars such as John Dominic Crossan, Marcus Borg, Richard Horsley, and E. P. Sanders. In addition to being informative, the interactive repartee in those conversations was quite entertaining. In a Greek class, we practiced rapid-fire questions made into a game about the language of a text.

Sometimes there are unplanned moments of humor. Once, a male student was enacting Simeon's blessing of the baby Jesus at the beginning of Luke's Gospel. The student held the child in his arms rather awkwardly as he pronounced Simeon's blessing, and then moved quickly to the next line. After he finished, I asked him rather playfully, "You don't have children, do you?" He replied, "No, why?" I said, "Good. Because you just dropped that baby on the floor!" We all laughed, because we had all reacted the same way. Then he told the story again with greater care for that child. It is a beautiful story.

We discovered in the class devoted to performing biblical passages that there is a lot of humor inherent in Scripture that becomes apparent when you perform it. I recall a woman doing the creation story in a way that was very faithful and yet set the audience to repeated laughter. One student enacted the passage in First Corinthians that portrays the community as various parts of the body; and he had us in uproarious laughter. He got the point across much better than if he had played it straight. Another student portrayed the humor involved with the denseness of the disciples and Jesus's exasperation with them in Mark. The dialogues of misunderstanding in John where Jesus and other characters talk past each other—like Abbott and Costello's routine about "Who's on First?"—were also quite funny. Paul's remark in Philemon to the effect that Philemon better do what Paul asks because "After all, you do owe me your life!" always brings laughter of relief in the midst of a tense message. And on and on. I have learned from students that joy and humor were surely an important dimension of ancient biblical storytelling and epistolary oratory. The humor that is already implicit in the biblical compositions emerges in the act of performing—and ends up engaging us and bonding us together, as it must have done in the early church.

On one occasion, I was giving a brief lecture on the historical Jesus when the cell phone of one of the students went off. The woman was somewhat embarrassed. So I stopped my lecture and said jokingly, "That better be Jesus." We all laughed. When she got her cell phone from her purse to turn it off, she looked at it and said, "It *is* Jesus!" That brought considerably more laughter. Then she added, "That's my husband's name." That brought down the house! You cannot make this stuff up. Sometimes the conversation of the class just lends itself to such banter back and forth, and it is often around the subject matter.

Love and Laughter

You have to love your students and love your subject to have fun. Forcing humor does not work. It just happens, but we can be ready for it.

21

The New Testament and Education

Part 1

ONE WAY TO ENHANCE student reflection on education is to encourage them to think about the relationship between the subject matter of the course and the contemporary educational process. For my classes, the question was this: What might the New Testament have to say about education in general and about the experience of learning in particular?

INCREDIBLE DIVERSITY

Of course, this question is too broad, as if the whole New Testament had one thing to say about any given matter. Such an approach ends up reducing the insights from the New Testament to the lowest common denominator. It is a bit like asking: What would Jesus do?—when there are twenty-seven different writings in the New Testament, including four different portrayals of Jesus, that would each answer this question in a somewhat different way. It is much better to differentiate each of the writings in the New Testament and then ask: What might Mark have to say about the learning process? What might John have to say about education? How could Paul's Letter to the Galatians relate to the classroom experience? And so on.

Of course, none of the New Testament writings addresses contemporary life directly, and certainly not in relation to the issue of education. Nevertheless, the writings do deal with a new proclamation, conversion and transformation, knowledge, means of knowing, ethical templates, and visions for society, with the possibility of drawing out implications for learning from these writings. Once we have offered an interpretation of a given writing in its original context, we can ask about its relevance for contemporary life (as preachers do in sermons). For example, we can ask: Given the dynamics of Mark's Gospel in the first century, what might Mark have to say today about life in the twenty-first century? In that context, how might Mark's perspective illuminate education and the learning process? Naturally, this is an act of imagination, a fact that, of course, makes it all the more fun to do—and all the more interesting.

So, what follows in this chapter and the next one are some thumbnail sketches I have used with students in the classroom to discuss education from the perspective of different writings in the New Testament. Each profile presents a depiction of the human condition in that writing and the means by which the message of that writing addresses that human condition. Then follow some implications that this sketch has for modern education. Please note that each of these all-too-brief profiles of New Testament writings is not intended to make the writings simplistic or to whitewash difficulties or to imply that this is the only legitimate interpretation of that writing. Rather, the sketches are designed for insights about education.

Among the many payoffs for this exercise is that it not only leads students to reflect on their educational experience, but it also teaches a valuable lesson about the New Testament—namely, that the New Testament is a collection of diverse writings with different points of view and approaches to any given situation and that these diverse approaches can certainly be brought to bear in reflection on contemporary situations.

THE GOSPEL OF MARK: A MAJOR THEME

The Gospel of Mark seeks to overcome fear and to foster courage that enables people to take risks in the course of being faithful.

Courage to Be Faithful

Mark addresses the fear of taking risks by engendering courage and faithfulness. In Mark, the disciples are limited in their understanding and in their capacity to follow Jesus faithfully because of their fear (e.g., Mark

9:32). Both Judean and Roman authorities are frightened of any threats to their power (6:20; 12:12). Jesus too is fearful of torture and death in his prayer at Gethsemane, but he overcomes his fear of death (14:32–42). The Gospel ends with the women running from the tomb, "for they were afraid" (16:8).

In its original context, Mark's Gospel sought to empower people to take risks for the good news about Jesus in spite of the threat of opposition and persecution. Mark's first audiences probably lived just after the Roman-Judean War of 66–70 CE. At that time, followers of Jesus were threatened by authorities on both sides of that war (13:9). On the one hand, they were persecuted by Judeans, many of whom thought of Jesus's followers as traitors because they had refused to fight in the war. On the other hand, they were persecuted by Romans who thought of them as revolutionaries because, after all, their leader had been executed by the Romans as a traitorous messianic claimant. The resulting fear among followers of Jesus likely led to inaction on their part. We can conclude from the Gospel that Mark believed people were avoiding risky actions on behalf of Jesus and the gospel out of fear, because good actions might involve sacrifice, loss, rejection, risk, and even persecution and death. Mark's Gospel leads followers of Jesus to face their fear and to act in spite of it because of their commitment to Jesus and the kingdom of God (8:34–35).

Mark also believed that it was because of their fearfulness that people were driven to do evil by dominating others. Out of fear, people want to save or secure their lives by accumulating wealth at the expense of others (8:34–35), by seeking status while marginalizing others (9:33–34), by using power to control others (10:41–45), and by persecuting those who threaten their security. In Mark's portrayals, the Roman and Judean authorities reflect this fear, and so, in limited ways, do the disciples (14:1—16:8). Mark took a critical stance against such behavior because such self-securing actions generated a society of exploitation, domination, marginalization, and persecution by the powerful over against the vulnerable. Such attitudes and actions on the part of those with power constituted imperial domination.

Mark believed that if people overcame their fearful need to secure themselves, they could create a society in which people served each other: "Whoever wants to be great among you is to be your servant" (10:43). By inviting people into the sphere of the kingdom/rule of God, Jesus was calling people to live for others—to relinquish wealth to the poor, to be willing to be least as a means to elevate others, to use power to serve, and to be faithful to the rule of God in spite of the fact that those actions might result in loss, persecution, and death (14:36). Only by being faithful and taking such risks would they spread to others the message of power in serving: "Those who will save/secure their lives will lose them, but those who will lose/risk their lives for me and the good news will save/secure them" (8:34–35) The rhetoric of Mark's story seeks to empower hearers to have courage—in the face of very legitimate fears—to act on behalf of establishing God's kingdom by taking healing to the sick, liberation to the possessed, bread to the hungry, belonging to the marginalized, and hope to the least.

Courage to Learn

How might Mark's Gospel give us insights into the learning process today? The extreme situation of persecution and the threat of death for Mark's audience is an analogue for less extreme situations in which the quest to live fully is thwarted by fear. As such, in our time, the avoidance of "death" due to fear can be seen as a metaphor for any event that threatens to diminish someone's personal security—by shame or embarrassment ("I thought I'd die"), loss of financial well-being ("I'm finished"), lowering of status ("They treated me as if I did not exist"), or loss of control over others ("I count for nothing"). In order to avoid these negative experiences, we will also end up avoiding the faithful risks we might take in living.

Given this analogue, we might ask: How much does fear limit your learning? For example, in the classroom, students often keep their learning process in safe confines, saying little and risking little, so as to avoid embarrassment or rejection by teachers and by fellow students. Students often use learning as a means to secure themselves—what others think of them, their grades, and their job prospects. In so doing, they avoid negative (deathlike) experiences by refusing to stick out or by being unwilling to take risks that may affect their popularity or their grade. There is a lot at stake in the learning process, and if students play it safe, they will never become independent thinkers and will never form a community of assertive learners.

Based on Mark, we might challenge students to overcome their fear. Of course, their risks are of a different order. Nevertheless, by overcoming their fear (perhaps by trust in God's security), they could take responsibility for their own learning, risk speaking up in class, try out their own ideas, do things that do not fit the mold, put learning above grades—all in the service of getting, at whatever risk, a real education. Mark's rhetoric could empower students to be faithful to a vocation of assertive learning out of a larger commitment to create a better world. When students do this, they will also be practicing the courage they will need later in life to relinquish wealth, status, and power in service to others and to have the courage to be moral agents in the creation of a humane society.

THE GOSPEL OF MATTHEW: A MAJOR THEME

Matthew exposes dynamics of hypocrisy and engenders integrity in the quest to be righteous humans.

Live with Integrity

One of Matthew's goals is to tell a story about Jesus that will lead people to be truly righteous. Matthew understands true righteousness to involve *integrity*; that is, he seeks to engender in people an integrity of thought, word, and action—all oriented toward fulfilling God's will. Matthew calls people to "be perfect as your heavenly Father is perfect" (Matt 5:38). To be perfect, in Matthew's view, is to be thoroughly single minded, to have purity of heart in both attitudes and actions (5:8) in the consistent expression of goodness and love for others—not only for family and friends but also for enemies as well (5:43–47). Matthew seeks to demonstrate an interpretation of the Judean law in which the true goal of the law would be fulfilled; namely, so that it would result in integrity in service to God's will (5:17).

Matthew opposes people who are not single-minded but who are double-minded or hypocritical (6:2). He is referring to people who have the right actions but the wrong motives; for example, they pray to God in order to be seen and glorified by people (6:5–6). Or people who have the right actions but who have the wrong reasons for those actions; for example, they do acts of charity in order to impress people (6:1–4). Or people whose inner attitudes don't match their outward appearance; for example, they do not commit adultery outwardly, but inwardly they lust (5:27–30). Or people who are not consistent in love of others; for example, they love their friends but not their enemies (5:43–48). Or people who are forgiven by God but who will not forgive others (18:23–35). Matthew's Sermon on the Mount (chs. 5–7) provides a positive portrayal of righteous people living in the blessings of the beatitudes, with a penetrating moral exposé of hypocrisy, with example after example of double-mindedness, along with guidance to live with wisdom and integrity. Matthew's woes on the Pharisees (ch. 23) provide a powerful critique of those who have failed to live by integrity.

Matthew's target is not only the crass hypocrisy of those who intentionally say one thing and do another. Rather, he aims also to enlighten those who have *blind* hypocrisy, those who believe themselves to be good but who have deceived themselves about the ways in which they fail to live up to the very standards they espouse. As Jesus says, "Do whatever they teach you, and follow it; but do not do as they do" (23:2–3). Matthew's rhetoric challenges people to have depth of character—with the integrity according to the high moral standards that God wills, the willingness to examine oneself, the powerful blessings of God for those who seek goodness, the death of Jesus bringing forgiveness when people fail, and the empowering relationship with the risen Jesus. In fostering such a relationship with God and Jesus, Matthew seeks nothing less than to engender in his audience a willingness to do a fearless moral inventory and a capacity to strive for moral excellence so that they can fulfill their true purpose as human beings—to be like good trees bearing good fruit.

Learning with Integrity

How might Matthew's point of view inform contemporary education? Through Matthew's eyes, students might be challenged to avoid hypocrisy in the learning process—not to do assignments just in order to complete them, not to take classes just in order to fill a requirement or to get a grade, not to get an education for the purpose of making money or gaining status, not to learn just in order to accumulate knowledge, never to cheat or cut corners as a means to do well. Students should act in the conviction that all learning has moral dimensions.

Based on Matthew's Gospel, students are urged to have radical integrity in the learning process—to read for insight, to take classes in order to grow in understanding, consistently to use the opportunities of every class as a means to learn, to do more than just what is expected or required, to get a degree so as to be a better person in whatever job one does, and to learn in order to become "wise" so that knowledge might be used in the service of morality. Reading Matthew might challenge students to seek *excellence* in education in the confidence that any failure in this effort will be forgiven and accepted by God—with the result that anyone can rise from failure and try for excellence again. To be true to Matthew, we would want education to serve character development, so that graduates will contribute to the well-being of society with honesty, with uprightness, and with wisdom in consonance with God's will. Matthew's ultimate hope is that people will act with this integrity so naturally that they will not even be aware of doing it. They will be like those who show compassion to the hungry, the naked, those in prison so that, unbeknownst to them, "just as you did it unto the least of these members of my family, you did it to me" (23:40).

THE GOSPEL OF LUKE: A MAJOR THEME

Luke condemns societies that do not show mercy toward the poor, and Luke works to generate communities of compassion.

Live to Liberate Others

More than any of the other Gospels, Luke's story of Jesus focuses on the injustices in society as a whole and how to address them. Luke depicts a society with great inequities between the rich and the poor, the elites and the marginalized, the powerful and the oppressed. Luke's Gospel calls people to counter a society that lives for money, that loves honor, and that uses power over people. It is a prophetic call for people to repent of their injustices and to transform society through acts of generosity, humility, and service.

Luke has an alternative vision for society, a society driven by mercy. "Be merciful," Jesus says, "just as your Father is merciful" (Luke 6:36). Luke writes to liberate victims of this society who are gripped by poverty, degradation, marginalization, and oppression. "The Spirit of the Lord is upon me," says Jesus, "because God has anointed me to bring good news to the poor, to recover sight to the blind, to free those who are oppressed, to announce the year of the Lord's favor" (4:16–21). As such, Jesus "came to seek and to save the lost" (19:10). In this regard, Luke's Gospel is filled with a cavalcade of characters who get lifted up in the story—lepers, the sick, the Samaritan stopping by the roadside, the poor beggar Lazarus, the bent woman, the woman who anoints Jesus with her tears, the tax collector Zacchaeus, the widow of Nain, and the thief on the cross, among others. Luke's Jesus seeks to liberate such characters from their downtrodden circumstances and to restore them to health and dignity and empowerment in community.

Luke's Gospel bears a portrait of God who is determined to "bring down the powerful" and "lift up the lowly," by feeding "the hungry with good things" and sending "the rich away empty handed" (1:52–53). In Luke, Jesus challenges the wealthy and powerful to join him in liberating the downtrodden. Luke calls for people to repent and receive the Spirit of God, which will empower them to share their wealth and to oppose oppression and thereby to provide a countercultural community that models what the world *should* be like. Such an alternative life is depicted in the Acts of the Apostles (a second volume also written by the author of Luke) as a community that shares possessions and gives authority for the oppressed to be the leaders (Acts 2:43–47).

Learn to Liberate Others

What about the implications of Luke for contemporary education? Based on Luke, learning means nothing if it does not liberate people from deprivation, impoverishment, marginalization, discrimination, and oppression. There is a reason liberation theologians look to Luke as a kindred spirit. Luke's Gospel might (with Paulo Freire) call for learning to be a subversive activity that undercuts the societal status quo of oppression in all its expressions. Most education is organized by the leaders of society who seek to reinforce the current order of things and who do not want people to radically challenge the powers that be with a prophetic call to change society into a more just and merciful reality. Students may learn; but what do they learn *for*? Learning is not neutral. It supports one kind of society or another. Without a commitment to a just society, learning just adds information and maintains the status quo.

The Gospel of Luke might inspire students to decide what kind of society they stand for and to learn in order to make a difference—to be prophets who name injustice, who call for peace, who challenge the wealthy, who condemn institutional violence, who puncture the arrogance of the powerful, and who live in such a way as to give an alternative model for life together. If we look at education through Luke's eyes, we might work for education to be made readily available without cost for members of suppressed groups—the poor, people of color, people with disabilities, and people in prison, among others. Regardless of the social location of students and in whatever job or career they enter, graduates would choose to be in solidarity with the vulnerable in society. Such a commitment would not be an add-on to their education but one of the driving forces behind it. These students would be empowered by a sense of a human vocation in their learning, empowered by the Spirit to get an education in order to subvert the forces that diminish human life and in order to liberate and bring life to the lost, the sick, the rejected, the exploited, and the victims of discrimination and injustice.

THE GOSPEL OF JOHN

John's words bring the experience of eternal life (in the now) to humans alienated from the divine source of their being.

Living as Mystical Knowing

The Gospel of John was written to engender in hearers a profound religious experience of life in God through the risen Jesus. In John's view, Jesus came to bring this experience of life and to bring it abundantly (John 10:10). Referring to the experience of the Holy Spirit, Jesus says that "To one who believes in me . . . out of his heart shall flow rivers of living water" (John 10:10).

John believes that pedestrian knowledge of the world in itself is mundane and ultimately does not bring meaning, satisfaction, or morality to human beings. There is a kind of temporality and death in this mundane existence. One can drink water or eat bread but will grow thirsty and hungry again. One can have sunlight but not be illuminated. One can travel but not know the way/access to a full life.

Humans will come to fulfillment only if these created things become gateways to a deeper knowledge comprised of an intimate relationship with the Force at the origin of life. Hence wine, water, bread, light, vines, pastures, gates, and paths become signs and metaphors leading to the more profound experience of the risen Jesus through the Holy Spirit:

the true wine (2:1–11), the temple (3:1–22), the water of life (4:7–15), the real vine (5:1–11), the bread of life (6:25–40), the good shepherd (10:7–18), the door to life (10:7), the light of the world (12:35–16), and the way, the truth, and the life (14:6)—all of which point to and bear the reality of God and Jesus that lies behind and within these created things. This deeper reality, in John's view, is pure love. And in relation to this reality, "No one has greater love than this, to lay down one's life for one's friends" (10:11; 15:13).

John believes that the Word active in creation became flesh/human in the person of Jesus. Jesus came from God to restore the relationship between human beings and the Creator. His role was to bring creation to fulfillment in a harmonious interrelationship between creatures and Creator. Because all creation bears the imprint of the Creator and of the Word, therefore all created things potentially mediate the restoring of this relationship. Human relationship with the creative power of life itself involves an epistemology that goes beyond theories about knowing on a literal level and opens up a capacity to know at a deeper level—for people to "abide in God" and for God to "abide in" people (17:20–24; 15:1–11). John seeks for people not just to know *about* God but to "know" the source of life intimately and existentially—in a way that is transformative and profoundly meaningful. For John, this *is* eternal life—"to *know* God and Jesus Christ whom you sent" (17:3). People who come into relationship with Jesus have *already* passed from death into the life of the new aeon (5:24)—not only an everlasting reality but the *fullness* of life, *now*. Eternal/aeon life refers to a quality of life that is profoundly meaningful and fulfilling *in the present* and that endures into the future. An experience like this is nothing less than a rebirth into this fullness of life (3:3). In light of this experience, the whole created order manifests itself as a vehicle for intimacy with the source of life.

Learning as Mystical Knowing

The Gospel of John might lead us to question the exclusive emphasis on factual knowledge and practical training that people acquire in schools and to consider it to be limited and limiting. John's Gospel instead (or in addition) promotes mystical knowledge as the foundation for life. What would education be about if it included "knowing" the creative forces of life? Without it, without a rootedness in love, factual knowledge and practical training might be misunderstood and misused.

As such, the Gospel of John may lead us to question the entire educational enterprise in the West. Based on John, all learning is ultimately meaningless unless one knows the source of life—intimately, spiritually, mystically. Just as John's Jesus was surprised that Nicodemus, a teacher of Israel, did not know about being born from above or about the Spirit that blows where it wills (3:1–21), so, similarly, we should perhaps be shocked to think that the educational system does not seek to engender a knowledge that goes beyond cognitive knowledge to involve a deeper rootedness in the creative forces of life. One cannot *make* this experience happen, but John's whole Gospel shows what can happen when teachers seek to engender such an experience of God or the life Force with metaphors, analogies, signs, and stories that are designed to trigger the experience of "life abundant." Meditation, reflection on nature as witness to the Creator, the exploration of metaphor as a sign for the interior life, and acts of love as events that can evoke love in others—all these would be means to foster this deeper knowledge. I can imagine John might advocate for art, poetry, story, nature, and music as integral to the education experience, because they are often evocative of deeper realities.

From this perspective, a relationship with love, manifested in Jesus, should be the basis for the proper understanding and moral use of learned knowledge such as economics, politics, and management. Otherwise, they become technological fixes that do not involve the fundamental transformation necessary for genuine human development. Also, the relationship with the source of life would lead those rooted in love to cease violence and live for others. John knew that those who pursued such mystical knowledge could have had their lives deepened in the first century. This might also be true in the contemporary church and in the world. Though perhaps small in numbers, their alternative life together itself would be a witness that could lead others to similar experiences.

A VITAL DIVERSITY

These four brief profiles of the Gospel writers witness to the explosion of creative reflection and transformation that went on in the first century in response to the Jesus event. This vital diversity, this ductility, this capacity of the Christian movement to speak to diverse and changing circumstances, may be the single most important reason Christianity thrived and spread so quickly and has endured for so many centuries in such diverse cultures. The diversity also provides us in the twenty-first century with a rich plethora of visions with which to consider the life and work of God in our own time—and our response and responsibility to it. The challenge before us is how to determine the relevance of these visions and how to determine which ones are most appropriate to the issues we face at various times and different places. In the next chapter, we will consider three other writings in the New Testament and then offer some overall implications for education in our time.

22

The New Testament and Education

Part 2

This chapter is a continuation of the sketches of some selected New Testament writings and their potential implications for contemporary education. Here we examine Paul's Letter to the Galatians, the Epistle of James, and the book of Revelation. At the end, there are some general reflections on the overall process.

THE LETTER TO THE GALATIANS: A MAJOR THEME

Paul seeks to free people by showing them that they are justified by God's grace, thus liberating them from the struggle and harm that come when they seek to justify themselves.

Living Out of Grace

Paul develops a somewhat different theology in each of his letters in order to address the particular identity and circumstances of the diverse communities. In several letters (Galatians, Philippians, and Romans), he develops the concept of justification by grace through faith, albeit in a slightly different way in each letter. It is this concept, drawn primarily from Galatians, that we will examine. In Galatians, Paul contrasts those who seek to justify themselves by their own identity/effort with those who consider themselves to be justified by grace through an act of God in Jesus.

Paul argues that people tend to justify their existence before God and in the eyes of others based on that which is human (flesh)—either by dint of birth (such as nationality, family, inheritance [Phil 3:2–11]) or achievement (such as moral goodness, legal adherence, wisdom, or bravery [1 Cor 1:22; Gal 2:15; 5:4; Phil 3:2–11]). This justification is based on human traits and/or human efforts. It sets up standards that people either meet or fail to meet. The result is that these standards become the basis for determining whether people have justified themselves or not, whether or not they are fundamentally acceptable as human beings and acceptable to God. It is a transactional relationship with God: if I am a good person, then God will accept me.

In Galatians, Paul is countering gentiles who thought they had to justify their existence before God by adopting and measuring up to the standards of the Jewish Torah rather than by accepting their justification *as Galatians* (and not by becoming Judeans) based on God's free gift of grace (Gal 1:6–9; 3:1–14). Paul believes that self-justification is a prime source of evil in the world (5:26). Paul claims that divisions, discrimination, and violence among humans occur as a result of these dynamics. Justifying one's existence out of one's own identity or accomplishments leads to comparison, competition, and conflict between individuals, ethnic groups, genders, and nations (3:28). The consequence is either arrogance (for those who meet the standards) or envy/jealousy (for those who have failed to meet the standards [5:26]). Furthermore, Paul argues, when we seek to justify ourselves, we manipulate other people to prove our worth. We are interested in people only insofar as they serve our project to justify ourselves (6:13). We do good actions mainly in order to benefit ourselves or our group. We love others for our benefit rather than for their sake. The key is this: love of others for their sake is not possible when our so-called "loving actions" are motivated by a self-oriented desire to prove *our* own worth.

Paul applies this analysis primarily to the standard of the Torah, the law that expressed the will of God in Judean culture. Paul praises the goodness that the law was meant to engender, but he says that we err when we use that law as a standard to justify or condemn ourselves and others based on our efforts to live up to it. Paul refers to many standards of human identity and achievement by which people seek to justify themselves. These human standards should never be used as a basis for determining that one's existence as a human being is justified or condemned. When they are, they serve as bondage for ourselves and others seeking to live up to those standards (4:8–11)—not just for individuals but also for families, races, nations, and other social groupings. People who claim human standards as a basis for justification will seek to dominate others and impose these standards upon them. Or they will lose their identity in efforts to assimilate into a dominant culture. All these destructive human patterns emerge when justification is based on standards that measure human worth on the basis of human traits or achievements.

By contrast, a whole different life is possible when justification comes from God as a gift apart from human achievement or failure (3:1–5). Paul claims that, in Christ, God has justified people freely by grace. People are called to rely on this act of God and to live out of the freedom given (5:1–13)—freedom from the burden of having to *be someone* or to *do something* before we can be acceptable before God and others. In Paul's view, when we are all equally justified by an act done outside of ourselves by God's grace, then there is no basis for us to boast in ourselves, no basis for us to be envious (1 Cor 1:26–31), and no basis for discrimination. And if we live out of the security of God's justification of us, we do not need to manipulate others in projects designed to prove our worth—because we have *already* been justified.

There are therefore no standards based on human attributions or achievements that are legitimate bases for our fundamental self-worth. Race or ethnicity or gender or family or work status or appearance or health or ability or nationality or economic status cannot be the basis for arrogance or envy, for in Christ, "there is no longer Jew nor Greek, no longer slave nor free, no male and female" (3:28). Nor can any "standards" be a legitimate basis for dominating others in an effort to make others become like us. Individuals and groups and nations are free to pursue their God-given identity without assimilation into dominant groups. None can be the basis for the justification of our existence.

The consequence of justification is a freedom from the project to justify oneself and one's group, freedom from the need to be self-oriented. Because people are already justified, they can be interested in others for the sake of the other. They can love others for the sake of the other. There are no grounds or even need for arrogance or envy. There is no need to dominate or assimilate. People are free to discern their own identity before God and to express it in ways that are consonant with the grace and love given in the original act of justifying grace from God in Christ. Communities of mutuality rather than hierarchy and subordination are now possible—communities in which people are humble, consider others better than themselves, and look to the interests and needs of the others (Gal 5:22–26; Phil 2:2–4). When a community lives out of a trust in justification by God's grace, community members express their love for one another out of security and freedom. When people live out of an abiding sense of self-worth already given, with no need to prove anything, then true goodness and mercy are rendered possible and can be freely given.

Learning out of Grace

In light of this, what might Paul teach us about the contemporary educational process? Sometimes, when I returned the first papers seminary students have submitted for a course, I would say to them, "Remember, you are justified by grace, not by grades!" Virtually all students understood me to be offering consolation to those who made poor grades. But, I quickly added: "I am saying this *not* mainly to those of you who are not pleased with your grades but to those of you who did well and are proud of your grades. You are not justified by your grade!" Individually, it means that the burden is removed from those who invested so much in their academic work that they staked their identity and self-worth on it. They are under bondage to their works. But when they realize that they have already been justified, the high-achieving students would be free to love learning for its own sake, to take risks, and to put other, more important priorities above their academic performance at times, because they have nothing to prove. When we live by grace, learning would become an expression of who we are rather than a means to prove we are someone. The students would not be justified by success nor unjustified by failure.

Moreover, this point is not just relevant to the individual but to the class members as a community—especially with regard to the competitive social pressure to do well and to make good grades. Because God would be the source of justification, there would be no cause for competition among students, no reason to be arrogant or envious. They could cooperate in the educational process so that they could help each other bear the burden of learning, able both to give and to receive support gracefully. They could take responsibility for themselves and also celebrate when others do well, accept and assist the students who are struggling, and create an atmosphere of mutual trust and accountability—so that together in a spirit of freedom they could be the best they can be as a community of learners. And they would know that I as a teacher give love and respect to them because they are valuable as human beings whether they perform well academically or not.

THE LETTER OF JAMES: A MAJOR THEME

James shows people that destructive communities result when people compete for the *limited* resources of life. Conversely, communities of peace and justice result when people depend on the *unlimited* resources from God.

Countercultural Living

James works with a zero-sum understanding of the resources of this world. The resources are clearly limited and in short supply. There is only so much wealth or honor or power or control to go around. So if one person or group gains, then another person or group loses. Hence there is a never-ending fight to get control and to keep control of these things for oneself and one's group (Jas 4:1–4). The mentality of scarcity dominates. Envy and ambition prevail. These attitudes lead to destructive behavior: gossip (3:1–12), false accusations (4:11), theft, withholding of wages (5:4), discriminating against the poor (2:1–7), and murder and war (4:1–4), among other things. When James warns readers to "keep themselves unstained by the world," it is this mentality and this destructive behavior against which he warns. The self-centered "wisdom of this world" results in domination, oppression, marginalization, discrimination, poverty, and deprivation (3:13–16).

From James's point of view, although the resources of the world are limited, the resources from heaven, from God, are unlimited. James encourages people to get out of the zero-sum game by looking to God as the source of every good and perfect gift (1:17). From God, grace pours forth like summer rain to bring growth and harvest (5:18). From God, there are honor and status and power and true wealth. But even beyond this, James understands that God is seeking to rectify the inequalities in the world that result from the mentality of limited goods. Because Jesus lived and died and rose for all, particularly for the poor, the members of the community are to honor the poor (2:1–7), feed the hungry and clothe the naked (2:14–17), use the tongue for good (3:1–12), return good for evil, and seek peace in all matters (3:17–18). This commitment to the most vulnerable is why James defines true religion as caring for "the widows and the orphans" (1:27). When every good thing is from above, there is no need to protect or to grasp. Rather, there are ample resources to turn the tide of evil and to produce a harvest of righteousness for the world, especially for the downtrodden and the vulnerable. The "wisdom from above" is peaceable and gentle, and it results in righteousness (3:17–18). This wisdom from above meets human needs and legitimate wants, because grace from above leads to sharing.

The wisdom that leads to righteous action and peace for human beings is discerned through acute observation of the natural world of creation. James uses analogies from every corner of creation—waves of the sea, flowers in the desert, birth, light and shadow, ships, forest fires, fresh and brackish water, seasonal rains, fertile fields, and much more. These are lively and vivid analogies. But they are more. They tap into the age-old Judean tradition that nature is God's realm and that there are analogies between human nature and the rest of the natural world. Careful observation of nature will teach not only the pitfalls of human existence but also the profound possibilities for humans to bear the fruit of righteousness. The wisdom from above includes the knowledge of how God works and how life manifests itself in the natural world for human good.

Furthermore, James makes it clear that right belief is useless unless it is followed by action (2:14). What good is it if a brother or sister is in need and you do not do something about it? In James's view, belief apart from works is barren, dead (2:18–26). Just as a tree was made to bear fruit, so humans were made to bear good actions. If they do not, they fail to fulfill the purpose for which they were created. The actions James has in mind are related to the love of neighbor, particularly the vulnerable—not only the orphan and the widow but also the poor, the naked, the marginalized, and the sick (5:14–16).

Countercultural Learning

In relation to contemporary education, James's letter might encourage us to emphasize not knowledge but wisdom. What good is learning unless it leads to wisdom that changes the world? Following James, education might teach people an alternative way of thinking about the culture—to wage peace rather than war, to control the tongue, to love the neighbor before oneself, to strengthen the weak rather than secure the strong, to advocate in solidarity with the poor. Education might emphasize the wisdom of knowing that the limited resources in life are shared fairly when we draw upon the unlimited resources of grace and wisdom. In all of this, James would insist that the best learning about human life comes from close and careful observation of nature.

Furthermore, looking through the eyes of James, we would closely attend to the relationship between learning and action. What good is learning if it does not lead to action? If the rhetoric and purpose of James are designed to lead people to be generous, then acts of generosity would *be* its interpretation! Correspondingly, what if every interpretive paper was accompanied by a social action? In seminary, we tend to think of field education as practice for ministry. What about field education when an implementation of a biblical writing is viewed as an interpretation of it? What about the idea that students engage in community service and reflect on it in relation to biblical values? In James's view, learning without action is dead.

THE BOOK OF REVELATION: A MAJOR THEME

Revelation exposes the idols that people worship in the illusion that the idols will bring them life; and Revelation offers the true God as the source of life for a new world.

Living to Resist the Idols

Revelation is perhaps the most politically radical of all the writings in the New Testament. Its purpose is to unmask the Roman Empire so that people no longer see it as a powerful and wealthy empire blessed by God that cannot be opposed. The prophet John exposes Rome as a cruel beast (Rev 13:1–18) and a seductive whore, acting on the authority of Satan (17:1–18). This empire has established itself by fear and intimidation, by the death and destruction of all who would stand in opposition to it. At the same time, this empire has also established itself by seductive and deceptive efforts to lure the kings and merchants of earth into cooperating in order to receive the wealth and glory of the empire (18:1–20). The sins of the Roman Empire, which are "heaped as high as heaven" (18:5), are enforced by the imperial demand to worship the emperor and to give unconditional allegiance to this self-proclaimed "eternal" realm. John's gruesome imagery and graphic portrayals are designed to unmask the beast so that people can see it for what it truly is.

John calls for people to withdraw from the Roman Empire (18:4)—by refusing to engage in economic activity that has anything to do with the empire and its coinage, by ceasing all participation in social festivals that honor the empire or that provide meat offered to idols, and by refusing to worship the emperor—even if these actions result in persecution and death (2:1—3:22). Such tragic results were likely in light of the fact that local officials in Asia Minor where Revelation was presented expected their residents to give unfettered allegiance to Rome as a basis for receiving many benefits from the empire for their cities and region. They would suppress all who stood against this allegiance to Rome. Nevertheless, in John's view, the withdrawal of Christians from anything having to do with the Roman Empire is urgent, because God is about to bring this destructive empire to an end (11:18). Since God will ultimately prevail, people must choose against Rome now, so that it is clear in the end where their allegiance lies. John even portrays in imagination the burning of Rome and the grief of kings and merchants over its loss (18:8–19) as a way to lead the hearers of Revelation to detach from their relationship with and their dependence upon Rome.

In place of allegiance to the Roman Empire, John wants his hearers to give allegiance and worship to the God of all creation, who is in process not only of ending the old order by "destroying the destroyers of the earth" (11:18) but also of creating a renewed heaven and earth (21:1—22:5). In the Jerusalem of this new world order, God will dwell on earth amid God's people; and there will be no more grief or crying or pain. There will be justice and peace. And there will be harmony with nature. The river of the water of life will flow clear as crystal down the middle of the city streets, available to all free of charge. The tree of life will produce fruit all year round to assure that no one goes hungry. The leaves of the trees will be a cure for the nations. John enables his hearers to imagine this new world and to live even now in such a way as to worship God, to celebrate the coming of this new world, and to live in the present by its values of truth and justice.

Learning to Resist Idols

Students of Revelation might create an educational system that challenges the political, economic, and social status quo and that calls into question those values of society that lead to destruction. They would seek to treat all subject matter in the class as an opportunity to expose the dark side of the systems of this world; for example, the way our economic system exploits people and nature, the way our political system can crush those who oppose our core values, the way the prosperity of some is dependent on the poverty of others, the ways the dominant culture discriminates against minority groups, the way we demand unfettered allegiance to our capitalist and democratic institutions, the way corporations are profit driven at the expense of workers and consumers. This educational approach would ferret out the power dynamics of every entity under study, including nations, corporations, even the church, as well as the educational system itself, in order to discern any imperial dynamics that are at work in our institutions.

A new educational approach might expose the deceptive and seductive ways by which the purveyors of "empire" lure ordinary folks into seeing only the benefits and thereby ignoring the injustice and exploitation of the system. This educational system would not be politically neutral. It might encourage students to act on what they were learning so that they find ways to withdraw from the exploitative and destructive dynamics in which they themselves participate.

At the same time, an educational experience inspired by Revelation might foster the imagination of an alternative vision of justice and peace. We could make a distinction here between the prophetic and the apocalyptic. Prophets speak truth to power as a means to change the system and redirect the nation/empire. John does this. However, John also embraces an even more radical approach. John is apocalyptic; that is, he not only condemns the present system, he also imagines its end and the onset of a new world. He offers the vision of a different world and invites people to live *now* as if that world were a present reality. Insofar as people live that way now, the vision would in a sense be a *present reality*. This is truly contra-imperial.

Such an educational system might invite people not only to withdraw from empire where they expose it but to create pockets of communities that embrace alternative values and realities. How could we imagine different economic dynamics, alternative political realities, and social relations that are humane and constructive rather than dehumanizing and destructive? Perhaps the classroom itself could be a laboratory for such experimentation.

Furthermore, the vision of the new Jerusalem in John moves readers/listeners toward a restoration of the whole creation. Students would be encouraged to see nature and earth themselves as the sites of God's creativity. It is time in all of our subjects and disciplines, across the curriculum, to express concern over our contemporary degradation of earth and to integrate a commitment to restore creation for future generations. As this education would expose injustices toward people, it would also reveal our horrendous exploitation of earth and its resources. It would reveal how interwoven are the attitudes and actions that devastate the earth.

REFLECTIONS ON DIVERSITY

These two chapters of reflection offer sketches of the ways in which some writings of the New Testament might be relevant to the contemporary educational experience. As acts of imagination, both the interpretation of the ancient texts and their modern appropriations can be done in many ways. As for diversity, there are twenty-one additional writings in the New Testament to explore! Nevertheless, the exercise with these seven writings may be sufficient to show students how attending to the diverse visions of the New Testament can shape their current endeavors in education.

We have done this exercise with the educational experience in mind as a point of comparison. This exercise can be done with other subjects as well. In one class, for example, students reflected on Hurricane Katrina, asking how different writings of the New Testament might look at the dynamics of that event and its aftermath. Students often get stuck thinking there is only one gospel or one Christian theology or one Christian ethic or one Christian way of relating to the world, when in fact diversity was *constitutive* of the Christian movement from its inception at Pentecost. This exercise is meant to loosen up those assumptions, to stimulate the imagination, and also, as in our examples here, to enhance the educational process.

Another occasion that generated diverse biblical reflections on contemporary culture came with the opportunity to team teach with fellow

New Testament scholar Robert Jewett. We taught a course three times on The New Testament and Contemporary Film. This was not a course about films whose subject matter had to do with Jesus or any part of the ancient world. Rather, students chose a book or passage from the diverse New Testament writings and then related that selection to a relevant contemporary film dealing with current cultural issues. For example, a theme of liberation in the Gospel of Luke was related to *Boyz n the Hood*. The freedom from self-centeredness in Galatians was correlated with the same theme in *Rain Man*. The servanthood motif in Mark led to insights on *The Piano*. As it turned out, the films invariably also informed our thinking about the biblical selections. So, the process became a genuine dialogue between the New Testament and contemporary culture. While these films are now dated, you can get an idea how the process worked by consulting two books of reflections that Bob Jewett published: *Saint Paul at the Movies: The Apostle's Dialogue with Contemporary Culture* and *Saint Paul Returns to the Movies: Triumph over Shame* in which he dealt with deep human issues raised by classic films such as *Amadeus*, *Ordinary People*, and *Dead Poets Society*.

IMPLICATIONS

Here are four general implications of New Testament studies for the educational process today. All of them suggest ways in which the exercise of imagining the relevance of different New Testament writings might foster transformation through dialogue as we enter into conversation with the biblical texts regarding the educational experience. In so doing, we open ourselves to personal transformation as well as to the transformation of the education system itself.

Intertextual Dialogue

First of all, we can highlight the experience of placing such unlikely texts—here the writings of the New Testament—side by side with the modern classroom. The exercise shows the power of intertextuality, the possibilities that open up when we place (often unlikely) texts next to each other—in this case, the possibilities for insight that are opened up when we place a text from early Christianity next to the "text" of a classroom. Curious interrelations appear. Connections hitherto unseen pop up. Fresh ideas and new angles of vision suggest themselves. Our understanding of the dynamics of education is deepened and expanded.

Letting the Texts Transform Us

Second, it is interesting that the study of New Testament texts involves not just an interpretation of the meaning of a text but also the implied rhetorical impact of the text upon readers/hearers. We often think that the writings were mainly meant to get us to *believe* a certain way or to be persuaded by the author's point of view, when in fact the possibilities are much greater, and they move in the direction of human transformation. The implied rhetorical impacts include such things as overcoming fear (Mark), generating the capacity to recognize our hypocrisy (Matthew), leading people to share their wealth (Luke), evoking the experience of eternal life (John), liberating people from the need to justify themselves (Galatians), and so on. Each of the writings seeks to transform whole persons in some fundamental ways—such that they have a new identity, a different sense of purpose, a new set of relationships, or a fresh sense of power for moral living.

But there is more. These writings address communities. They are not individualistic in their orientation. They are seeking to engender certain kinds of alternative communities—including educational institutions—with certain beliefs, attitudes, moral compasses, and sets of relationships. As we have seen, these visions for community differ somewhat with each of the writings of the New Testament. Furthermore, in the largest sense, each of the New Testament writings projects a vision not just for a community but for the world—and seeks to generate that new world by empowering people to enact it. As Gandhi said, "Become the change you envision."

Our Actions Are Interpretations

Third, the question to be asked is this: What kind of pedagogy is appropriate to writings that are meant to generate such powerful rhetorical impacts? Does not our classroom need to consider the concreteness of the potential outcomes of these writings? I have on a few occasions struggled with this question and sought to try some experiments. Here are some examples of assignments I have given in an effort to take account of the rhetorical force of different writings.

- Think like Mark during the time of this course. Read the newspaper, attend to programs on television, and notice events around you from a Markan perspective and with the lens of Markan values and relationships—and report on your reflections each week (Mark).
- In the manner of the Sermon on the Mount, do a fearless moral inventory of your life, examining comprehensively (but privately) the ways in which you might see more clearly the personal and public hypocrisy in your life (Matthew).
- Give away something of value this week to someone in need. Reflect on your experience and what it might imply for your lifestyle (Luke).
- Meditate for a half hour on a symbol of life, such as water, trees, fruit, light, or some other aspect of nature. Seek to understand that symbol as a pathway to deeper knowledge. Share your experience with someone (John).
- List all the things of which you are ashamed or guilty and declare in relation to each one, "This does not unjustify me. I am justified by God's grace." Then list all the things for which you feel righteous and proud, and declare in relation to each one, "This does not justify me. I am justified by God's grace" (Galatians). What happens to you as a result of this exercise?
- Cross a social boundary and interact in a significant way with someone who is marginalized by society. Share the ways you were changed by this interaction (James).
- The vision of the new Jerusalem integrates human life and justice, the presence of God, and the riches of nature in the tree of life and the water of life. What might a modern ecological vision of human life in a city look like? And what would we have to change in our personal habits and our social systems in order to bring that vision about? (Revelation).

The point of these assignments is the following: it may not be enough simply to do a verbal analysis of the meaning of New Testament texts. Since the New Testament writings were seeking to have an impact on the world, why not consider pedagogies that experiment with enacting these visions in some way? After all, the purpose of preparing people to be citizens of the world should lead to action and participation. And the purpose of preparing pastors and lay leaders in the church is to help them see how they can engender transformation in their parishioners—through sermons and Bible study and Christian education. So why not provide that bridge in the seminary classroom?

Engaging Now, in the Classroom

Fourth, since the rhetoric of the different New Testament writings is designed to change people, then the class ought to consider this outcome for itself. Early in each class, I tell seminary students: "I have just gone over the course syllabus with you. The information in the syllabus is comprised of the readings and assignments and papers and conversations we will be doing for this New Testament class. But the real thing that is going on, likely the most important thing that is going on, is the way you yourself are impacted and changed by your engagement with the writings of the New Testament. For if *you* are not changed by the writings of the New Testament, then you will not really be prepared to expect *others* to change as a result of your future ministry."

I recall the following experience I had when I was a pastor in the parish. I went to a retreat and heard a really dynamic speaker. He told some wonderful stories and gave some terrific examples. All I could think about was: "I cannot wait until I preach next Sunday so I can tell these stories to my parishioners. They will really be changed by them." Suddenly I realized that I had missed a very important step. I was so eager to use the stories on/with others that I had neglected to ask the fundamental question: "How are these stories changing *me*?" I backed up and worked through that. And not until I had wrested a blessing and a challenge from those stories in relation to myself was I ready to share those stories in my church. The same is true for me as a teacher.

So how can we incorporate into the educational process itself the kind of transformations engendered by the writings we study? These things are not graded. We cannot expect such a thing to be public knowledge except as the student wishes to share. We cannot make such a thing happen. But we can encourage it. We can give assignments that engender it. We can give space for students to reflect on it. We can even provide an opportunity on student evaluations of the class for students to reflect on how the course has impacted them. And we can model the process by sharing those moments when we ourselves have been challenged and transformed and provoked into new life by the writings we are studying.

Given the nature of seminaries, we who teach will be preparing students to do something later in their lives after they have graduated. But that is such a deferred fulfillment both for them *and for us*. The students already have a life and a vocation *as a student*, and they have relationships *now*. My teaching vocation is *now*. I seek to make the teaching/learning experience of the New Testament as meaningful and life changing as I can for the students, even while we as seminary faculty are preparing them in a challenging way, with high standards, to be the wisest, best informed, most compassionate, and most effective citizens of society and leaders of the church that they can be.

MAKING THE NEW TESTAMENT WRITINGS RELEVANT IN CONTEMPORARY LIFE

The relationship of ancient texts to modern contexts is highly complex because of the cross-cultural nature of the texts as well as the difference between the ancient context/circumstances of each writing and our own particular circumstances. The challenge is to relate the texts creatively and appropriately. And who determines what is appropriate? And by what criteria? Furthermore, given the diverse nature of so many different New Testament (indeed, biblical) writings, how do we adjudicate which vision or gospel among them addresses a current circumstance or situation with the most integrity and authority, and in what way? And without harm to one group or another? Christians are faced with this every day. Pastors are faced with it every Sunday in preaching. Clearly, all of our efforts are tentative and conditional. While I have broached these issues in my classes through the years, I did not consistently carry out an examination of these critical issues of interpretation and appropriation. I should have done so more—and done it in collaboration with faculty and students in other fields of study in the seminary in an open and ongoing way.

23

Teaching Outside the Curriculum

Greening the Seminary

Despite the fact that faculty have their hands full with teaching, advising students, perhaps supervising grad students, serving on committees and trying to do research, many faculty members also have some distinctive passion that they pursue on their own initiative because they believe it expresses a critical dimension of their vocation and because it may serve an important purpose in the overall life of their institution. Sometimes these "extra" commitments become part of a person's workload or, with financial support, develop into a program or a center.

It would be mistaken to think that faculty members were not teaching in the process of carrying out these extracurricular activities. They are teaching by example—modeling how to administer a center, organize a conference, demonstrate a commitment to justice, or build community. These forms of teaching can have a major impact upon students.

My own efforts in this regard were directed toward fostering a commitment to care for creation. I began teaching at LSTC in 1988 when care for creation was not on the seminary radar. Nevertheless, I had a vision that the seminary might incorporate care for creation into our life on campus and into our educational mission to prepare leaders for the church in service to the world. No small task! Greening the seminary did indeed turn out to be a long process, but a process that eventually made creation care an integral part of the seminary's identity and purpose.

This reflection was substantially completed shortly after I retired some years ago. I have not been closely involved in the life of the seminary since that time and do not know how much of the commitment to creation care has been carried on. Nevertheless, I am convinced that the learning that occurred has not been lost on the members of the seminary community who participated in this endeavor over the years.

This reflection highlights some of the pedagogical lessons we learned together in the process of community organizing—including some steps, principles, and strategies that helped to make it happen. As can be seen from the broad chronological sketch that follows, the movement involved three major methods of teaching: modeling a community-organizing process; involving students in the process; and developing slogans or mantras that encapsulated our learnings.

Launching a Movement

At the beginning, as I learned about environmental issues, I struggled with the overwhelming nature of the crises that the world was facing. I felt that neither fear nor guilt nor anger nor grief would motivate me or the students who became involved to make good decisions or lead us to persist in this movement for the long haul. Rather, I came to see and embrace the unconditional and unlimited grace of God present everywhere in creation as the enduring source of a faithful commitment, what Gerard Manley Hopkins referred to as "the dearest freshness deep down things." I was eager for the grace of God to be the sustaining force in our efforts as a community at the seminary. So our first lesson, which I repeated frequently, was this:

> We do this freely and with joy out of the abundance of God's grace in all creation.

I began by gathering a few students who would be willing to work on the task of greening the seminary. We decided to think of the seminary as a "Green Zone," which we defined as an earth-friendly space with earth-friendly people. I learned that it was important to:

> have a name that gives people a sense of identity.

Green Zone was an appellation that was easily remembered and that became a moniker for the seminary as a whole and for the group within the seminary who worked on these issues. The goal of the committee was to promote care for creation throughout the life of the seminary and to engage as many people as we could in that endeavor, even, and especially, if they were not part of the committee. That way:

> Everyone should take ownership for the care of creation.

Early on, there were usually only three or four to ten or so people present for our meetings. We discovered, however, that an enormous amount could be done with a small group. As such, two of our principles were:

> It only takes a few.
> Never let those who are not there keep those who are there from having a party!

Often our efforts were meager, but little by little they began to contribute to a sense of purpose and identity. Throughout the entire process, ecological efforts were student driven, with more and more faculty and staff supporting us and adding contributions as we went along. And we were helped in those early years by some angels who gave us financial support. For example, the denominational church offices offered small grants for specific projects, and the seminary supported two student workers to serve as Green Zone leaders under faculty supervision. It was never our intention for the committee to do all the ecological projects ourselves. Rather, our purpose was broader:

> The Green Zone Committee was a catalyst to make the whole seminary a Green Zone.

So we would find out what other individuals, committees, centers, programs, and offices were doing and ask if they might incorporate care for creation into their programs and activities. We requested those in charge of a lecture series to invite a speaker to address the environment. We asked the worship committee to provide creation-care resources for worship planners. We proposed a sustainability workshop for the stewardship requirement. We asked the LSTC building and grounds staff for a recycling program to be set up for the living units. We suggested subjects for articles in the school publications and website. We proposed ideas for ecological gifts that the senior class might give to the seminary upon graduation. The purpose was to piggyback on and invest in efforts already underway and to get as many people and offices involved as we could.

Another principle was this:

> Don't worry about what we don't get done; just celebrate what we do get done.

When you have a huge long-term issue, this adage helped us to focus in a positive way by celebrating the things we completed. It was important that we not be overwhelmed by all the things that could be done or by the urgency of the earth's problems.

In addition, it was not our job to complain or to criticize or to promote "ecological correctness," because, as we said often,

> We are not the environmental police.

Rather, it was our pleasure to do what we could and to delight in it—and invite others to join the effort. Not only did this approach help to support our group and our fledgling efforts, but it also worked well with the rest of the seminary community, who were responsive to positive efforts rather than to negative criticism.

Maintaining the Process

For the first ten or so years, we developed an overall vision of greening throughout seminary life, and each year we reminded ourselves of this vision. Occasionally, we would imagine what a seminary with care for creation might look like in twenty years, and then we identified what needed to be done to make it happen. We found it critical to have a comprehensive vision before us:

> Keep the big picture in mind.
> Without vision, the people don't get much done!

Without a comprehensive vision, our efforts would likely be scattershot and short-lived. It would have been too easy to think of our environmental committee simply as an interest group that does some things from year to year rather than a long-term movement designed to transform the core identity of the institution. In this way, the greening of the seminary could serve as a laboratory for students as they prepared to green their future parishes.

The goals of the vision that we embraced related to five areas of the Green Zone model we developed:

1. Promote transformation through worship.

2. Engender engagement through education.
3. Maintain buildings and grounds as an earth-keeping model.
4. Foster earth-keeping practices among LSTC members in their personal lives.
5. Exercise public ministry to church and society.

Each year, our Green Zone group would choose projects in several of these areas and carry them out on behalf of the community: for example, a special worship service, an eco-fair, the sponsorship of a lecture, an environmentalist-in-residence, or the sale of green cleaning products in the campus bookstore.

To choose our projects, it was important that we assess the passions and gifts of students who were active in any given year (asset-based organizing) and what needs and opportunities arose at the seminary (opportunity-based organizing). Our principle was this:

> What we have energy for and what opportunities are present, let's do that.

Though these steps were often small, they accumulated through time to make a significant impact on the identity and activities of the seminary.

One obstacle hindering continuity was the turnover of students that make up the seminary community. Each year, two-thirds of the seminary community changes. One-third of the students graduate, and another third head off to internship. Meanwhile, a third return from internship, and a third is comprised of new first-year students. We found ourselves having to reorganize the Green Zone Committee at the beginning of each fall, often taking weeks to develop new leadership. Eventually, we came up with a plan to offset this. We decided on this organizing principle:

> Set the student leadership of the Green Zone group for the next year in the previous spring.

In this way, the Green Zone leaders could develop plans to hit the road running when fall arrived. The committee planned ahead for the orientation of new students and an early fall meeting that would include new and returning students. This solved the transition problem. Continuity was also helped by the fact that I or another faculty person continued as the point person for the seminary throughout the twenty-two years I was there. It is critical to have a committed member of the faculty or the staff of the seminary who will be there from year to year to stay involved and to keep the continuity going. For LSTC, this meant that there were consistent and enduring efforts every year, throughout the year, to keep on greening the seminary.

Another related principle we followed was this:

> Institutionalize it.

At first, many of our projects were done on a volunteer basis. If we wanted to have a composting system in the courtyard of one of the apartment areas or to hold an Earth Day worship service, it was necessary for student volunteers to keep the system going each year. What we discovered was that volunteer efforts were limited. New students came in each year, and there was not always the same initiating energy from year to year to keep up the composting or to assure that certain worship services would take place. So we worked with the building and grounds manager to incorporate the composting system into the work of the maintenance crew at the seminary. And we worked with the chapel office to make sure that creation care worship services automatically appeared on the worship calendar for each year. This way the things that we had begun were incorporated into the life of the seminary in a way that would enable them to continue without having to be renewed or reinvented every year.

Creation Care in the Curriculum

Of course, one important purpose of all these efforts was to train students to give leadership in the congregations they would serve after graduation and in the communities in which their congregations were located. And so we pursued a number of avenues to incorporate care for creation into the curriculum of the seminary. Faculty offered elective courses such as Bible and Ecology, Greening Your Congregation, and The Future of Creation. Regular Stewardship of Creation workshops were made available. Many faculty members incorporated an eco-justice component into their survey courses. The fieldwork director found some environmental agencies to serve as internship sites, and students were encouraged to do their parish internship project on environmental issues. In addition, the Green Zone proposed an environmental ministry emphasis (the first of eight emphases now at LSTC). Unlike a major, an emphasis means that students take a few specialized courses and also write relevant papers in their regular classes, have fieldwork experiences, meet together regularly as a group, and do a senior project. At least a handful of students were engaged in the environmental ministry emphasis in any given year.

We also found it very helpful to:

> repeat a regular series of events every year.

Eventually, our annual schedule looked something like this:

- Orientation in September: Introduce the Green Zone to new and returning students.
- Opening meeting or workshop with leading speakers: Get students active early on.
- Fall worship at chapel during a week in mid-October: Monday: Blessing of the animals; Wednesday: Making a covenant with creation; Thursday: Creation care student sermon
- Monthly Green Zone Committee meetings open to all: Including an educational component and project planning
- Senior dinner in early spring for graduates, with speaker and the distribution of materials for use in the parish after graduation
- Earth Week Celebration at chapel in April: Monday: faculty preacher on creation care; Tuesday: an interfaith creation-care service; Wednesday: full communion with care for creation liturgy and preaching; Thursday: a Native American service or other creation-care liturgy

These activities became a regular part of our life together as a seminary, and they involved students, faculty, and staff. The repeated events gave a rhythm and an ongoing presence to our earth-care commitments.

As these things were developing, we learned another important lesson:

> Look for the thresholds, and make the leap forward.

One amazing aspect in these efforts was how the small things we did would accumulate. More people and groups of the community would become involved, and they would initiate efforts out of their own commitments. A greater sense of LSTC's identity as a Green Zone was taking hold. More and more students were arriving with creation-care commitments.

In light of this, we watched every year for what could be identified as thresholds that brought us to a new level, either overall or in one area of seminary life—an advancing stage in which certain things were now possible that had not been possible before. It was extremely important to identify these thresholds and to take advantage of the new and bolder opportunities made possible by them. One example was the critical mass of faculty who had published articles and preached sermons on the environment. When we realized how many there were, we brought their works together in a spiral notebook called *Creation and the Future of Humanity: LSTC Writings on the Environment*. This collection became a staple that we distributed to students and visitors. It gave us a chance to promote the faculty and seminary commitment to ecological justice.

Fulfilling Our Comprehensive Vision

Throughout this time, the seminary was building on the five areas of the Green Zone model.

1. Worship

New liturgies. Blessing of the animals. New chapel design with floor-to-ceiling windows and a solar-powered baptismal font. Trees and air-purifying plants in the worship space.

2. Education in the Life of the Seminary

Courses, lectures, and conferences. Hosting environmentalists-in-residence. Sponsoring students to attend environmental conferences.

3. Building and Grounds as a Model

Energy audits. Retrofitting lights. Placing energy-efficient lights inside and outside the main buildings. Engaging students to place energy-efficient lights in student living units. Standard recycling and composting as well as disposal sites for batteries and cell phones. Acquisition of chinaware for dinners and receptions (to cut down on paper and Styrofoam). A major insulation project in all living units.

4. *Lifestyle of Members of the Seminary Community*

Community members making a personal covenant with creation. A brochure explaining the practices and products needed to *Green Your LSTC Apartment*. Students writing a devotional booklet *The Stewardship of Creation: A Thirty-Day Discipline*. Dinner groups devoted to simple living.

5. *Public Witness*

Collaboration with other seminaries. About thirty interested faculty from nearby seminaries formed the Chicago Theological Initiative for Eco-Justice Ministry to foster developments in seminary education. ACTS for Eco-Justice, a cross-seminary student group, met for several years. In both cases, students learned that some programs rise, serve a purpose, and then go out of existence. We move on to other initiatives.

Serving Church and Society

Part of the role of a seminary is to provide new and innovative resources for the church and the world. So we set out to provide resources for parishes. Students collected materials for *Care of the Earth: A Manual for Church Leaders*, edited by Tina Krause. We set up an ecumenical website called the Web of Creation and populated it with congregational resources for creation care. Two students were paid from year to year to organize the website, gather information, and manage the site. Students in the course Greening Your Congregation wrote chapters for a spiral notebook on congregational properties, edited by David Glover and myself: *Environmental Guide for Congregations, Their Buildings, and Grounds*.

From the gathered resources, we put together another spiral notebook, *The Green Congregation Training Manual*, and established the Green Congregation Program and held Green Congregation workshops. Seminary students planned and helped to carry out two workshops in the local synod. For the students, the experience of managing the website and planning the workshops became an important part of their seminary preparation, namely to:

> Prepare to be leaders in congregations and society.

Furthermore, a graduate student helped me to collect and edit a book of sermons by scholars and environmentalists, *Earth and Word: Classic Sermons on Saving the Planet*. Also, along with some good friends and colleagues, we helped to spawn several new organizations: the Green Seminary Initiative, organized with colleagues from other seminaries, a wonderful ecumenical interfaith organization committed to taking earth care into the life of seminary preparation across the country; Lutherans Restoring Creation, dedicated to bringing care for creation into the full life and mission of the ELCA; and Let All Creation Praise, an ecumenical website offering care-for-creation worship for the church year, including resources to celebrate a Season of Creation.

These efforts were designed to provide resources for parishes in their communal life and in their witness to society, all meant to convey the message that

> the church exists for the sake of the world.

In all of this, the Green Zone sought to keep the greening activities of LSTC in front of the seminary community so that there was a growing awareness of our institutional commitment. Here was a critical mantra:

> Promotion, promotion, promotion

Our publicity office reported relevant events and had feature articles in the LSTC magazine. We had regular reports, testimonials, and advocacy appeals in the in-house newsletter. We established a section of the seminary website about "LSTC as a Green Seminary." We developed a promotional brochure with the admissions office on *LSTC as a Green Seminary*. And the LSTC administration incorporated care for creation into the distinguishing marks of the seminary that expresses our commitment to global concerns.

Solidifying the Identity

Eventually, all of this caught fire. The offices came on board and began to take their own initiative. The seminary was attracting more than a handful of students each year who considered these ecological commitments to be a decisive factor in their decision to come to LSTC. Faculty searches were attracting candidates who shared our environmental concerns. The dean was encouraging courses in creation care. The manager of the physical plant continued to propose eco-friendly projects. The communications office sought out stories and reports to share in publications. The development office approached us about formulating proposals to submit to foundations for funding. The Stewardship and Tithing Foundation at LSTC offered several grants. The Language Resource and Writing Center sponsored ecological reports from international students. And so on. After two decades of growing efforts, LSTC as a Green Zone was taking off.

Earth Year at LSTC

All of this came to a climax in the celebration of Earth Year at LSTC in 2009–10, a yearlong emphasis on social, cultural, political, and global issues related to ecology that engaged the entire community. And the impact of this immersion lasted well beyond that year. As one of our professors said, "I think it's now in our DNA."

WHAT SEMINARIANS NEED TO KNOW ABOUT CARING FOR CREATION

Later in my time at LSTC, it made sense to formulate a list of the critical things that seminarians should learn about care for creation in order to be prepared to offer leadership in parish and society. These included: the environmental state of the world; the justice issues involved in creation care, including environmental racism; the personal and systemic changes needed to address the problems; familiarity with relevant laws and policies; awareness of denominational stance; and what congregations can do to become creation-care centers. These were the things that, as a seminary, through a variety of means and venues, formal and informal, we were hoping that our students would learn.

HOPE FOR THE FUTURE

It is not easy to measure how much students are learning from this effort when the instruction is informal, ad hoc, and indirect, based mainly on modeling, partnership, and participation. I could see how the engaged students learned about community organizing, carrying out projects, managing computer programs, and working with others. They also learned about the ecological state of the world and our faith commitment to care for creation. As we said at the top, the goal of this movement was to bring creation care into the full life and mission of the seminary so that it would become part of the ethos of our life together. My hope was that, whether in classes or at worship or from community events or as part of informal conversations, students at LSTC would be exposed to these issues—and that they would be able to offer leadership around issues of ecology and faith in their future roles in church and society.

Postscript

For New Teachers

WHETHER YOU ARE TEACHING college students or graduate students or high school students or laity in a parish, this is a vocation. Teaching is a high calling. The act of teaching is inviting you into its space. Embrace it. Live out of that vocation from your deepest self. And try to reclaim your calling from semester to semester.

Love your subject matter. Be passionate about your field of study and let that passion be contagious. Keep current and contribute. Be intellectually courageous. Cultivate a large appetite for learning. Nurture an insatiable curiosity and let it be obvious. Learn how to expand your mind and how to change your mind. Let your subject matter be a delight for your students.

Develop a heart-centered intention to be an effective teacher. Be humble. Live with gratitude and grace. You are there to serve the students. They are in your trust. Partner with students in developing the learning process. Learn from them how best they learn. Don't ever be arrogant or use your position to aggrandize yourself. Don't overwhelm students with your knowledge. Let them find their way. Don't place your identity in degrees or titles. Your authority lies in your grasp of your subject matter, your moral integrity, and your respect for all. Take the students seriously. But never take yourself too seriously. Practice a sense of humor.

Beyond teaching your subject matter, how you relate to the students and how they relate to each other is integral to what you are teaching. Practice hospitality. Make the classroom a safe place to learn and grow. Treat students with respect and always be fair. Do not choose favorites. Do not neglect a single student. Never humiliate anyone. Discuss the values you try to live by and how you seek to engender them in the learning process. Do not just limit yourself to lecturing or other standard ways of teaching. Engage your imagination to see how it might be done other ways. Experiment and then recover from your mistakes and go at it again. Discover your gifts and use them.

Care for your students. Care about each one, while always maintaining boundaries. Know their names. Think about them as more than your experience of them in the classroom. They are real persons with their own hopes, fears, goals, wants, and needs. Treat them as such. Talk to them about your aspirations for them and what you are trying to teach them. Share your hopes and dreams for them, and invite them to join with you in the process of embracing those hopes and dreams. Let them find in the classroom a community of learners developing attitudes and skills for life. Provide the support they need without compromising your standards. Challenge them to do well and provide the encouragement to do that.

Prepare them for a career, for their vocation. Help them nurture their sense of calling. More than that, prepare your students to be contributing citizens of the world. And even more than this, show them how to be better human beings. There are so many issues facing the world today that seek to upend us. We so need people who are open to others who disagree, who are compassionate toward the vulnerable, who stand with the oppressed, who pursue justice and peace, who are part of the struggle to preserve the sanctity of earth. Let the classroom be for you and for them a laboratory for life together. And relish it!

Appendix 1

Scripture by Heart: Course Description

This appendix is an extended reflection on a course that focuses on understanding scriptural passages by learning and telling them, and as a way for others to hear them. When there were repeated requests from students to learn how to memorize and perform biblical passages, it made sense to offer an entire course on it. This was a semester-long course in three-hour blocks of time one evening each week. There could be only twelve students in the class. Otherwise, we would not have had enough time for all to share/practice their stories each week. I taught the class five times. Here is the description of the course.

> *Scripture by Heart.* The purpose of this course is to train future parish leaders in the memorization and presentation of biblical stories for congregational life. A major focus is on the life-changing power of these stories. Students have opportunities to perform biblical selections in class and in public presentations. They also learn how to incorporate biblical storytelling into preaching, worship, Bible study, and pastoral care.

WHAT IS SCRIPTURE BY HEART?

The title of the course, Scripture by Heart, conveyed the importance of rote memorization. Students were to do word-for-word memorization, because that precision is critical for interpretation. Also, if these future pastors and lay professionals were to perform these stories as the Scripture lessons in worship, they needed to get it right.

This meant that students were expected to learn the stories as they appeared in the text of Scripture; but, more importantly, it meant that they were to learn passages so well that they came from their heart—like songs or hymns they know well, or poetry they can recite readily, or stories they have never forgotten. We all know some songs so well we can sing them by heart. And when we think about them as we sing them, we make the words of the composer and of the singer *our* words, and it is *we* who are now expressing the thoughts and feelings and commitments manifest in the lyrics and the melody of the song. If we could learn passages of the Bible so well that they became *ours*, then it would indeed be *Scripture from the heart*.

In our culture, the heart is the seat of the emotions. In the Bible, the bowels are the seat of emotions, and the heart is the center of thinking and willing. I wanted students to experience a story with heart, mind, will, and guts—the emotions of the story and the potential change in thinking that may result, as well as the shifts in behavior called forth by any given story. All these dynamics are crucial, because stories do not affect just our emotions; they also change our thinking, our will, our imagination, and our actions. So the issue is not just memorizing and telling but taking it in, ingesting it, being changed by it, and sharing it with others.

The point here is that words and stories change people at the mysterious heart level or, as we might say today, at a subconscious as well as a conscious level. By means of stories, therefore, God gives us a new heart—a new way of thinking, a new will, and new emotions to empower us to act. In this way, the class was more than a mechanical telling of stories; and it included opportunities for students to share what was happening to them in the course of learning and telling and hearing biblical stories.

Students were not permitted to turn in written work for the class! For students, this was unheard of. It changed the entire way the students related to the learning process. In addition to performing biblical passages, students also performed liturgies and discussed the oral dynamics of preaching. And they learned how to train lectors in reading/performing Scripture in worship.

A TASTE OF TRADITIONAL ORAL CULTURES

In biblical times, the Mediterranean world was composed of predominantly oral cultures in which 85 percent to 98 percent of the population were nonliterate. All the writings now collected in the Bible were originally performed and received by audiences in an oral venue. To give that ethos some contemporary connection, we read Tex Sample's little book on rural settings, *Ministry in an Oral Culture*. Sample draws on Walter Ong's work on oral cultures, *Orality and Literacy*, to show how the ethos of an oral culture differs from that of a print culture. Here are some features of oral cultures that shaped the learning context in our classroom:

- Teach and learn by apprenticeship
- Make decisions by consensus
- Express an empathic core
- Practice communal ethics
- Do lots of storytelling
- Learn or create some proverbs to help us learn

I sought to be intentional and explicit about our efforts to adopt these approaches. Some African American students, Native American students, most international students, and a few students with rural backgrounds, who had lived closer than others to the ethos of an oral culture, resonated especially well with the experience.

THE POWER OF STORIES

Also, we spent a good bit of time talking about the power of stories. We read Tom Boomershine's book, *Story Journey*, which shows a number of ways to learn and teach Bible stories, how the experience of performance can help to interpret the stories, and how stories can be used in various venues of Christian ministry. Out of this, I asked students to brainstorm together a list of all the different ways in which stories might be important for the ministry of clergy and laity in a congregation. In addition to the importance of stories in preaching, education, hospital care, pastoral care, and the quest for social peace and justice, students also suggested that different families could learn stories and share them in a storytelling event, that a church could adopt a Bible story related to its own identity and everyone could learn it, that members could set up a chain ministry to call the next person and tell them a story, and that children could learn stories and tell them together or act them out in worship, among other ideas. I introduced them to the Network of Biblical Storytellers,

International, an organization devoted to small-group ministry in congregations in which Bible study groups learn a story each month, share it with others, and report back their experiences.

More than this, we talked about the power of stories to transform individual lives, communities, and cultures. Stories are integral to what it means to be human. Stories are not only a delightful add-on to life, an illustration for a point, a source of entertainment, or a way to enliven a sermon or discussion. By themselves, those approaches diminish the power of stories in an incredibly reductionist way. The American novelist Reynolds Price once said to me that "next to food and shelter, stories are necessary for human life." Life itself has a narrative quality. Storying is how we make sense of our lives, our daily activities, the span of our life and its meaning. It is the only way we talk about anything. In this sense, narrative is constitutive of sanity and wholeness. Furthermore, we swim in the larger stories of our culture, which we seek to live out or perhaps act against. Stories are like the air we breathe. Students were to ask which stories we live by personally and collectively and how we might challenge and perhaps change those stories in light of the biblical stories.

Examining Our Personal and Communal Stories

I stressed that each of us is in the middle of a story or of multiple stories that make sense of our lives. Usually, we live so as to make our story come out as we might hope. Often it is the case that while we say we are living one story, say, a Christian story about losing our life for others, in actuality we may be living the American dream by securing our lives financially and socially. It takes courage to examine the stories we claim for ourselves and the personal and social stories we may be caught up in. However, unless we are consciously aware of the stories we are living out, it is unlikely that we will be open to changing our stories.

How could the course lead students to examine their stories? Students reflected on some questions: What has been your story up to this point in life? How would you like it to turn out? If someone were to write a story about you, how might they describe the story of your life? Whose lives do you seek to emulate? How are you trying to live out their stories in your life? When have you changed your story? How did that happen? How might you change your story now? It is not easy in a class to entertain these profound reflections. It takes a large measure of self-examination and a lot of trust.

It helped that we read Robert Coles's *The Call of Stories* as a means to see how that might happen. This is a collection of many transcripts of Coles's conversations with his students and clients as they were examining their lives and changing their personal stories—as they read short stories and novels that transformed their lives. By seeing their own lives mirrored in these published stories and by their identification with various characters, the people in Coles's book were discovering new ways to think of themselves and the courage to behave in new ways. As we in the class read stories about people in the Bible who are changing, we reflected on the possibilities of transformation in our own lives. Then we would also reflect on the biblical stories we were memorizing and telling—stories we were seeking to make an integral part of our lives—and we would ask how these stories might change us.

FOSTERING AN ETHOS OF TRUST

As the class was having these discussions, we were also doing weekly performances of biblical stories. And this was the most challenging part. Here a crucial ingredient was an atmosphere of trust. For students to be able to tell stories and engage in mutual critique required a safe atmosphere. How could I establish trust for this process?

First, I taught the course pass-fail. The main expectation was that the student would make a significant effort to participate in all the activities of the class. This approach removed the anxiety about grades. Besides, the cooperative nature of the course in giving each other feedback and in planning together a public presentation by the group was intrinsic motivation to do well. Add to this the motivation to perform well before one's classmates and before the larger community. There was certainly incentive enough built into the class to elicit excellent work! Having removed anxiety about a grade, I as a teacher and the fellow students could work together to the benefit of all in an atmosphere of mutual trust.

Also, I sought to engender trust by the choice of the classroom where we met. It had to be a place of privacy (no windows into the classroom where others could observe), a quiet place where there was no outside noise and where there would be no interruptions. Part of the room was set up for performing, with chairs in one semicircle and an open space in front for the presenter. Also, I placed a lectern to the side where they could place the script. "You do not need to perform 'free fall' without a text. Always work with a safety net. It is not a problem to consult a text and then continue."

In addition, as a means to engender trust, the students needed some time at the first class to get to know each other and share any personal experiences of memorizing and performing (good, bad, or indifferent) they might like to share. For those who could name their hurts from bad experiences in the past, I asked them to pray for the healing of their memories before the next class.

Modeling the Process

As a further means to relieve anxiety about the class, I also began by demystifying the process of memory work. They chose a story in one of the Gospels for me to memorize right then and there before them—a story that I had not already learned. They could see that I had to go line by line, repeating it several times, that I struggled to remember, that I did have a process, and that I needed to work at it. In this first experience, watching me, they invariably said, "*I* can do that." They corrected me when I made mistakes, and they quickly wanted to try it for themselves. I then gave them guidelines for learning passages. You will see these guidelines in appendix 2.

Later in the course, I asked them to describe for the benefit of other class members how they went about memorizing and preparing to perform: some used a tape recorder; some learned it generally and then went back and got the details down; others had to "see" it first in their imagination; and some used key words to help with the recall. I also supplied them with a process for interpreting a narrative, so that they better understood the passage they were learning—the role of the narrator, the plot, characters, settings, rhetorical devices, and norms of judgment. Detailed guidelines for this can be found in *Mark as Story: An Introduction to the Narrative of a Gospel* (edited by Rhoads et al.). They learned how to stumble in performing. When they performed and forgot, we simply waited for them to recover on their own without prompting them. Recovery from forgetting, when it occurred, became a normal part of the presentation.

GETTING STARTED

For each of the first several weeks, each student chose a different passage to learn and perform from the Gospel of Luke. The first week, they chose from a list of parables. The next week we did healing stories, and then the following week we did controversy stories. Then they learned sequential portions of the Lukan birth narrative. Each week, they signed up for the passage they wanted to do for the following week.

During the first week in which they presented, I allowed for time after each presentation for other students to jot down one thing they liked and thought was effective. After all the presentations had been completed, we shared these comments in conversation. It was always amazing to see how they learned from watching each other and from getting feedback. In the second week, they went a step further. For each performance, they jotted down one affirming comment and one constructive suggestion that might make the presentation more effective. By the third week, they wrote down their overall feedback for each presentation, and then we distributed all these written evaluations so that each person could see all the comments and suggestions by all the other class members for her or his performance. After reading these, they shared in small groups and spoke about how they might do their performance differently the next time. This process fostered great solidarity among the class and developed relationships of support and encouragement.

The whole class process was a matter of coaching students through practice and feedback, practice and feedback, so that ultimately they were able to memorize and perform independently of the constructive suggestions offered by me and the other students.

LEARNING TO PERFORM

It was important that the students presented in storytelling mode rather than in some artificial performance mode. My goal for them was that they could present the passages in a way that was *natural* for them and in a way that was *meaningful* for their audience. The idea was that they were to imagine that they had actually seen the event they were telling about and that they were telling it to someone with the seriousness and excitement and animation appropriate to what they had witnessed. They found their own style in doing this.

At the same time, they learned techniques drawn from the contemporary art of oral interpretation of literature. We used a text to help with this, *Performance Studies*, by Ronald Pelias. Students were to "see" whatever episode they were recounting in their mind's eye and to "show" the audience what they were seeing. To do this, they learned to develop onstage and offstage focus, how to provide different voices for different characters, the use of gestures in suggestive and natural ways, the use of pace and inflection, pauses and emphases, how to portray conversations between two characters without having to turn sideways, and the importance of being aware of the "subtext"—that is, the message they were conveying by *how* they said a line. It was often necessary at first for students to practice performing in somewhat exaggerated ways and in different ways so as to stretch and expand the range of what seemed natural to them and then settle back into a meaningful way to tell their story without emoting or being artificial.

In this process, I related to the students as I did in no other class—as director and coach. In other classes, the students are mainly doing work for the teacher and for other students. In this class, I coached the students, working with one individual after another in front of the whole group in such a way that all the students could apply to their own performing the suggestions made for each student. I told them to try it this way or that. I asked them what impact they wanted their passage to have. Even though I was evaluating their work (in terms of effectiveness, not grades), my relationship to them was different than it was in other pedagogical contexts. They were preparing for public presentations, and I was helping them to do it well. We were in this together.

PERFORMANCES FOR THE COMMUNITY

The outcome of their work involved two storytelling performances for the seminary community, one as a midterm presentation and one at the end of the course. We set up the community lounge or the chapel for these presentations. Usually thirty to fifty people attended, mostly families and friends. The students gave performances of passages that ranged in time from five to nine minutes. That was quite a challenge. The students each chose their own passage to present from the Old or the New Testament. Here are some examples from a program for a midterm storytelling performance:

- The Samaritan Woman (John 4:1–2)
- Jesus's Teaching (Luke 6:27–36)
- Rom 5–8 (abbreviated)
- The Story of Jonah
- Jesus's Words to His Disciples (John 14:1—15:17)
- Rahab's Story (Josh 2; Jas 2:14–26)
- First Thessalonians (Abbreviated)
- Jacob's Story (Gen 27)

Here is a selection from an end-of-term set of presentations:

- The Presence of God (Ps 139)
- Dry Bones Rising (Ezek 37:1–14)
- Mary and the Birth of Jesus (Luke 1:39–57; 2:1–7)
- Wealth and Poverty in the Kingdom of God (selections from Luke)
- The Bread of Life (John 6)
- Washing the Feet of the Disciples (John 13:1–30)
- The Raising of Lazarus (John 11)
- Resurrection Stories (John 21)

After each performance, the members of the class reflected together on why each one had chosen the passage they had presented. This was always illuminating. For example, one person chose Jonah because it expressed their resistance to their chosen vocation, another chose the call of Moses because of their lack of self-confidence, another did the "light of the world" passage in John because they suffered from seasonal affective disorder, another did a passage from Romans to overcome the experience of having had this passage "shoved down his throat" in his youth, and so on.

For most students in this class, what they learned had a high impact on their ministries. There was a new appreciation for the possibilities of presenting Scripture in worship. After graduating, many of them prepared to preach by memorizing the passage at the beginning of the week and repeating it throughout the week. By Sunday, they knew it well enough to present it by heart for the congregation. That way, the "reading" of Scripture becomes a high moment in the worship service.

Those preparing to preach also reported that their sermons seem to emerge organically out of their intimate knowledge of the passage and from the fact that they were living with the passage throughout the week in interaction with their daily lives. Students in the class also learned a portion of liturgy by heart so that they could transfer what they had learned about Scripture to the way they might conduct worship. In this way, the liturgy was no longer a ritual they were going through with their congregation but an actual dialogue of transformation between priest and parishioners.

FEEDBACK AND OUTCOMES

There was positive feedback from the students throughout the course and at the end. But I wondered what long-term impact the course had on the students. As I repeated the class, I kept track of the students who had taken it. Later, I sent a set of questions to the alumni of these Scripture by Heart classes after they had been in ministry for several years. Here are some verbatim quotes of the responses I received, organized by subject.

About the Class

- Students felt comfortable enough to take some risks and really explore the range of what they could do with voice and gesture and still make the telling respectful and authentic. The class didn't just teach me to tell Bible stories; it also taught me how to teach!
- As a result of this course, a classmate and I offered a practicum for other students who wanted to learn the art of telling Scripture by Heart.
- After both [public performance] occasions, the feedback from the seminary community by those who had attended was tremendously positive. For weeks afterward people would approach us and tell us how meaningful it had been for them to hear the stories presented orally and how it had transformed their own relationship with Scripture and been deeply moving.
- I recall learning a lot about the art and skill of presentation. In developing a presentation, we are interpreting the Scriptures. Body language, movement, facial expression, gesture, tone, inflection, etc.

are all a part of that interpretation. These things have given me great comfort and confidence in presenting the Gospel or preaching on the text each Sunday as well as attempting dramatic presentations with costumes.

- Teaching a clear methodical way of memorization enabled me to participate without a lot of anxiety. Never before had I learned a technique for memorizing.
- This class was like none other that I took at LSTC. I remember being in a small group of people who became friends through a unique experience of sharing of ourselves and sharing Scripture with one another. We grew closer to each other because we were doing something that was not only risky (to tell entire passages of Scripture by heart!) but something that was, in a way, deeply personal (in terms of which passages we chose for the midterm and final).
- Hearing my classmates perform, learning their insights, and sharing were wonderful ways of unpacking the Scripture; and I often felt covered with God's grace in response.
- It was amazing to see how classmates who seemed quiet and timid in other classes appeared more vibrant, excited, vulnerable, and genuine in this class. As a result, stronger relationships between classmates seemed to be formed in this class.

Relating to Scripture

- What amazed me was the discovery of how much impact the process of learning and telling the stories would have on me. I found myself experiencing the passages from new angles, through the eyes of different characters, and focusing more on the story world—what it might have smelled, felt, sounded and tasted like to the people in it. It is an amazing thing when Scripture gets into your heart and very being.
- It had a profound effect. In some ways for the very first time, Scripture became me or should I say, "I became Scripture." I ate the Scripture and digested it. It became a part of me. This has truly been a wonderful gift.

- I was immersed in Scripture, really, for the first time, having to know every jot and tittle (so to speak!) of the passages I was performing. It caused me to ask questions of the text, learn more about the text and its characters and themes, in order to present it faithfully to the audience, being inclusive of mood, different characters, and the overall message of the text.

Personal Growth

- It was, in many ways, a spiritual dawning as I discovered the passion I have for the Story.
- This class has formed and shaped me as a child of God and as a pastor equal to or more than any other class. So often I heard classmates say something like, "Theology is great but I long for more spiritual formation." This class certainly involves theological thought. But more than any other class, it involves spiritual formation.
- This class helped reconnect me spiritually and satisfied my longing to be back in a personal relationship with our Lord. It helped me not lose my sense of vocation in the busy-ness of graduate work. It is the class that I probably remember the most keenly because of its powerful impact on my life at that time.

Regarding Worship and Preaching

- I was very eager to try it in a parish setting. It was overwhelmingly received in an affirmative manner. I have loved this process of Scripture by Heart and have continued with it in my ministry of four years.
- Amazingly, the weeks I took the time to first learn the text—deeply learn it so that I breathed it—the sermon would come on its own. To this day, when I find myself feeling "stuck" and the creative well is running dry, I will stop and learn the story; and when I do, the rest follows.
- My hope is to expose as many people as possible to Scripture in this way. I am gratified to see how people light up when they discover, or rediscover, Scripture this way.

- I have continued with presenting Scripture by heart each Sunday for four years now. I continue to hear things like, "I heard the Word differently" or "I hear the gospel of Christ much better" or "It becomes so much more real." I have even had congregants invite others to worship just to hear the Scriptures presented by memory.
- Memorizing Scripture helped me preach better, in the sense that I had developed a practice of asking deeper questions of the text; and, by telling the Gospel lesson by heart, the story came alive to the congregation.

Appendix 2

Guidelines for Learning and Performing Biblical Stories

THE GOALS OF THE following exercises are: 1) to experience the Gospel in a new medium, its original oral medium; 2) to increase understanding of the Gospel and its potential impacts; and 3) to have a powerful encounter with the story as a contemporary experience. Here are several ways that performances of biblical stories can be done with a class.

1. Students can be invited to learn an episode of their choice and present it to the group.
2. Students can learn and perform a series of episodes in a row, such as the opening stories of a Gospel or a section of a Gospel such as the journey to Jerusalem or the crucifixion narrative or one of the shorter epistles.
3. Divide a Gospel into sections according to the number of students in the class for performing or for reading, then set aside a time of two and a half to three hours for experiencing a Gospel in its entirety with opportunity for discussion afterward.
4. One of the first three choices can be done as a presentation for an audience beyond the classroom, such as your academic community, a church event, or in a local theater.

1. BECOME FAMILIAR WITH THE STORY

Note: You may find the narrative exercises in appendix 2 of *Mark as Story: An Introduction to the Narrative of a Gospel* (edited by Rhoads et al.) as means to know the episode well.

Here are the key steps to learning an episode by heart.

Step One

Do the following exercise in pairs (or individually):

- Read the passage silently and study it. Then have one of your pair tell the story as closely as possible to the wording, while the other person listens without following the book. Then look and see what you missed.
- Repeat the above, but reverse roles.
- Ask questions line by line without answering them.

Step Two

Tell the story from the point of view of each character by changing the relevant pronouns. Invest yourself in the feelings and tone of each character. This exercise will help you say the dialogue lines and the interactions of characters with each other.

Step Three

Follow the story, line by line, for causation and connection from one action and/or dialogue to the next. Ask how and why each detail follows the previous one. This exercise will help you remember what comes next.

Step Four

Imagine the progression within the single episode as a series of very brief moments of action and dialogue. Imagine where the characters will stand as they act and speak. This exercise will help you visualize the story as you tell it—so you can, in a sense, tell/show the audience "what you have seen."

Step Five

Act out the story. Remember that you are embodying the story with your whole self. This exercise will help you remember the story with your entire body.

2. LEARN THE STORY BY HEART

- Learn each line one after the other by repeating each line five times without looking. Keep checking to see what you might have added, omitted, or changed. After you know the first line, do the second line five times. Then do the first two lines together and so on to the end.
- Repeat the whole episode often until you know it by heart. Carry a printed copy of the story with you so you can relearn parts you might have forgotten.
- Find your own way to learn the story—telling others, making an audiotape and listening repeatedly to it, acting it out, or setting it out on paper in configurations that will help you remember it.
- Say it quickly so as to get the words down. Once you know it well, you can slow down and concentrate on *how* you will tell it.

3. TELL IT

- Tell it to a friend in a natural way appropriate to the nature of the story. Do this apart from a performance setting. You may want to tell it in a plain and straightforward way. Or tell what you have "seen" with the appropriate animation and emotion.
- Now do it as a presentation to a group, as you did it with the friend, as if you were addressing just one or two persons. The goal is to tell the story in ways that most appropriately convey its meaning and potential impact.
- Experiment with how you will tell it. How will you stand? What will your gestures be? How will you inflect the dialogue of the characters? Where and how will you place the emphasis? How will you pace the story?

4. PERFORMANCE EXERCISES

There are many ways to tell a story. The tone and inflection of your voice, the volume and pace of the telling, your gestures and facial expressions, as well as your body posture and movement all contribute to a distinctive way to share the story. The goal is to gain an understanding of the passage and its potential impact, and then seek to find ways to present it that are faithful to that interpretation. You are performing the passage. However, think of yourself less as an actor and more as a storyteller. After you have learned the story well, here are some exercises that may help you refine and stretch your experience of performing the passage.

Voice

In your telling, think about tone of voice, inflection, volume, and pace. The "subtext" is the message you give based on *how* you say a line. You can convey seriousness, accusation, sarcasm, puzzlement, and so on simply by the way you deliver a line. As an exercise, take each line and say it in different ways. Then settle on the most effective way you can say it so as to convey the meaning you think it has and the impact you want it to make.

Facial Expressions and Gestures

You do not need to find a gesture to match every line. Be sparing. Use gestures in a suggestive rather than a dramatic way. Be natural. Gestures and facial expressions are not add-ons. Rather they are an integral part of conveying the meaning and impact of a line.

Physical Movement

You may want to move around the performance space to convey some change of scenery or move closer or further from the audience to manifest some aspect or impact of the story. Again, make this movement integral to the telling rather than something that is wooden or mechanical.

Characterizations

You may want to provide slightly different presentations of yourself for each of the characters when you as the narrator switch to saying their lines.

- Determine the goal and purpose of the character speaking and give the appropriate inflection.
- As you portray dialogue, do not try to turn 180 degrees to the right and then to the left as you imagine dialogue between two people. Rather, turn very slightly to the right or left to convey two different characters in dialogue.
- You may want to direct all lines, including the characters you portray, *offstage* to the audience. Or, when you give the dialogue line of a character, you may want to direct it *onstage* to the imaginary character or characters you are addressing in front of you.

Emotions

Feelings may range from urgency to amazement to laughter. Express emotions in ways that are appropriate to the story or teaching you are telling. Do not exaggerate.

Tips

Do stretching and relaxation exercises before you practice and perform your passage. Keep a copy of the text nearby and consult it if needed. Look for a storytelling guide or a performance study as a way to increase your ability.

5. REFLECTION QUESTIONS FOR CONVERSATION AFTER THE PERFORMANCE

For the Performer

- What was your process of learning the story, and how did it work?

- What did you learn about the passage and the Gospel [or the letter] in which it appears?
- What was it like being the narrator and taking the role of different characters?
- What did you understand to be the potential impact(s) of the passage on the audience?

For the Hearers

- In what ways is it different to hear the passage in contrast to reading it?
- What did you understand in a new way about the passage and the book in which it appears?
- Did you feel led or impelled to think differently or to do something? How did the performance engender that response?
- What feelings did you have while listening? And what was it about the story and the way it was told that evoked these emotions?

For Performers and Hearers

- In what ways does this experience change the way you think about the origins of the Gospels (and the New Testament) in the predominantly oral cultures of the first century?
- Were there aspects of the story that you found profoundly meaningful or that you resisted?
- How does this experience lead you to think differently about your relationship to Scripture? Would you like to see this happen more often?

Note: For examples of and opportunities for biblical storytelling, look up the Network of Biblical Storytellers, International (https://nbsint.org).

Selected Bibliography

Aleshire, Daniel. *Earthen Vessels: Hopeful Reflections on the Work and Future of Theological Schools*. Grand Rapids: Eerdmans, 2008.

Austin, J. L. *How To Do Things with Words*. 2nd ed. 1975. Repr., Cambridge: Harvard University Press, 2018.

Bailey, Randall C. "The Danger of Ignoring One's Own Cultural Bias in Interpreting the Text." In *The Postcolonial Bible*, edited by R. S. Sugirtharajah, 66–90. The Bible and Postcolonialism 1. Sheffield: Sheffield Academic, 1998.

Bain, Ken. *What the Best College Teachers Do*. Cambridge: Harvard University Press, 2004.

Baker, Sheridan. *The Practical Stylist: With Readings and Handbook*. 8th ed. Harlow, UK: Longman, 1997.

Becker, Ernest. *The Denial of Death*. Tampa, FL: Free, 1997.

Belenkey, Mary Field, et al. *Women's Ways of Knowing: The Development of Self, Voice, and Mind*. New York: Basic Books, 1986.

Berger, Peter, and Thomas Luckman. *The Social Construction of Reality: A Treatise on the Sociology of Knowledge*. Garden City, NY: Doubleday, 1966.

Berling, Judith. *Understanding Other Religions: A Guide for Interreligious Education*. Maryknoll, NY: Orbis, 2004.

Bevans, Stephen. *Models of Contextual Theology*. Maryknoll, NY: Orbis, 1992.

Boomershine, Thomas. *Story Journey: An Invitation to the Gospel as Storytelling*. Nashville: Abingdon, 1988.

Boys, Mary C. *Educating in the Faith: Maps and Visions*. Harrisburg, PA: Trinity, 1998.

———. "Engaged Pedagogy: Dialogue and Critical Reflection." *Teaching Theology and Religion* 2 (2000) 129–36.

Brache, John, and Karen Tye. *Teaching the Bible in the Church*. St. Louis: Chalice, 2000.

Bruffee, Kenneth. *Collaborative Learning: Higher Education, Independence, and the Authority of Knowledge*. 2nd ed. Baltimore: Johns Hopkins University Press, 1999.

Cannon, Katie G. "Studying the Bible from the Perspective of the Racially and Economically Oppressed." In *Scripture: The WORD beyond the Word*. New York: United Methodist, 1985.

Chopp, Rebecca S. *Feminist Practices of Theological Education*. Louisville: Westminster John Knox, 1995.

Coles, Robert. *The Call of Stories: Teaching and the Moral Imagination*. New York: Houghton Mifflin, 1990.

Crossan, John Dominic. *Dark Interval: Toward a Theology of Story*. 1975. Reprint, Temecula, CA: Polebridge, 1994.

Csikszentmihalyi, Mihaly. *Finding Flow: The Psychology of Engagement*. New York: Basic Books, 1997.

———. *Flow: The Psychology of Optimal Experience*. New York: Harper & Row, 1990.

Davis, Barbara Gross. *Tools for Teaching*. 2nd ed. San Francisco: Jossey-Bass, 1993.

Dube, Musa W. "Toward a Post-Colonial Feminist Interpretation of the Bible." *Semeia* 78 (1997) 11–26.

Dunne, John S. *The Way of All the Earth: Experiments in Truth and Religion*. Notre Dame, IN: University of Notre Dame Press, 1978.

Elliott, Neil. *Liberating Paul: The Justice of God and the Politics of the Apostle*. 1994. Minneapolis: Fortress, 2005.

Erskine, Noel Leo. *Black Theology and Pedagogy*. New York: Palgrave MacMillan, 2008.

Everding, Edward, et al. *Viewpoints: Perspectives of Faith and Christian Nurture*. Harrisburg, PA: Trinity, 1998.

Farley, Edward. *Theologia: The Fragmentation and Unity of Theological Education*. Philadelphia: Fortress, 1983.

Finkel, Donald L. *Teaching with Your Mouth Shut*. Portsmouth, NH: Heinemann, 2000.

Foley, John Miles. *Teaching Oral Traditions*. New York: Modern Language Association, 1998.

Foster, Charles R., et al. *Educating Clergy: Teaching Practices and Practical Imagination*. San Francisco: Jossey-Bass, 2006.

Foster, Michele. *Black Teachers on Teaching*. New York: New York Press, 1997.

Freire, Paulo. *Pedagogy of Hope*. New York: Continuum, 1994.

———. *Pedagogy of the Oppressed*. New York: Herder & Herder, 1970.

———. *Teachers as Cultural Workers*. Boulder, CO: Westview, 1998.

Gardner, Howard. *Frames of Mind: The Theory of Multiple Intelligences*. New York: Basic Books, 1983.

———. *Intelligence Reframed: Multiple Intelligences for the 21st Century*. New York: Basic Books, 1999.

Gelb, Michael. *How to Think Like Leonardo: Seven Steps to Genius Every Day*. New York: Dell, 1998.

Gittins, Anthony. *Bread for the Journey: The Mission of Transformation and the Transformation of Mission*. Maryknoll, NY: Orbis, 1993.

Glover, David, and David Rhoads, eds. *Environmental Guide for Congregations, Their Buildings, and Grounds*. Chicago: Web of Creation, 2004.

Goldberger, Nancy Rule, et al., eds. *Knowledge, Difference, and Power: Essays Inspired by Women's Ways of Knowing*. New York: Basic Books, 1996.

González, Justo L. *Out of Every Tribe and Nation: Christian Theology at the Ethnic Roundtable*. Nashville: Abingdon, 1992.

Greene, Maxine. *Releasing the Imagination: Essays on Education, the Arts, and Social Change*. San Francisco: Jossey-Bass, 1995.

———. *Teacher as Stranger: Educational Philosophy for the Modern Age*. Belmont, CA: Wadsworth, 1973.

Guardiola-Saenz, Letitia. "Borderless Women and Borderless Texts: A Cultural Reading of Matthew 15:21–28." *Semeia* 78 (1997) 69–81.

Halliday, M. A. K. *Explorations in the Functions of Language*. Explorations in Language Study. Cambridge, MA: Elsevier Science, 1977.

Harris, Maria. *Teaching and Religious Imagination: An Essay in the Theology of Teaching.* San Francisco: Harper & Row, 1987.

Herzog, William R., II. *Parables and Subversive Speech: Jesus as Pedagogue of the Oppressed.* Louisville: Westminster John Knox, 1994.

Hess, Mary, and Stephen Brookfield, eds. *Teaching Reflectively in Theological Contexts: Promises and Contradictions.* Malabar, FL: Krieger, 2008.

hooks, bell. *Teaching to Transgress: Education as the Practice of Freedom.* New York: Routledge, 1994.

Hopkins, Gerard Manley. "God's Grandeur." Poets, [1877]. https://poets.org/poem/gods-grandeur.

Howe, Randy, ed. *The Quotable Teacher.* Guilford, CT: Lyons, 2003.

Jewett, Robert. *Saint Paul at the Movies: The Apostle's Dialogue with American Culture.* Louisville: Westminster John Knox, 1993.

———. *Saint Paul Returns to the Movies: Triumph over Shame.* Grand Rapids: Eerdmans, 1998.

Jones, L. Gregory, and Stephanie Paulsell, eds. *The Scope of Our Art: The Vocation of the Theological Teacher.* Grand Rapids: Eerdmans, 2002.

Kim, Jean Kyoung. "A Korean Feminist Reading of John 4:1–42." *Semeia* 78 (1997) 109–19.

Knowles, Malcolm Shepherd. *The Adult Learner: A Neglected Species.* Houston: Gulf, 1990.

Krause, Tina, ed. *Care of the Earth: A Manual for Church Leaders.* Chicago: Web of Creation, 1996.

Kwok, Pui-Lan. "Discovering the Bible in the Non-Biblical World." In *Discovering the Bible in the Non-Biblical World*, 8–20. 1995. Reprint, Eugene, OR: Wipf & Stock, 2003.

Law, Eric H. F. *The Wolf Shall Dwell with the Lamb: A Spirituality for Leadership in a Multicultural Community.* St. Louis: Chalice, 1993.

Lee, Spike, dir. *Do the Right Thing.* Universal City, CA: Universal, 1989.

Martin-Schramm, James B., and Robert L. Schriver. *Christian Environmental Ethics: A Case Method Approach.* Maryknoll, NY: Orbis, 2003.

McCowen, Alec. *Personal Mark.* New York: HarperCollins, 1985.

McLuhan, Marshall, and Quentin Fiori. *The Medium Is the Massage: An Inventory of Effects.* Richmond, CA: Gingko, 2001.

Merriam, Sharan B., and Associates. *Non-Western Perspectives on Learning and Knowing.* Malabar, FL: Krieger, 2007.

Moore, Mary Elizabeth Mullino. *Teaching from the Heart: Theology and Educational Method.* 2nd ed. Harrisburg, PA: Trinity, 1998.

Ong, Walter J. J. *Orality and Literacy: The Technologizing of the Word.* New Accents. New York: Methuen, 1982.

Palmer, Parker J. *The Courage to Teach: Exploring the Inner Landscape of a Teacher's Life.* San Francisco: Jossey-Bass, 1998.

Parenti, Michael. *Democracy for the Few.* 9th ed. Independence, KY: Cengage, 2010.

Patte, Daniel, et al., eds. *Global Bible Commentary.* Nashville: Abingdon, 2004.

Pelias, Ronald J. *Performance Studies: The Interpretation of Aesthetic Texts.* New York: St. Martins, 1991.

Pobee, John, ed. *Towards Viable Theological Education.* Geneva: WCC,1997.

Postman, Neil, and Charles Weingartner. *Teaching as a Subversive Activity*. New York: Delacorte, 1969.

Reinhartz, Adele. "A Nice Jewish Girl Reads the Gospel of John." *Semeia* 77 (1997) 177–93.

Rhoads, David. *The Challenge of Diversity: The Witness of Paul and the Gospels*. Minneapolis: Fortress, 1996.

———, ed. *Creation and the Future of Humanity: LSTC Writings on the Environment*. Chicago: Web of Creation, 2006.

———, ed. *Earth and Word: Classic Sermons on Saving the Planet*. New York: Continuum, 2007.

———, ed. *From Every People and Nation: Reading the Book of Revelation in Intercultural Perspective*. Minneapolis: Fortress, 2005.

———, ed. *The Green Congregation Training Manual*. Chicago: Web of Creation, 2005.

———. *Israel in Revolution 6–74 C.E.: A Political History Based on the Writings of Josephus*. Philadelphia: Fortress, 1976.

———. "Performance Criticism: An Emerging Methodology in Second Testament Studies—Part I." *Biblical Theology Bulletin* 36 (2006) 118–33.

———. "Performance Criticism: An Emerging Methodology in Second Testament Studies—Part II." *Biblical Theology Bulletin* 36 (2006) 164–84.

Rhoads, David, et al. *Mark as Story: An Introduction to the Narrative of a Gospel*. 3rd ed. Minneapolis: Fortress, 2012.

Roncace, Mark, and Patrick Gray, eds. *Teaching the Bible: Practical Strategies for Classroom Instruction*. Resources for Biblical Study. Atlanta: Society of Biblical Literature, 2005.

Salinger, J. D. *Franny and Zooey*. New York: Little, Brown, 1991.

Sample, Tex. *Ministry in an Oral Culture: Will Rogers, Uncle Remus, and Minnie Pearl*. Louisville: Westminster John Knox, 1994.

Sanders, Cheryl J. *Empowerment Ethics for a Liberated People: A Path to African American Social Transformation*. Minneapolis: Fortress, 1995.

Schreiter, Robert J. *The New Catholicity: Theology Between the Global and the Local*. Maryknoll, NY: Orbis, 1997.

Segovia, Fernando F., and Mary Ann Tolbert, eds. *Teaching the Bible: The Discourses and Politics of Biblical Pedagogy*. Maryknoll, NY: Orbis, 1998.

Seymour, Jack L., and Donald E. Miller, eds. *Theological Approaches to Christian Education*. Nashville: Abingdon, 1990.

Shor, Ira, and Paulo Freire. *A Pedagogy for Liberation: Dialogues on Transforming Education*. Westport, CT: Bergin & Garvey, 1987.

Sugirtharajah, R. S. "Biblical Studies After the Empire: From a Colonial to a Postcolonial Mode of Interpretation." In *The Postcolonial Bible*, edited by R. S. Sugirtharajah, 12–22. The Bible and Postcolonialism 1. Sheffield: Sheffield Academic, 1998.

Tennyson, Alfred Lord. "In Memoriam A. H. H." In *Selected Poems*, 96–198. Penguin Classics. London: Penguin, 2008.

Tolbert, Mary Ann. "Reading for Liberation." In *Social Location and Biblical Interpretation in the United States*, edited by Fernando F. Segovia and Mary Ann Tolbert, 263–76. *Reading from This Place*, vol. 1. Minneapolis: Fortress, 1996.

Weaver, Jace. "From I-Hermeneutics to We-Hermeneutics: Native Americans and the Post-Colonial." *Semeia* 75 (1995) 153–76.

Weston, Anthony. *How to Re-Imagine the World: A Pocket Guide for Practical Visionaries.* Gabriola Island, Canada: New Society, 2007.

Wolf, Anthony E. *Get Out of My Life, But First Will You Drive Me and Cheryl to the Mall.* Rev. ed. New York: Farrar, Strauss & Giroux, 2002.

www.ingramcontent.com/pod-product-compliance
Lightning Source LLC
LaVergne TN
LVHW091112080826
845145LV00008B/1878

* 9 7 8 1 6 2 0 3 2 8 7 9 8 *